Lost in Transition

LOST IN TRANSITION

Removing, Resettling, and Renewing Appalachia

EDITED BY AARON D. PURCELL

The University of Tennessee Press / Knoxville

Library of Congress Cataloging-in-Publication Data

Names: Purcell, Aaron D., 1972- editor.
Title: Lost in transition : removing, resettling, and renewing Appalachia /
    edited by Aaron D. Purcell.
Description: First edition. | Knoxville : The University of Tennessee
    Press, [2021] | Includes bibliographical references and index. |
    Summary: "Volume editor Aaron D. Purcell presents this thematic and
    chronological exploration of twentieth-century removal and resettlement
    projects across southern Appalachia. The work's seven case studies,
    addressing public land removal actions in Virginia, Kentucky, the
    Carolinas, and Tennessee from the 1930s through the 1960s, reveal
    confrontations between past and present, federal agencies and citizens,
    and original accounts and contemporary interpretations. The result is a
    critical analysis of fact, mythology, and storytelling that illustrates
    the important role of place in southern Appalachian history"—Provided
    by publisher.
Identifiers: LCCN 2021031026 (print) | LCCN 2021031027 (ebook) | ISBN
    9781621905899 (hardcover ; alkaline paper) | ISBN 9781621905905 (PDF) |
    ISBN 9781621905912 (Kindle edition)
Subjects: LCSH: Appalachians (People)—Relocation—History—20th century. |
    Appalachians (People)—Relocation—Case studies. | Appalachians
    (People)—Ethnic identity. | Persons displaced by eminent
    domain—Appalachian Region, Southern—Case studies. | Public
    lands—Appalachian Region, Southern—20th century. | Public
    lands—Social aspects—Appalachian Region, Southern.
Classification: LCC F210 .L67 2021 (print) | LCC F210 (ebook) | DDC
    975—dc23
LC record available at https://lccn.loc.gov/2021031026
LC ebook record available at https://lccn.loc.gov/2021031027

They built a dam in '55
And it brought light to strangers lives
But some of us got left behind
Like the Little Tennessee

—Highland Travelers, "The Little Tennessee," 2018

Contents

Illustrations

Acknowledgments

The genesis of this book occurred during my tenure at the University of Tennessee. From 2000 to 2007, I called Knoxville home, the James D. Hoskins Library my place of work, and the History Department my academic incubator. At the end of many workdays as I left the Hoskins Library I could see the downtown TVA towers. Even though I seldom set foot in the buildings, the towers served as a distant reminder of my research interest. I spent many of those years studying TVA and trying to better understand if the agency shaped the region for the better, or if some of the outcomes were for the worse.

Being in or near the place you are studying often informs your thinking. In March 2004, I prepared for my comprehensive doctoral examinations. A week before the written examination in the general field of American history, I rented a cabin at Norris Dam State Park to mentally prepare. Maybe I had seen *The Paper Chase* too many times, or maybe I just need a break of sorts. That week I spent each morning organizing piles of books and articles, reading as much as I could, and writing outlines for possible essay questions. By the early afternoon of each day I was ready to take a break and reflect on readings and writings of the morning. I took long walks on the nearby hiking trails, which were totally empty.

The walks cleared my head to focus on the upcoming task at hand, but it also made me think about those who once called the hilly woods and dark coves their homes. Exactly what and who had occupied the spaces before the federal government took control in the 1930s was an ever-present theme, especially when I looked out of my cabin's window and saw the water's edge of Norris Lake sparkling in the sun. During my daily walks I passed by cemeteries (some of which had been decorated in recent times). These cemeteries were on the higher ground and were not part of TVA's reinterment program, which removed and reinterred hundreds of graves that would have been covered by the rising waters of TVA lakes. The headstones marked the final resting places of families who farmed the ridges, sent their children to one-room schools, and sold their crops in small towns that dotted the now inundated valleys.

The idea of removal as cultural loss resurfaced a few years later. In spring 2007, I helped organize an exhibit and lecture series for the Special Collections Library. That spring, the campus embraced an initiative called the Appalachian Semester to help celebrate and investigate the culture of the region. As part of that initiative, I planned an exhibit of original items and three public lectures around the theme of "Appalachian Removals and Relocations." Lectures on the Cherokee Removal and the founding of the Rugby Colony were well attended and well received. The third and final lecture in the series was led by Dr. W. Bruce Wheeler—my dissertation advisor, mentor, and friend. His past work on TVA's controversial Tellico Dam project of the 1970s, deep knowledge of the agency's history, and infectious presentation style made him an ideal speaker. He always draws a crowd and for good reason.

Over the course of the forty-five minutes that followed, Dr. Wheeler described the removal of families to make way for the Great Smoky Mountains National Park and the dams for the Tennessee Valley Authority. He explained that electricity and tourist dollars contributed to the economic and agricultural development of the region, even if the benefits of change were uneven. His argument was that these federal removals improved the region more than it harmed it. That simple conclusion seemed uncontroversial, but little did I know that several of the audience members, who were visibly bothered throughout the lecture, were descendants of those directly removed as a result of creating the Great Smoky Mountains National Park or TVA projects. Once the applause stopped, the questions began. Several attendees expressed anger that the federal government used its power to rob hardworking Tennesseans of their land, heritage, and homeplace. He responded with no alarm and explained that "we moderns" cannot fully comprehend life in the region before the Great Smoky Mountains National Park and TVA, the same way that the generations before would not understand how we, the moderns, lived. The debate continued for a few more questions, but ended quietly with casual conversations while snacking on fruit and cheese. The importance of the contested memory of those removals, however, stuck with me, and over the years I witnessed emotional reactions from descendants to the loss of family lands at the hands of the federal government.

I left East Tennessee in fall 2007 for Southwest Virginia. In the decade that followed, I frequently encountered the unaddressed theme of loss in my research, reading, and editing. As I reviewed article and book manuscripts focused on TVA, I consistently suggested that the authors discuss what was lost in the TVA's processes and programs. No authors accepted my challenge. In 2011, I attended a presentation by Virginia Tech professor of English Katrina M. Powell about the difficult removals of families for the creation of the Shenandoah National Park in the 1930s. Her focus on the challenges of displacement spoke directly to the theme of loss, and she was eager to write more on the topic. A few years later, I discovered a master's thesis focused on the "Road to Nowhere" controversy in Western North Carolina. I approached the author, Matthew Chisholm, about developing a shorter article for a journal that I edit, *The Journal of East Tennessee History*. Following that article, I asked if he had more to say about the removal of residents on the North Shore of Fontana Lake. He agreed.

By 2018, I assembled a group of scholars to write about the issue of loss in the Appalachian South by exploring specific federal relocation projects of the 1920s through the 1960s. Their chapters describe examples from the mountains of Southwest Virginia, Western North Carolina, East Tennessee, Western Kentucky, and Northwestern South Carolina. The authors grapple with questions about regional development, the importance of Appalachian culture in the face of change, the power of the federal government, and how the process of displacement created loss and gains throughout the region. Each author has spent perhaps more hours in libraries and archives than in the natural spaces they describe, and a few of them have family connections to the places redefined by removal.

I must first thank my all-star lineup for their willingness and patience with me to present this story. I pledged to let them write in the directions they wanted to, and I kept my red pen mostly capped. As one result, the chapters vary in length and approach, but collectively they tell the larger story of loss during a significant period of transition for the region. The contributors quickly tuned in to my vision for the volume, which made it much easier to get buy-in from Scot Danforth at the University of Tennessee Press. As usual, Scot provided feedback and ongoing support. He read my first outline for this project and recognized the need for this book. The external reviewers also suggested directions into the importance of changing memory and the use of oral histories to tell varied perspectives. Finally, I must thank my family—Laura, Sam, and Caroline. They gave me the time I needed to shape this project; without their support this would have never come to fruition. I dedicate this book to them.

Abbreviations

ALCOA	Aluminum Company of America
APC	Appalachian Power Company
ARC	Appalachian Regional Commission
CCC	Civilian Conservation Corps
DOI	Department of the Interior
FPC	Federal Power Commission
GSMNP	Great Smoky Mountains National Park
KNPC	Kentucky National Park Commission
MCNPA	Mammoth Cave National Park Association
MED	Manhattan Engineer District
NARA	National Archives and Records Administration
NCNR	National Committee for the New River
NPS	National Park Service
SANPC	Southern Appalachian National Park Commission
TVA	Tennessee Valley Authority
WPA	Works Progress Administration

Introduction
The Permanent Enjoyment of the Past

AARON D. PURCELL

On September 2, 1940, President Franklin D. Roosevelt addressed a crowd of hundreds of spectators at the Rockefeller Monument high atop Newfound Gap. His purpose was to officially dedicate the Great Smoky Mountains National Park (GSMNP) "for the permanent enjoyment of the people."[1] The massive park included over a half-million acres of extraordinary biodiversity straddling Tennessee and North Carolina. From an elevation of over five thousand feet above sea level, Roosevelt announced: "Here in the Great Smokies, we have come together to dedicate these mountains, streams, and forests, to the service of the millions of American people." He explained the historical context and significance of the region by saying: "The old frontier, that put the hard fibre in the American spirit and the long muscles on the American backs, lives and will live in these untamed mountains to give to the future generations a sense of the land from which their forefathers hewed their homes." In essence, Roosevelt emphasized the importance of protecting fragile land and preserving a piece of the past for later generations to enjoy. The use of the word "permanent" in his speech emphasized an irreversible break with the past as well as the preservation of a specific past for the modern world.[2]

Roosevelt's speech, which was more focused on the dangers of fascist regimes in Europe, barely hinted at the challenges of creating the Great Smoky Mountains National Park. The vast expanse, which to many attendees sounded like an uncharted wilderness, had been inhabited for centuries, first by the Cherokee and then by white settlers. Beginning in 1928, the federal government in cooperation with state and local officials began the lengthy process of removing hundreds of families from their property and communities in order to create the park. Displacement created a variety of challenges for mountain families. For many, leaving the old homeplace represented various forms of loss, not just in terms of land and houses, but the destruction of communities and familial networks. As Roosevelt predicted, their sacrifice of property and place brought enjoyment to the millions of visitors who followed, but at the time it was unclear whether the new park was truly meant for the removed or their descendants.

The Whaleys from the Greenbrier area were just one of many families removed to create the Great Smoky Mountains National Park. Local lore about their removal experience makes the plight of the Whaley family unique. According to the oral narrative, the family left its Greenbrier property sometime in the late 1920s and used their settlement money to purchase or perhaps rent farmland just north of Knoxville, in either Anderson or Union County. Their dreams of farming in the Clinch River Basin ended in the early 1930s with the announcement of the building of Norris Dam, which required the removal of approximately thirty-five hundred families. Thus, the Whaley family experienced a second removal, this time by the Tennessee Valley Authority (TVA).[3]

As the story goes, the Whaleys relinquished their property in the Norris Basin and moved to farmland further southwest in either Anderson or Roane County. That dream also ended. In the early 1940s, the Army Corps of Engineers acquired thousands of acres for a top secret endeavor, which would later be known as the Manhattan Project, and ultimately as the "secret city" of Oak Ridge. The Army Corps moved quickly with their removal process, sometimes giving families only two weeks to vacate. In the process, the Whaleys and hundreds of other families were forced to surrender their property. Following the third removal, the Whaley family returned to the Pigeon Forge area just on the edge of the Great Smoky Mountains National Park.[4]

The story of the Whaley family's triple removal at the hands of the federal government is perhaps more legend than truth.[5] Oral histories and stories passed down through generations abound with tales of removal of the same East Tennessee family more than once during this period. Even if exaggerated, embellished, or fabricated, the real value of the Whaley family's story is that what may have happened represented the worst aspects of removal and the human costs of regional change. The Whaley family experienced a constant state of sudden change, and their story indicates the scale of loss across the Appalachian South that began in the 1920s and continued for several decades.

President Franklin D. Roosevelt at Newfound Gap, dedicating the Great Smoky Mountains National Park, September 2, 1940. "Franklin D. Roosevelt, Newfound Gap," by Thompson Brothers, Thompson Brothers Commercial Photographers, Calvin M. McClung Historical Collection, East Tennessee History Center, Knoxville.

The saga of the Whaley family connects well with the groundbreaking work of oral historian Alessandro Portelli. In *The Death of Luigi Trastulli and Other Stories* (1991), Portelli identified three main points about oral histories: they contrast with written sources, they change over time and take on new meaning, and they contribute to the formation of memory.[6] Similarly, the sense of loss due to a forced relocation changes because of time, memory, and the creation of new sources. In the case of federal removals that physically separated families from their land, oral history became one of the few ways to return to spaces now lost to time or submerged by shimmering lakes. As an example of this changing narrative, government relocation workers provided ample evidence that most residents were happy to move, but many later oral history interviews with those removed suggested a deep sense of regret and loss when they left their homeplace. Further, interviews with the descendants of removed families demonstrated that the removal story changed over time, and that those descendants created a mythology about a way of life that they never experienced. This creation of memory allowed later generations to express their loss, which centered on broken promises and separation from their buried ancestors. Over time, the Whaleys' epic story became amplified to near mythic proportions and holds enormous power and value to help analyze the theme of loss.

The Whaley family represented the memory of—or an idealized traditional way of—mountain life that by the 1920s had been forced to change. From old to new, from traditional to modern—these are the pathways of change. Whether cultural, social, economic, or political, change takes time and transition. Sudden change is the most difficult. When change directly affects people, institutions, or communities there is a period of panic, denial, and resistance before acceptance. Some may never fully accept the change, while others embrace it quickly and move on with their lives. Other types of change, such as environmental and cultural changes, are less obvious or take much longer to manifest. Change creates both positive and negative memories for those directly affected. Such memories are not static. Memories of both real and imagined events become part of the historical narrative. Later generations not directly affected by the initial change often adopt and then adapt that narrative to construct different memories. Many of these narratives focus on what was lost, instead of gained, in the process of transition from old to new, from traditional to modern.

The sense of loss due to significant and rapid change is a striking part of the history of the Appalachian South, especially during the mid-twentieth century. From the 1920s through the 1960s, the federal government sponsored an unprecedented number of removal and relocation projects. With limited opposition from those directly affected, the government claimed thousands of acres of privately held land in the mountains of Southwest Virginia, East Tennessee, Western Kentucky, Western North Carolina, and Northwestern South Carolina to create now beloved public spaces like the Great Smoky Mountains National Park and Mammoth Cave National Park. Other spaces were claimed for government needs such as electric power production and top secret research. The purposes behind these projects were as complex as the projects themselves—provide flood control, support the war effort during the early 1940s, employ thousands of workers, generate electricity, eradicate malaria, protect fragile ecosystems, promote tourism, stimulate economic growth, and even build the components of the first nuclear weapons. From a regional perspective, federal removal projects were intended to revitalize and modernize an area long affected by poverty, limited opportunities, and environmental destruction. These incursions swept thousands of families from their property and created preserved areas for recreation, motor tours, government research, camping, and other public or shared uses. Although the projects differed, many of the results, including the creation of new communities and shared natural spaces with limited occupants, were the same.

Federal removal projects had the joint objective of attempting to improve the lives of those relocated and to preserve the physical spaces as cultural reminders of a past with little if any evidence of the removed inhabitants. The extent of this near-paternalism and preservation varied with each project, leaving later generations, especially from the descendants of those affected by the removals, to question the benefits. A new, more sentimental, narrative about living in Appalachia during a "simpler and better time" emerged just as postwar cynicism toward the federal government spiked. The growth of the environmental movement, as well as the backlash against the environmental movement, heightened the debate over whom the reclaimed lands were for. For some of the projects, the federal government created spaces that did not have the long-lasting benefits for nearby communities, or they simply failed to keep their promises. As a result, in many mountain counties the large amount of land owned by the federal government decimated the tax base and created new pockets of poverty. Other projects that uprooted residents resulted in millions of annual tourist dollars to once struggling communities, but often only service-based jobs remained in the communities while the millions flowed to outside investors.

Loss is a reoccurring theme when studying any of the government-sponsored removal projects in the Appalachian South during the mid-twentieth century. By creating national parks, scientific laboratories, protected forests, wilderness areas, and watershed-control systems, the federal government took much more than land. Some would argue that the removals created a loss of Appalachian culture and even threatened personal independence. Those removed from their land had the most obvious initial loss. These Appalachians were not a monolithic group; rather they were quite diverse and scattered in many directions following removal. The majority were farmers, both Black and white. They owned homes and significant property, worked for their families, rented land, were sharecroppers, or in some cases were squatters, but all faced a significant challenge to their way of life. Some of those directly affected also received many of the benefits of federal intervention, especially when compared to other nearby regions which did not have large-scale removal projects, while others suffered. Thus, the losses and the potential gains that occurred afterward help to get closer to answering the question of whether the losses of these removals were worth the benefits.

Scholars in the humanities and social sciences have discussed the significance of federal removals by examining specific projects and communities. Durwood Dunn's *Cades Cove* (1988) was one of the landmark books in this genre. Dunn analyzed the historical development of a small mountain community and how the creation of the Great Smoky Mountains National Park led to the removal of the residents, many of whom resisted the process. Most importantly he traced the conscious effort to preserve the look and feel of the community, minus the residents, for millions of tourists to view from the confines of their automobiles. Ron Foresta's *The Land Between the Lakes* (2013) told a somewhat opposite story of how government planners designed a massive recreational space in Western Kentucky and West Tennessee which intentionally contained little if any historical traces of past inhabitants. Foresta explained that a majority of the residents were happy to leave their property to make way for the public recreation area. Most strikingly, only small numbers of tourists, and their wallets, followed the siren's song to the park. The most popular parts of the park were in fact the few areas that had structures of evidence of past historical occupation. The government's many promises of economic growth never materialized, and the Land Between the Lakes project ultimately created a protected public space that was difficult to manage and sustain.[7]

Other scholars mentioned the significance of removals from an environmental and conservation-history perspective. In *Blue Ridge Commons* (2012), Kathryn Newfont discussed how the US Forest Service removed families to create a network of protected forests in the eastern mountains. The study focused on the role of activists in preventing both private development and government seizure of property. She portrayed the residents who faced removal as stewards of the land who viewed federal protection of land as both elitist and environmentally irresponsible. Sara M. Gregg's *Managing the Mountains* (2010) took an even broader view of how New Deal programs approached conservation in the Blue Ridge Mountains of Virginia and the Green Mountains of Vermont. The book explained that, during the 1930s, the federal government attempted to return the eastern mountains into a primeval forest through excessive land acquisition. By carrying out this vision of conservation, sometimes known as "greenwashing," the federal government displaced thousands of families and took their farms out of production. Similar to Newfont, Gregg argued that mountain residents opposed government land-use policies and spoke out against the type of recreational forest commons that followed.[8]

These sources are part of a growing body of scholarly literature on federal removal projects in the Appalachian South. Absent from these studies, however, is a deep discussion of the loss associated with regional removal initiatives. The closest analysis of loss was in Michael J. McDonald and John Muldowny's *TVA and the Dispossessed* (1982). This data-heavy book explored the displacement of thirty-five hundred families in the Norris Basin by TVA during the early 1930s. Their focus was TVA's haphazard process of removal and the infant agency's short-lived efforts to assist with relocation of those affected. The authors argued that the majority of the removed families recognized the advantages of leaving their homeplace, but for most relocation created a remembered connection to older cultural values associated with a poorer, hard way of life. Their book demonstrated that certain types of loss occurred because of the building of Norris Dam, but the authors were more focused on TVA's removal processes and determining success of the agency's initiatives.[9]

As a remedy to this significant omission in the historical literature on modern Appalachian history, this book is focused on the theme of loss during a rapid period of transition. It examines a group of specific removal projects either led or sponsored by the federal government in the Appalachian South during the mid-twentieth century. Through agencies such as the Tennessee Valley Authority and the National Park Service, the federal government reshaped the landscape and land-use patterns of many areas of this mountainous region. These projects all represented some attempt at improvement and perhaps economic and social renewal. The initial challenge, however, was actually removing the occupants to start the process. While many of those slated for removal helped prepare the spaces for future generations of tourists or campers, they were not necessarily the intended audience for what would be created. The preservation of the spaces and what was lost in the process inform the larger narrative about Appalachian culture, how it was presented, received, and remembered.

The concept of loss unifies a diverse range of federal relocation projects in the Appalachian South and has modern-day relevance. Removal created a severed past for those directly affected. Just as important, the descendants of the removed often created an imagined past of removal based on a loss of place, culture, and heritage. This intersection of historical memory and change is best explored through the theme of loss. The decades-old choices of policy makers, politicians, and community leaders often define the history and potential of post-removal sites, communities, and the descendants of those removed.

Each of the following chapters focuses on a specific removal project. The removal sites include the Great Smoky Mountains National Park in Tennessee and North Carolina, the Norris Dam and Basin in East Tennessee, the Shenandoah National Park in Virginia, Mammoth Cave National Park in Western Kentucky, Oak Ridge National Laboratories in East Tennessee, the Fontana Dam and Lake in Western North Carolina, and the Keowee-Toxaway hydroelectric project in the mountains of Northwestern South Carolina. A final chapter on the significance of memory and loss ties together all of the related removal projects throughout the mountains of the Appalachian South. The chapters, however, are not designed to be definitive histories of removal at each location. Instead, they look at the theme of loss before, during, and after the removals took place. Further, the focus is on the people and families dislocated and not the resistance to removal through legal challenges.

The authors are demonstrated experts on specific removal projects. Their chapters review the spaces and culture before removal, the people affected, the removal process, short-term achievements, what long-term promises came to fruition, memory of the removals and pre-removals, and the overall assessment of what was gained and what was lost. In many cases, the stories continue until present day with descendants of the removed returning to a homeplace, either real or imaginary, that they never knew. These created memories shaped a different narrative of Appalachia and contribute to the modern identity of the region and its people.

▲▲

This book is focused on the twentieth century, but it would be a significant oversight for a study of removals and loss in the Appalachian South not to mention the forceable removal of Native Americans in the nineteenth century. In many ways the history of federal removals in this region begins with the Cherokee Removal. Throughout the early nineteenth century, white politicians, speculators, and settlers in search of inexpensive land urged new western settlement into vast territories occupied by Native Americans. Discovery of gold in the Georgia mountains in the late 1820s accelerated efforts to dislodge the residents of the Cherokee Nation from their ancestral homeland in the eastern mountains. In the early 1830s, President Andrew Jackson pushed for the removal of the Cherokee from the Eastern United States to make way for white settlement. The controversial Treaty of New Echota (1835) promised $5 million to the Cherokee Nation in exchange for abandoning their lands east of the Mississippi River. Jackson's efforts to remove the Cherokee Nation came to fruition in 1838. Several thousand Cherokee died during the forced Trail of Tears march to Oklahoma. Not all of the Cherokee left the mountains in the nineteenth century. Those who remained later organized the Eastern Band of the Cherokee in Western North Carolina.[10]

The Cherokee Removal represented an early precedent of forcible removal by the federal government. It also paved the way for white settlers to occupy newly available lands, many of them modest farmers who then put down deep roots. Treaties and legislation are used to enact removals or annex lands, but the power of federal and state governments to relocate landowners is grounded in the final clause of the Fifth Amendment of the US Constitution. The Fifth Amendment guarantees personal protections and most famously connects citizens to their rights of life, liberty, and property. The final portion of the Fifth Amendment, known as the "takings clause," states: "nor shall private property be taken for public use without just compensation." Thus, while the Fifth Amendment protects individuals' property, it also acknowledges the principal of eminent domain, which allows state and federal governments to take private property for public use with the qualification that the owner be compensated accordingly.[11]

Eminent domain is used for a variety of public purposes—building a highway, a city park, a railroad spur, a power plant, or a reservoir. Sometimes public and individual opposition to a proposed project and the taking of land is effective, especially when groups have resources to legally challenge the project or offer a more agreeable solution. Other times, the individual or communities affected are unable to reverse the decision and a project proceeds.

The process by which government entities acquire land from private landowners and determine compensation is known as condemnation (not to be confused with condemning a structure) or appropriation. During the condemnation process, affected residents and communities may reject the compensation offer, counter with a higher asking price for their land, challenge the information collected about their property, or file other lawsuits. Such opposition can slow down removal projects for years if not decades. In the majority of cases, however, condemnation proceedings result in the transfer of property from private individuals to federal, state, or city governments.

During the twentieth century, politicians and business leaders expanded the intent of eminent domain from "public use" to "public good." A common abuse of eminent domain is the use of government authority for private business interests. For example, during the second half of the twentieth century, many city leaders invested in downtown or riverfront revitalization projects. Such efforts were designed to bring more residents and tourists into the city center outside of regular business hours. Thus, business owners and developers recognized the economic potential of these projects and argued that the general public benefited from seizure of private property. Often, the communities most affected, especially with interstate highway construction, were people of color. The passage of restrictive zoning laws were yet another way to reclassify private property for public use. In many cases, the affected residents had minimal resources to oppose the projects or legally challenge the taking of their property through eminent domain. In the process, even the most successful urban revitalization projects severed or destroyed existing communities which previously occupied those spaces.[12]

Federal agencies such as TVA have specific powers related to eminent domain. The *United States Code* gives TVA and other federal agencies like the National Park Service the power of eminent domain and the acquisition of real estate through condemnation proceedings. Specifically, it gives TVA the "power to acquire real estate for the construction of dams, reservoirs, transmission lines, power houses, and other structures, and navigation projects at any point along the Tennessee River, or any of its tributaries." Further, if landowners do not comply and refuse to sell for a reasonable price, then TVA can initiate condemnation proceedings to purchase the land. This broad set of powers allowed TVA to move quickly in the 1930s and 1940s to complete a massive water control system along the Tennessee River watershed.[13]

Another interpretation of eminent domain is that "public use" can be applied to the "public enjoyment" of natural or historic areas. President Roosevelt's sentiments in 1940 that the Great Smoky Mountains should be protected and shared with all Americans echoed that sense of public good, even if families and communities had to be uprooted as part of the process. Much of the government's interest in protecting the natural environment and cultural heritage sites began with FDR's cousin President Theodore Roosevelt. The elder Roosevelt took a leading role in the conservation movement of the early twentieth century. During his presidency, 1901–9, Roosevelt established the US Forest Service, worked to establish or expand six national parks, created 150 national forests, and signed the Act for the Preservation of American Antiquities, which gave the president the power to create "national monuments." It total, Roosevelt approved legislation that protected approximately 230 million acres of public land.[14]

In the two decades that followed Theodore Roosevelt's "green revolution," federal politicians made larger efforts to protect natural spaces from development. In 1916, President Woodrow Wilson established the National Park Service to help manage a growing number of designated national parks and national monuments. In 1933, after only a few months in the White House, President Franklin Roosevelt centralized all national parks and monuments under the jurisdiction of the Park Service. That action resulted in the Park Service managing sixty-four individual sites.[15]

While his cousin Teddy gets the most credit for spurring the conservation movement, there is clear evidence that Franklin Roosevelt made preservation of natural spaces a top priority. In *Rightful Heritage: Franklin D. Roosevelt and the Land of America* (2016), Douglas Brinkley demonstrated Roosevelt's commitment to conservation. He argued that Roosevelt accelerated the use of eminent domain to protect the land from private use and preserve it for public enjoyment. During his presidency, 1933–45, Roosevelt established or modified 115 national forests, created eight national parks, established twenty national monuments, and created 140 national wildlife refuges. While a majority of the protected spaces were located in the West, many of Roosevelt's New Deal programs were focused on poverty-stricken areas in the southern mountains. His regional development and water control projects were yet another type of conservation, which resulted in millions of privately held acres claimed for the public to use, to benefit from, and enjoy.[16]

During the 1940 dedication ceremony at Newfound Gap, Roosevelt pledged to make natural areas available to future generations. The Great Smoky Mountains National Park, Shenandoah National Park, and other projects described in this book attract millions of visitors each year. These sites celebrate a specific past which minimizes the importance of the previous occupants of the land. Many of the displaced families were the "common man" that Roosevelt's New Dealers were trying to help. In the decades that followed, regional development was tied to water control projects or federal control of endangered natural spaces.[17]

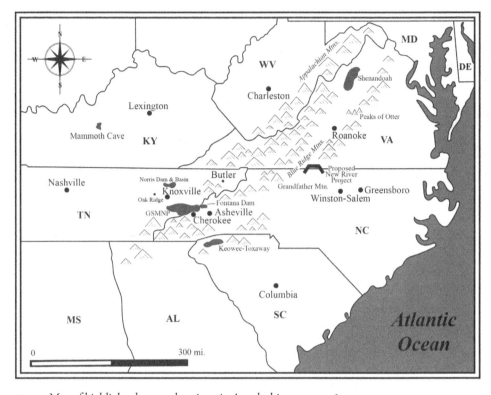

MAP 1. Map of highlighted removal projects in Appalachia, 1920s–1960s.

This trend of federally sponsored regional development was especially common in the Appalachian South, where a series of removal projects from the 1920s through the 1960s displaced thousands of families, erased their local communities, and ignored their culture. These families gave up their land for the promises of a better future, a better farm, or for the prospect that one day their children and grandchildren might enjoy natural spaces and the benefits of a more modern world. Those coordinating the removals often accused the affected families of being unwilling to move because of a fear of progress. Further, the administrators of removal believed that removals were a necessary price to pay for progress. Today, however, the managers of these protected spaces are reinterpreting and recognizing the past occupants of the land. This acknowledgment connects to the purpose, and title, of this book—to better understand what was lost in the transition of small mountain communities to publicly shared and federally controlled natural spaces that define the region.

The image on the cover of the book reflects the intersection of traditional and modern, as well as the hubris of many federal removal projects in the Appalachian South. In the late 1930s or early 1940s, a government photographer set out to document how TVA's electrical power program was transforming the region. The setting was a traditional cabin on a farm most likely in Tennessee. Pictured in the distance was a farmer in overalls and a group of well dressed women (perhaps visitors from a nearby town or church congregation) investigating the landscape. In the foreground, a young woman in a white dress, with her back turned to the camera, stares at a young barefoot boy in overalls playing with puppy on the front porch of the cabin. The young boy ignores her glaze and stares down the photographer with a look of disdain, distrust, and bewilderment. The photographer, however, was not concerned with the people or rural landscape. Instead their focus was capturing the electric powerlines, massive transmission tower (which was built extraordinarily close to the cabin), and electric power meter on the side of the cabin. TVA believed that electricity would modernize the region. The lengthy caption for the image summarized the goal of electrification:

> General planning. This photograph is included in the series as a vivid document on the impingement of the Twentieth Century technology upon the neglected and backward rural scene. The meter on the wall of the rural shack indicates that is now receives its share of electricity from the power carried overland by the huge TVA (Tennessee Valley Authority) transmission line. TVA program must resolve the conflict between modern and ancient ways of life so that individuals, similar to those which are show in the picture, will be benefited.[18]

The cover image is a visual representation of both transition and what was lost during the process.

The chapters that follow describe a range of removal projects across five states united by loss, geography, and memory. The authors take different paths to get to the issue of loss in Appalachia, but their main focus is on the people who were removed. Related removal processes, such as reinterment, archaeological investigations, road and railway rerouting, dam construction, and reservoir clearance are included as a secondary part of the story. Similarly, the political aspects of each project are mentioned, but only as context for how those decisions affected the removal of families.

The journey is somewhat chronological and begins with Margaret Lynn Brown's analysis of loss due to the creation and expansion of the Great Smoky Mountains National Park. Part wilderness conservation project and part tourist trap, the GSMNP became a model for how government officials and business owners collaborated to create an enormous protected space occupied by only a handful of permanent residents. Brown discusses the different removal experiences in Cades Cove and along the North Shore of Fontana Lake.

The second chapter, by Aaron D. Purcell, looks at removals in the Norris Basin during the mid-1930s. Building Norris Dam was the Tennessee Valley Authority's first major project, which included the displacement of approximately thirty-five hundred families. The chapter discusses the agency's removal process, what losses occurred because of removal, and how vanished communities such as Loyston are remembered. It also explains how the constructed memory of such lost places have become a permanent part of the history of TVA and the Appalachian South.

Chapter 3 explores the creation of the Shenandoah National Park in the Blue Ridge Mountains of Virginia. Katrina M. Powell and Savannah Paige Murray explain how the federal government's conservation approach conflicted with pre-removal land-use patterns and the tradition of environmental stewardship. They also address a later example of residents in the New River Valley in Virginia, who through effective activism successfully halted efforts by the Army Corps of Engineers to further develop the waterway.

The following chapter also has a focus on local opposition and land-use patterns. In chapter 4, Alyssa D. Warrick describes the creation of Mammoth Cave National Park in Western Kentucky. While many might not think of these natural wonders as part of the Appalachian South, the Mammoth Cave region aligns well with the economic and cultural realities of the other projects described in this volume. Further, the Appalachian Regional Commission identifies Edmonson and Hart counties, two of the three counties that Mammoth Cave is part of, as part of the Appalachian Region.[19] Warrick argues that displacement to make way for the creation of Mammoth Cave National Park resulted in significant changes to the local economy, the natural environment, land-use patterns, and community networks. These changes brought an end to many facets of the local Appalachian culture.

Wartime needs of the early 1940s resulted in several removal projects in the region. In chapter 5, Russell Olwell examines the various layers of loss connected to the city of Oak Ridge, Tennessee. Wartime Oak Ridge was intentionally designed with racial segregation in housing and other parts of society. Those divisions continued after the war. Olwell explores the city's fractured history beginning with the pre-removal communities, its development as a Cold War outpost, and the current efforts to open up once restricted areas to tourists with an interest in the region's atomic past.

A complex TVA removal story is the focus of chapter 6. Matthew Chisholm chronicles the removal efforts for the building of Fontana Dam during World War II. He focuses on the various promises and deals made to construct a paved road to the past that ultimately went only seven miles and ended in disappointment. As with other removal stories, Chisholm explains that the memory of the physical community has enormous emotional power, even if the memories were imagined.

In chapter 7, Austin Gregory describes a later removal project in the mountains of South Carolina. The Keowee-Toxaway Project represented how a powerful private company, Duke Power, collaborated with government officials to greenlight a massive hydroelectric and nuclear project which displaced hundreds of families. He argues that, by the 1960s, powerful private interests had significant influence over government officials to promote removal initiatives in poverty-stricken areas.

The conclusion, by Stephen Wallace Taylor, is focused on the significance of memory and removal in the Appalachian South. He ties together the common themes of removal projects in the region and offers observations on how those affected and their descendants remembered the actual losses. Taylor explains that many times those memories have been adapted and reimagined to tell a far different story of life before removal.

The selected removal projects in this book fall into two main categories, both of which were predicated on the removal, if not complete erasure, of the inhabitants of the spaces. The first category of removal projects focused on preserving existing natural spaces. Three of the described projects, the Great Smoky Mountains,

Shenandoah, and Mammoth Cave attained national park status, the gold standard of environmental protection for natural spaces. For national parks, the natural features of the landscape are the focus. As part of the process of preparing the spaces for visitors, the federal government sculpted the physical landscape with specific purposes in mind. In addition to preserving the natural spaces, the National Park Service wanted to create the experience of exploring a pristine wilderness with little traces of human occupation. Their main audience was middle-class tourists with cars and disposable income, which created a tourist-based economic model. Removing the people who occupied the natural spaces was a short-term challenge, and there was little if any interest by park designers to integrate the preexisting culture into the master plan. Only decades later did Park Service leaders change their perspective on recognizing the former occupants of federal lands.

The second category of removal projects focused on creating intentional natural spaces with obscured industrial purposes. The Norris Basin, Fontana Lake and its North Shore, and the lakes of the Keowee-Toxaway Project are intentional natural spaces created by planners and engineers. These spaces have multiple purposes, especially industrial uses such as electric power production and flood control. But these sites, which are often state parks or public lands, resemble the look and feel of national parks by emphasizing natural features and supporting recreational tourism. These sites were designed to draw middle-class tourists to a more controlled natural experience with restrictions on certain types of use. Such designed natural spaces were often more exclusive, and in some cases the managers permitted private development and land ownership. Removing inhabitants from these sites was a priority and an uneven process because elements of the pre-removal culture was not part of the "new" multipurpose landscape.

The Oak Ridge community which supported the Manhattan Project combines aspects of both categories of removal projects. Similar to projects in the second category, Oak Ridge was an intentional community molded from a rural setting. Oak Ridge was an industrial site to support the work of atomic research and development of a nuclear weapon, so planners were less concerned about whom they were removing and had few long-term objectives for how the space would be accessible to later generations and how it would look. In 2015, however, Oak Ridge joined Los Alamos in New Mexico and Hanford in Washington as part of the Manhattan Project National Historical Site, managed by the National Park Service and the Department of Energy. With that designation, Oak Ridge represents a removal project that emphasizes a preexisting environment (the historic scientific research buildings), even though that industrial environment was built by humans.

Further, efforts to detoxify the natural environment after decades of contamination indicate efforts to return the landscape to a natural environment. Like many national historic sites, portions of Oak Ridge will have no evidence of any layer of human habitation. Exactly how tourists will experience the built environment of atomic research facilities has yet to be determined, but with the recently opened K-25 Interpretative Center there is better acknowledgment of the communities displaced nearly eight decades ago.[20]

In hindsight, it is easy to assume that federal removal projects in the Appalachian South were connected and carried out in a similar way. The resulting projects across the region were complimentary in supporting recreation, tourism, and perhaps environmental protection, but the removal practices and policies varied by project and agency. Federal agencies worked together to prepare spaces for new purposes, but often they invented or adapted their own policies and practices for removal because of the uniqueness of each project. For example, TVA had a master plan for regional development through hydroelectric power development, flood control, and agricultural improvements. The agency worked with other federal entities to put that plan into action. With the Norris project in the early 1930s, TVA developed a detailed process to remove residents. However, by the time the agency prepared the North Shore for the Fontana Dam in the early 1940s, many of the removal practices used at Norris had been dropped or significantly adapted because of the different conditions at the location and the urgency of World War II. Removal efforts by the National Park Service for various projects were less coordinated, and often the removal process depended on local governments and private entities to complete the work. In the case of the Keowee-Toxaway Project, a private company partnered closely with local and state government to carry out the removal process. Even though there was overlap between projects and interplay between agencies, the uniqueness of each project made the creation and adaptation of policies and practices necessary.

These removal projects occurred separately, but they each shared common threads and outcomes. Despite the lack of coordination, each project shared a common purpose—to redesign natural spaces for the benefit of a region. The chapters describe the importance of the environment, the availability or lack of farmland, growing federal authority, the power of government to take private property for the "greater good," the erasure and creation of communities, the influence of private interests over public lands, opposition and resistance to sudden change, the complexities of preparing natural spaces for new purposes, the shadow of Native American occupation in many of the removal zones and their removal experience, and the desire of former residents and their descendants to connect with their deceased ancestors and lost homeplaces. For many of these removals, there are present-day efforts to recognize and memorialize the displaced people and lost communities.

As part of the removal process, many cultural elements were lost during the transition to a more modern region. This book is an assessment of who benefited the most from removal and why. It traces the complex narrative of how loss and memory of that loss changed over time. The chapters that follow are designed to bring into fuller focus whether the losses of removal were worth the gains.

1 Loss, Betrayal, and the Power of Stories

Healing Lost Communities in the Great Smoky Mountains

MARGARET LYNN BROWN

In his classic work, *Cades Cove: The Life and Death of an Appalachian Community 1818–1937* (1988), historian Durwood Dunn tells the story of the Oliver family, who came to Cades Cove in the Great Smoky Mountains as early as 1819. Although Dunn himself was a descendent, he described the mountain-farm world they created with the cool eye of an anthropologist. He recreated a rich heritage of independently controlled Baptist churches; an economy of cattle and hog production in Blount County, Tennessee; a folk culture that includes tall tales of panthers and bears; and the importance of family life to the 708 people who lived in the cove by 1900.[1]

Anyone who reads Dunn's book cannot help but empathize with the plight of John Oliver, the grandchild of that first pioneer family who a century later witnessed the death of his beloved Cades Cove by eminent domain. In the late 1920s, the states of North Carolina and Tennessee used their constitutional taking power to buy this valley to create a national park in the Great Smoky Mountains. Cades Cove became one of eighteen small communities and an estimated fifteen thousand people who were forced to leave their homes. Before the land was turned over to the federal government, Oliver fought the right of states to absorb private land for a national park in court. "Cades Cove is the most beautiful spot in the world, six miles long and three miles wide, level as a floor and very fertile," described one of Oliver's neighbors, G. Walter Gregory. "It is very productive and a farming district. Its people are very prosperous and happy and do not want to give up their homes for park purposes."[2] Gregory wrote to the philanthropist John D. Rockefeller Jr., in an effort to dissuade him from providing money for the land purchases. In the end, the North Carolina Park Commission paid twenty to thirty dollars per acre for farmland; Oliver (in Tennessee) was originally offered twenty dollars per acre.[3] Gregory expressed a palpable feeling of *loss* in the letter: "We most respectfully ask, beg, and implore you to request the park people to leave us outside the park area or you will withdraw the Rockefeller donation."[4]

John Oliver ran the Cades Cove Post Office, and he kept careful records of his small farm and tourist business as well as his church involvement and family genealogy. He assembled a good court case with multiple witnesses, but he could not fight the park boosters, who motivated Tennessee politicians with the belief that a national park would bring glory and tourism to Knoxville and their state. Oliver's actions show how the Cades Cove resident felt about this impending loss, but when the park became a reality he voiced something that might be closer to *betrayal:* "The state of Tennessee has been waging a most cruel, unjust unnecessary warfare against me for nearly seven years." He hoped the federal government, of which he was a faithful employee, would treat him better. Park rangers arrived in 1931 to begin management; the Civilian Conservation Corps (CCC) workers came a few years later to build trails, roads, and campgrounds; and Franklin D. Roosevelt dedicated the Great Smoky Mountains National Park in 1940. "Now in the evening of my life and in the winding up of this great Sacrifice in giving up our much loved homes I ask no special favors, but only wish to be treated as my neighbors have been. I want to suffer with them and I want to rejoice with them." Like many of the former residents of the park, Oliver rented back some of his own farmland and lived in Cades Cove as a lessee. He finally moved from his beloved Cove on Christmas Day 1937.[5]

Today, Cades Cove has become one of the most beloved valleys in one of the most heavily visited national parks in the United States. At present, the Great Smoky Mountains National Park fuels the economy of Blount, Cocke, and particularly Sevier County, Tennessee. The park attracts multiple businesses to Sevier County, including Dolly Parton's theme park, Dollywood, and the county claims to make $2 billion in tourism, almost twice that of the nearby urban area, Knoxville. A study released by the National Park Service estimated that 11.4 million visitors annually spend $953 million in communities near the park, which results in 13,737 jobs. Not only does Dollywood celebrate mountain living, but in 2006 Townsend, Tennessee, opened a Mountain Heritage Center in the same county as Cades Cove. The new facility, which is part museum and part event center, brings more visitors to the valley and celebrates the Smokies' mountain heritage. In addition, the Park Service operates six visitor centers, which of course provide restrooms, directions, and natural history, but also include the human story. This kind of celebration of history as well as job opportunities and general prosperity make a difference in how those who were displaced feel about the sacrifice they made; however, it is important not to confuse this kind of compensation with being "paid off."[6]

It is certainly *not* true that money will "soften the blow" if one suffers deep loss. For example, if a beloved parent dies, one feels grief no matter what the inheritance might be. What does make a difference is that the grief is publicly acknowledged, especially in the form of a ritual and storytelling (a funeral, obituary, and annual memorials); the wishes of the deceased for promised assets are accommodated (the will); the bereaved parties are fairly treated and promises kept (no maneuvering by relatives); and time allows for grief to run its course. Similarly, it appears that those former residents of the park who feel remembered, who were treated well by the park, and who were able to prosper as park promoters promised they would, have processed their loss most effectively. Notably, the East Tennesseans who have benefited from development and whose stories remain central to displays of mountain life, including restored farmhouses within the park, have found perspective on the past, whereas North Carolinians who have had less economic gain from the national park and fewer dollars to spend on heritage tourism, still express an almost unmediated "sting" about their ancestors' displacement.

It must be acknowledged here that no formal study has been completed of the diaspora of Smoky Mountain people, nor has the financial success of descendants been charted. Historians have looked closely at the treatment of the mountain people during the era of their removal. Communications professor Bruce J. Weaver and this author have looked at the rhetoric of the park promoters, elite citizens from Knoxville and Asheville, who portrayed them as ignorant and parochial. As Weaver notes, "Nowhere in the information produced by the campaign, however, is there any clear evidence that the leaders ever genuinely understood the problems raised by removing hundreds of people out of their homes."[7] After they were removed, the National Park Service restored a natural landscape with very little human history commemorated on it. Richard Starnes emphasized the loss of human history in the interpretation of the Great Smoky Mountains National Park by the National Park Service. "Their worlds were defined by kinship and community," he argued. "After the park's formation, the Smokies became a scripted place, where nature dominated the narrative and human history received selective attention."[8] Numerous historians have described bitterness toward the National Park Service in the early years of the park.

Considerable correspondence, oral histories, and studies of issues related to removal do exist. There is even a little evidence that some who left remote mountain areas found a *better* life. Some who were interviewed years later concluded that economic improvement, in particular access to doctors and higher education, allowed them to prosper. R. L. Noland migrated to the Shenandoah Valley in 1928 and developed a mixed-use mountain farm of milk cows, corn, hogs, beef cattle, and forestry. Two years later, he wrote his old neighbor in the Ravensford area to convince him to join him. He boasted of low taxes and low-priced land in Virginia. "I made last year 55 tons of hay on 24 acres. Also this is fine fruit section, so come down and see for yourself," he wrote.[9]

Others who left the hardscrabble mountain life for the city did not regret leaving behind the sunup-to-sundown work and listed "vacations" as a benefit gained by moving.[10] "Now my Daddy was one of the first ones that sold," Calvin Shields remembered. "The reason [was] he had four kids and one of them had done got his education. To get high school you had to come out [of Cades Cove] to Maryville and stay somewhere."[11]

Anecdotally, it appears that many people who left the Smokies stayed in the counties surrounding the national park. Linton Palmer, who left Cataloochee at age five, attested that "my memories come from other memories" and believed that the majority of Cataloochee residents ended up in Haywood County. The Palmers purchased land nearby in part so that they could also rent back their farm in Cataloochee and run two operations. "They loved it so well they stayed over there, but they had some member of the family or some relative that would live in the house and they would commute back and forth across the mountain by horse or wagon or vehicle." Until they left in 1938, the Palmers rented their old home in Cataloochee to tourists.[12]

The other thing that should be acknowledged here is that individuals vary tremendously in their ability to handle loss, to mediate change, to develop resilience. In 1989, I interviewed Zenith Whaley, whose family was removed from Greenbrier, and he said something I always remembered: "Some people will nurse a grudge to keep it alive." Remembering his childhood in Greenbrier, as he did on his porch that afternoon, had become a precious memory to him, and he did not wish to tarnish it with blame and regret. William Myers, a resident of Cades Cove, ran the Ekaneetlee Lodge for tourists long before a national park altered the economy toward tourism, and he even hosted at various times park promoters, including John D. Rockefeller Jr. Perhaps these connections gave him more time to adjust to the impending change, but Myers remained positive toward the Park Commission and the National Park Service in his correspondence. He did believe that people who were removed should get preference for employment by the Park Service: "I think the people who have sold their homes and those who live here should have the work for they need it." Myers, like Oliver and others, wanted to retain his life and connections as long as possible. A reply from David Chapman, head of the Great Smoky Mountains National Park Conservation Association, said that he will do what he can for Myers.[13]

Just as some individuals can be more accepting of change and loss than others, others reacted to loss with anger, outrage, and even violence. In the early 1930s, fire became commonplace. Although historians and scientists alike tend to associate forest fires with weather and the tremendous logging that took place in the early twentieth century, a study of the Smokies from 1931 to 1988 showed that spiteful people played a major role in fire starting. A full 41 percent of all incendiary fires in the Smokies occurred in the early days of the national park. Some former residents "felt cheated and bullied by park organizers," did not want to leave, and were unhappy with the prices they received for their land. They hated the loss of their lifestyle, which included hunting, fishing, harvesting ginseng and galax, and cutting down trees for housing and firewood. Of these activities, only recreational fishing could be permitted in the new national park. "As the park took shape, many rangers dreaded duty assignments in areas where relocated families lived in proximity to the park because there was such open hatred," stated scholar John Hays.[14] At times this hatred broke out into fire. Some of these fires were set to distract rangers from moonshine operations or hunting trips, and some also were retribution for new park regulations. "A hunter caught on park lands could have his rifle or fishing pole taken away, face a fine and possible federal court."[15] While this may not seem like a severe punishment to a modern person, as Hays pointed out, mountain men regarded their rifles as so personal an object that they sometimes named them. They knew the sound of their own gun miles away.

Significantly, Hays also found that, when the economy improved after World War II, incendiary fires decreased as well. Whereas there were 147 cases in those early years, between 1946 and 1973 there were only 46 cases. The postwar years brought a fourfold increase in service establishments in the areas surrounding the park, and visitation to the Smokies grew from one million visits in 1946 to ten million in 1988. So many gift shops, restaurants, and other amusements developed in the gateway cities that eventually a place like Gatlinburg, Tennessee, became a destination. Many visitors eventually came to see Gatlinburg and did not even drive into the park. "All this economic activity produced a notable decline in incendiary activity," Hays noted.[16] One might argue that the anger that produced it declined, too. There is a connection between economic benefits and the ability to process loss.

The age of residents at the time of removal—the variable of time—is more difficult to assess but must play a role in acceptance of loss. "I think my grandparents were about the last to leave [Cataloochee]," remembered Gladys Wright, whose father, Mark Hanna, worked for the National Park Service after his family left the valley. "They moved to Maggie Valley . . . but they didn't last long after they moved out of Cataloochee. They both died, one of them in 1942 and one in 1944. And they never were satisfied after they left Cataloochee."[17] From the other end of the age perspective, Lucille Beck, who lived in Smokemont until age four, believed "at that time it was a disaster." Interestingly, though, as an adult who had moved away, married, and prospered, she related the feeling of loss more closely with the economic hard times of the 1930s than the fact of displacement. "Because so many people were out of work, and they couldn't find any more work" during the Great Depression, removal seemed at first difficult. Interestingly, she later married a man who found employment in Smokemont with the Civilian Conservation Corps. Her oral history put loss in the past tense.[18]

Loss also relates to how the land is cared for and interpreted by the Park Service. William Eugene Lequire emphasized that, at the time of removal, his family mourned the well-developed farming community in Cades Cove. He described his father hauling out bales of hay, mules, milk cows, a pig, chickens, and "what furniture they had" in a Model T Ford truck over Rich Mountain Road. He felt comfortable with early Park Service interpretation of Cades Cove, which emphasized the pioneer valley and bucolic scenes with cattle grazing and maintained farms. As the Park Service moved in recent years toward ending the leases and allowing Cades Cove to return to native meadow plants and river cane, he expressed pain that his former homeplace will soon "look like any other wilderness," he stated. "[There will] not be much of any sign that any of us ever lived up there. That disturbs me."[19] On the other hand, since I first did my original research on the Great Smoky Mountains National Park, the park interpretation more openly discusses the removal of farm families in the Smokies. Park historians interviewed local residents, and they became the basis of articles in Great Smoky Mountains Natural History Association publications, and the Park Service–sponsored website which tells the story of removal in plain language and does not resort to stereotypes. Both Cades Cove and Oconaluftee visitors' centers host Pioneer Days to celebrate the skills of mountain living.

The park remains beloved for misty vistas, contact with wildlife, and what many people consider a wilderness. Inevitably, the removal of people and community structures to create these unobstructed views would break hearts. "They just couldn't adjust. I mean, that was their home," said Lucille Cooke, Gladys Wright's sister. "They had married and grown up there, and it was hard for them to give up that way of life."[20] It is difficult to discern how loss affected their father, Mark Hannah. In an oral history, Hannah told a remarkable story of dedication to the Cataloochee Valley. Prior to the park, Hannah thought he might take a job in the encroaching lumber camps. He walked over the mountain to take a job but found it was not for him. "Roughest place I've ever seen." He went home to farm but then faced removal for the future national park. An early park ranger, Hannah had to chase poachers and moonshiners that presumably had once been his neighbors. According to Gudger Palmer, whose father owned a store in Cataloochee, Hannah even had to destroy some of the old homeplaces. "[T]he orders came from headquarters in Gatlinburg that if he didn't get rid of those houses he would lose his job. So, they tore them down, burned them." No record exists about his feelings being put to this task. Did it heighten grief at the loss of his community? Or did it become a ritual that helped him complete the end of one world and the beginning of another?[21] In Mark Hannah's new life, he watched over an emptier Cataloochee Valley, raised his family, and even helped establish a one-room school for his daughters and the few other families that lived in the area.

Still, reoccurring folklore from oral histories describes unnamed persons who received a nominal price for land, and then while they were finding a new home and work the bank failed and wiped out their savings.[22] I have not found the details of a real case in which this happened, but that does not mean such a case does not exist. The fact that *the story* is repeated often, tells us something about the folklore or mythology of displacement. Folks believed that they had lost everything, because to them their family and community *were* everything. And folklore—the telling of stories that create meaning out of life—can be a legitimate way to deal with loss. Although she was a teenager when she had to move out of the Sugarlands area, Lucinda Ogle wrote about her childhood her entire life. She produced poems and short stories, published and performed, all of which were inspired by her early years in this community. Together they preserve a charming nostalgia for a freedom-loving childhood in the outdoors, though she only talked about removal in interviews and speeches. "We were quite bitter at the time," she said in her later years. "Now I am happy the park took our home places to preserve them [especially] when I see every inch of land outside the boundary being used to commercialize on." In another speech, she emphasized the comfortable lives and prosperity that came to local people through the development of the national park. "I sometimes think a higher power had been taking care of us. . . . [N]ow I think it would kill us to go back and live as we did then!"[23]

In 1900, the Noah Bud Ogle family lived in the Junglebrook area, on the Tennessee side of the Great Smoky Mountains National Park. Lucinda Ogle (fourth from the left on the front row) wrote a memoir about a childhood spent exploring the creeks and woods of the area. Because of her celebratory perspective, she became a popular speaker and spokesperson for those who had been removed. This is the family that lived at Junglebrook, ca. 1900, Negatives of the Great Smoky Mountains National Park, Great Smoky Mountains National Park.

Just as psychologists have noted the importance of ritual to overcoming grief, successful incorporation of loss for many former Smokies residents involves *remembering* through the southern ritual of Decoration Day. In what might be thought of as a precursor to Memorial Day, southerners for generations gathered during a Sunday in May to clean, mow, and decorate graves. According to scholars Alan Jabbour and Karen Singer, Decoration Day usually includes a procession of participants carrying flowers, followed by music and readings, and then the individual families disperse to tell stories and decorate individual graves. Everyone meets, in the end, for a dinner. Shirley Crisp, one of Jabbour's informants, explained that women and children mounded up the graves with dug-up grass and weeds and carefully arranged flowers. Men were responsible for mowing and cleaning. She recalled fried chicken, chicken and dumplings, green beans, and creamed corn at these dinners.[24] Jabbour and Singer called Decoration Day "collectively produced folk art" that shows how the participants value kinship and respect the deceased. Decoration Day also supports a "modest equality and inclusion," as every grave in the cemetery is decorated, even if no relative joins in the festivities. There is both individual freedom in how a grave is decorated and a reinforcement of the importance of community in the ritual. Participants "use the word beautiful to describe a decorated cemetery."[25]

At present, National Park Service records show some one hundred cemeteries within the Tennessee side of the park and eighty-four on the North Carolina side. (Twenty of the Tennessee cemeteries and eight of the North Carolina "cemeteries" include only one grave.)[26] The same records for 2019 indicate twenty-one annual Decoration Days, reunions, or Homecoming events at cemeteries—together, they incorporate every major valley of the Smokies. "The visitations to the cemeteries ... goes back into time immemorial, and it was something that you did," says Larry Vickery. "It was not questioned. You did it."[27] More than eighty years after the first park superintendent arrived, area residents feel obligated to continue the tradition, as Vickery claimed. All human beings deal with loss in their lives. However, this ritual of remembrance in the Appalachian South keeps the stories of the deceased and their hardships and their faith alive. In no place has Decoration Day been as lovingly observed as in the Fontana section of the Great Smoky Mountains National Park. On the far southwestern side of the Smokies in North Carolina, the Fontana communities have a different history, and, I would argue, this different history has led to a unique relationship with loss.

When World War II broke out in 1941, the Tennessee Valley Authority (TVA) pushed to build Fontana Dam to supply the power needs of the Aluminum

Decoration Day in the southern mountains was a common tradition as seen at Elkmont Cemetery in Sevier County during the early 1920s. Decoration Day still continues at many of the family cemeteries in the Great Smoky Mountains National Park, as a way for family to connect with their ancestors. Decoration day at Elkmont Cemetery, ca. 1920, Negatives of the Great Smoky Mountains National Park, Great Smoky Mountains National Park.

Company of America (ALCOA), which supplied the metal for aircraft. TVA also saw building Fontana Dam as an ideal way to bring economic opportunity to Swain County, North Carolina. The *Bryson City Times* and the *Jackson County Journal* depicted the dam as a great boon for the residents of the county. Project leaders hired 6,337 workers; a population greater than Swain County at the time. Community members in Fontana, Proctor, Bushnell, Judson, Almond, Stecoah, Brock, Tuckasegee, and Japan were visited by TVA caseworkers before the federal agency initiated land-condemnation proceedings. Only about 10 percent of Proctor, for instance, would be flooded, but the above-water lands would be cut off from Bryson City (twenty-five miles away), as the only road would be underwater. TVA engaged in a heavy purchase policy in order to make management of the land simple. Six residents challenged the taking power of TVA, but the US Supreme Court upheld the agency's takings power.[28] About 44,400 acres of land above the dam would be adjacent to the Great Smoky Mountains National Park, so TVA agreed to remove people from this area. The Department of Interior promised to construct a scenic road around the edge of the lake, which would grant the former residents access to cemeteries as well as aid tourism in North Carolina at some time in the future.[29]

This second diaspora appeared at first to be less eventful. North Shore residents seemed to accept the changes, and they went about their lives, finding jobs and raising children in other places. However, when environmentalists proposed giving a portion of the Great Smoky Mountains wilderness designation in the 1970s—a designation that park management saw as simpler and less expensive for remote areas—the former North Shore residents organized against it. The lack of a scenic road or a commitment to economic development at the southwest entrance was revealed as a sore point, and the pain and loss the issue touched would last the rest of the century. By the 1980s, more than a hundred Swain County residents whose ancestors rested in a cemetery within the former site of Proctor were ferried across Fontana Lake for Decoration Day. Local resident Helen Vance became president of the North Shore Cemetery Association, which soon attracted as many as seven hundred members and published a lively newsletter. The newsletter contained not only updates about the wilderness issue and the lack of a road (with addresses of congressmen for recipients to contact), it included schedules of Homecoming and Decoration Day celebrations, obituaries, recipes, photographs, poetry, and other writing:

> There was many things on Hazel Creek that we enjoyed.
> But then one day along came a gang called T.V.A.
> And our homes and land they destroyed.

And they forced all the people to move away.
We didn't have a lot of money or wealth.
But we cared for each other when we needed help.
But then came a time we all had to part.
And so many went away with a broken hearth. . . .
—Myrtle L. Laney, 1984[30]

Misunderstandings between environmentalists, who did not want to see more of the park developed, and the North Shore descendants continued to polarize in the succeeding years. "Every time I mention having something [like a scenic road]," Vance insisted, environmental groups claim that North Shore residents wanted development within the park, such as fast-food restaurants. "But we know they're not going to build anything on that road. We know that. The park's not going to let anything be built in the park. But they'll bring it up at every meeting." She emphasized that she and others who oppose wilderness designation do not want the land to change into a commercial district. "We don't want that to happen. None of us. And so we just want access and that's what we're asking for and that's all we're asking for."[31] Although the Park Service provides access across the lake by boat, this did not satisfy many of those involved with the North Shore Cemetery Association. They wanted a road built. Decoration Day became a rallying point for the cause.

In an article written by Ruth Chandler, the importance of Decoration Day is well described. "We went back!" She exclaims in the Cemetery Association newsletter. "Some two hundred of us made the nostalgic journey to Bone Valley and Hazel Creek on June 29th, to the graves of our kindred and friends." She described vans, Jeeps, trailers, and trucks provided by the Park Service; a short ceremony; and then a walk down the hill for lunch at the Coeburn Place, where the Park Service employees set up tables for rest and lunch. Despite this government care for remembrance—and the fact that the Park Service was not the only government agency responsible for this removal—she concluded: "It takes all the joy out of the trip, knowing we are being treated like the Indians were. Our Congressmen seem to be ruled by a group who know nothing and cares less about our feelings for our homeplaces and our heritage." The main concern expressed by writers in the North Shore Cemetery publication continued to be a road, connected to the 1943 agreement.[32] Because they attached a feeling of betrayal to the loss of a road and a proposed return to wilderness, those who lost land to TVA on the North Shore, and their descendants, expressed more and more anger as time went by. How the past is remembered—or not—matters to those who have suffered loss.

The highwater mark of their outrage seems to have been the 1980s and 1990s. "I wonder how those who oppose us would feel if they found markers at the head of their loved ones, rooted out of the ground?" North Shore Cemetery newsletter reporters also described the ugliness around the reservoir. "The lake will fall lower and lower. The eroded banks will become more ugly as the winter comes on. The wild hogs will take over in the cemeteries."[33] For these interviewees, a reservoir was not beautiful, and they complained bitterly about the inability to find and decorate cemeteries.

Not all of those displaced from the North Shore remained angry. Some of them express something more like the kind of nostalgia that Lucinda Ogle captured so well. "How my heart rejoices to go back in memory to those beautiful streams, wonderful mountains, and clean fresh air," wrote Alice Posey, who grew up in Proctor. "We seemed to have so much love for each other. Neighbors helped neighbors. When someone was real sick, friends would gather in and help take care of the patient all night and then go to their jobs the next morning." When the Ritter Lumber Company finished cutting timber in the area, the company left, but many people stayed and rented houses to those who purchased the property. If the subject of the 1943 agreement arose, however, Posey shifted from nostalgia to anger. "Oh Lord, people, if we can't trust our government who can we trust?"[34] In a similar vein, the Reverend George Britt wrote about Hazel Creek and Bone Valley (other North Shore communities): "I regret so much that my two children and two grandchildren could not know the happiness and beauty of living on Hazel Creek. It is hard for those who were deprived of this blessing to grasp the chasm between the beauty of life in the mountains and the rat race in the concrete jungles of our modern cities," wrote Britt. He remembered his first encounter with faith in the Bone Valley Church, the pranks of young people, and the beauty of the mountains as a backdrop for his childhood. Like a lot of older people, he associates his own childhood on Hazel Creek with a simpler and better time: "While a maniacal greed and a frenzied pursuit of sensuality have gripped this nation," he concluded, "here on the periphery of the land that was their former home is an endangered species, the salt of America, a little reservoir of the sturdy, honest, pious, moral, patriotic stock which made the greatness of America of the eighteenth and nineteenth centuries. To them it is very much like a religious pilgrimage to have access to return to their sacred home sites and cemeteries and reminisce about the America that used to be."[35]

Currently, the National Park Service maintains more than ninety historic structures, including cabins, homes, barns, outbuildings, churches, and schools within the Great Smoky Mountains National Park.[36] None of these are in the North Shore area, which apparently was not considered for the kind of historical interpretation that is done at the Oconaluftee Visitor Center, Cataloochee Valley, and Cades Cove. No doubt this has everything to do with the age of the buildings on the North Shore and their relative inaccessibility. It was probably difficult for anyone in the 1940s to think of buildings from their own decade as "historic," which of course they would be today.

The North Shore removals by TVA during the 1940s have a different trajectory from those wrought by North Carolina and Tennessee in the late 1920s and early 1930s. The most obvious difference was *time,* as the earlier removals have had more time for the former residents and their descendants to process loss. The second difference was that the economic development of particularly the Tennessee side has been much more dramatic. The third was that the interpretation has been more accessible, and the emphasis on heritage tourism has been greater in Tennessee. It appears difficult to overcome the perception of betrayal for North Shore ancestors. In July 2018, US Interior Secretary Ryan Zinke, along with US Senator Thom Tillis (R-NC), US Representative Mark Meadows (R-Asheville), state Senator Jim Davis (R-Franklin), and local politicians presented a check for $35.2 million to Swain County in order to settle the North Shore Road issue. Whereas numerous politicians, including Charles Taylor and Jesse Helms, had taken up the North Shore cause, Tillis, Meadows, and Davis hoped to end the seventy-year battle with the federal government over development promised by the 1943 agreement.[37] Soon, however, some voiced their complaints that this development does *not* include plans for a lakeshore road. It's a large check for development, but what general prosperity will come of it is in the hands of local politicians. This study suggests that remembrance and heritage tourism should be part of their plan.

Until the settlement was announced, the Swain County government website included the story of the North Shore residents under the heading "historical grief and trauma." The web page professed loss of identity, heritage, spiritual beliefs, and trust as part of its description of what they have lost: "We have lost faith in our own federal government."[38] Here the author also tapped into another current in American life, characterized by President Ronald Reagan's famous line, "government is not the solution to our problems, it is the problem." I write this not to diminish the feelings of "historical trauma," but to suggest that the loss of "identity, heritage, and spiritual beliefs" has as much to do with being immersed in a modern society that values the individual over community; the accumulation of things over relationships; and paid work over a relationship with the land. Grief can be like that: all of life's miseries swirl inside it.

It is also worth noting that the Great Smoky Mountains National Park rests adjacent to the Quallah Boundary of the Eastern Band of Cherokee, who suffered historical grief and trauma through the Trail of Tears. "We have a great deal of experience in giving up our land," noted Tribal Council member Bob Blankenship, wryly, referring to the fact that the Cherokee once claimed territory in eight eastern states. "By the grace of God and a white man by the name of Will Thomas, a few of our people were able to remain in their homeland." The Eastern Band sought North Carolina citizenship, and Thomas, who was the adopted son of Chief Drowning Bear, fought for their right to remain when the rest of the Indian Removal Act of 1838 forced the rest of the tribe to move to the Oklahoma Territory.[39] The Cherokee also were *not* removed for the creation of the Great Smoky Mountains National Park. However, in World War I they allowed Parsons's Pulp and Lumber Company to construct a sawmill and a railway on thirty-three thousand acres of Cherokee land. According to Blankenship, Cherokee sold the lumber as a matter of patriotic duty to support the war effort.[40]

Significantly, Blankenship recalled growing up in Cherokee, North Carolina, without electricity or telephones: "We couldn't afford to get shoes for school until after we sold our tobacco, and that was up around November. Frost on the ground. I remember herding them cows up out with frost on the ground, and my feet a'freezing." He contends that if it had not been for gaming—in particular, Harrah's Casino, built in 1997—"all Indian tribes would still be very poor." Blankenship served in the US Army in Vietnam and returned home to run several businesses in Cherokee, including a Kentucky Fried Chicken, a trout farm, and a campground. Blankenship still had very little good to say about the US government, but he emphasized a narrative in which Native people can no longer be described as victims. For the first time in history, Blankenship argued, Native Americans have become empowered with political influence. Because of casino money they have built a new hospital, school, and corrections center, and every Cherokee person can go to college and receive cash payments at age twenty-one from Harrah's. In 2004, the Cherokee managed to negotiate a land swap in which part of the national park was gained to build a state-of-the-art high school in exchange for a remote area becoming a part of the national park. Without being asked this question, Blankenship's account of his life and the economic development in Cherokee demonstrates that success and prosperity make a difference in dealing with loss. The Cherokee also teach their language, art, and music in that high school; support history in the

Cherokee Museum; and keep alive the story of the Trail of Tears in the annual outdoor drama *Unto These Hills.*

Meanwhile, Decoration Days continue for some North Shore Residents. *Waynesville Mountaineer* staff writer Joanita M. Nellenbach depicted crossing Fontana Lake to the cemeteries as a "journey" that begins with a twenty-five-minute boat ride: "The travelers, most of whom are in their 60s and 70s, climb the bank, helping each other and using walking sticks for support." At the trail-head, other park employees drive the residents in a Jeep fifteen minutes up the steep road. From here, they hike a shady, winding trail to Higdon Cemetery. They begin by putting silk flowers on the twenty-two graves and sharing stories about the person in each grave. The group stays at Higdon about a half-hour before hiking back down the trail for a picnic and service. Then they begin the two-hour trip home.[41]

"I was raised with bitterness about it," Larry Vickery said, "my father having been killed in an automobile accident at the time we were being forced to move out and left my mother, who had never worked outside the home with four children, me being the youngest of five. She ended up moving to Knoxville and getting work in wartime industries, and then, of course, at the end of the war, there were no more wartime industries." Vickery says he never misses a Decoration Day, and he delights in a memory of wading in Hazel Creek with his aunt and listening to stories about his father. "It gives me a feeling of belonging or something."[42] Perhaps this is the greatest hope for long-term healing in the southwestern corner of the Great Smoky Mountains National Park—the continuation of Decoration Day and the public celebration of loving memories of the past. Frank Lequire described his family, who lived on Fish Trap Branch near Judson as being like most mountain families:

> We raised most everything to eat. My mother canned vegetables and fruits, made all kinds of pickles, pickled beans and corn, made jellies and jams, always picked black-berries, which I hated to do, and had potatoes which we holed up in the winter. We had two or three milk cows, to have milk and butter, had chickens and eggs, and slaughtered two or three hogs in the fall or the winter, Dad would salt and smoke the meat so that it would keep through the winter, ground the trimmings into sausage, and cooked the fat and skins to have lard. I think they used everything but the squeal. We raised enough corn to feed the chickens, and grind the corn meal for us to eat. Sometimes he would plant cane to make molasses.[43]

The farm life that Lequire described is well remembered at Pioneer Days, held at the Oconaluftee Visitor Center each fall. Craftspeople in the area are employed to grind cornmeal and render molasses for tourists. Although this is not Judson, it is North Carolina, one county over from where Lequire lived. "I was about half-way through the third grade when we moved to Macon County," he said. "The TVA was cleaning land and tearing down houses, so like the other families we had to pack up and move out. I still live in Macon County about four miles out of Franklin. I still make a garden every summer. We raise vegetables, corn and pota-toes, do some canning and make jellies and pickles. So I guess some things haven't changed all that much." [44]

2 At the Bottom of the Loyston Sea

The Tennessee Valley Authority and Loss in the Norris Basin

AARON D. PURCELL

> Every day was an adventure and every field, hollow, ridge, and swimming hole,
> was an old friend. It was inconceivable that we soon would be leaving, forever,
> those many friendly haunts of our childhood.
>
> But young folks could look toward the future with enthusiastic optimism and
> quickly adjust. Old folks couldn't. They were, to some extent, living in the past,
> among the familiar hollows and ridges they had known all their lives. They lived
> among their relatives and neighbors and lived in their memories among their
> ancestors—their people.
> —John Rice Irwin, 1987

Tourists traveling through East Tennessee are still drawn to charming hamlet of
Norris. Originally built by the Tennessee Valley Authority (TVA) to provide housing to workers constructing the agency's first dam, the town took its name from
Nebraska Senator George Norris, the "father of TVA." From the car window, the
vision of a 1930s New Deal community is still alive in Norris. The town is a tranquil
collective of small homes, well maintained green spaces, and a central community
center. Paved walkways meander through the rolling hills to connect shared public spaces and residences. The electrified town was a New Deal showpiece and a
model of a modern rural community. The nearby Norris Dam, completed in 1936,
is equally impressive. Its giant powerhouse feeds a host of electric transmission
lines that march across the horizon.[1]

No trip to Norris is complete without a visit to the Museum of Appalachia,
located on the outskirts of town. In 1969, local resident John Rice Irwin founded
the living history museum as a way to document rural life in the Appalachian

South. The sprawling sixty-five-acre property includes a recreated Appalachian community with log cabins, barns, churches, school buildings, and gardens. Three buildings house over 250,000 artifacts, dozens of exhibits, a restaurant, and a requisite gift shop. The museum hosts living history events, provides tours to school groups, and is even available for weddings. Irwin dedicated the museum to both preserve the physical artifacts of an earlier time and to instill in the community a greater knowledge of and appreciation for Appalachian heritage. His work to preserve Appalachian culture earned him numerous awards, including a McArthur Foundation fellowship in 1989.[2]

The Museum of Appalachia and the town of Norris represent a sharp contrast of two cultures—one before and one after TVA. Irwin spent his life preserving and promoting Appalachian heritage, especially what came before the sweeping changes from New Deal agencies like TVA. His experience is part of the story of the transition between the old traditional ways and the new modern ways. Born in 1931 to Glenn and Ruth, John Rice lived on a farm owned by his grandparents John G. and Sarah J. Irwin. The Irwin family lived and worked on an 83-acre farm located one-and-a-half miles west of the nearby town of Loyston. They owned cattle, chickens, hogs, and a few horses, and raised corn, tobacco, and hay.[3]

The announcement of TVA's Norris Dam project in 1933 resulted in the swift removal of thirty-five hundred rural families in the affected river basin. In fall 1934, fieldworkers hired by TVA visited the Irwin family, which included three-year-old Rice, to discuss their plan for removal. The fieldworker noted that the "family has a nice big old fashioned house," and they expressed an interest in assistance with relocating through the University of Tennessee's Extension Division. By late 1935, the Irwin family had removed all of their personal items, razed their buildings, and moved about thirty-five miles down the same valley to Robertsville, known as the New Hope community. Then, in 1942, the US Army Corps began removing families in New Hope to build the scientific labs of the Manhattan Engineer District, later known as Oak Ridge. The Irwin family owned about 325 acres and had only two weeks to move. Following the two forced removals, the family resettled near the town of Norris, only a few miles from their original home in Union County.[4]

The Irwin homeplace and the town of Loyston disappeared into the waters of Norris Lake by 1936. Archival materials, oral histories, photographs, and memories are all that are left of the town, but today adventurous tourists can visualize the space where Loyston once occupied. Big Ridge State Park is located a few miles from the Museum of Appalachia, accessible by taking Route 61 eastward. Mostly developed by the Civilian Conservation Corps (CCC) in the 1930s as part of TVA's larger Norris Reservoir project, the park offers a variety of outdoor adventures such as camping, fishing, swimming, and hiking. One of the shortest and more difficult hikes is the Loyston Overlook Trail. This steep and rugged path only one-third of a mile from the visitors' center takes hikers to one of the highest elevations in the park, with an impressive sight. From the ridgeline, out-of-breath hikers are faced with a panoramic view of the widest part of Norris Lake.[5] TVA named this part of the reservoir "the Loyston Sea" because the physical remnants of the town are submerged beneath the deep waters. Hikers may spot small colorful dots on the water, which are motorboats and other pleasure craft out for a day of fishing.

There are no physical remnants of Loyston on the viewable landscape. What remains are the memories of former residents and documentary evidence collected by TVA on this lost community. In the early 1930s, TVA prepared the residents of Loyston to leave the bottomland and their traditional ways. A large number of affected residents founded the nearby community of New Loyston or resettled in nearby counties. Through the multiyear removal process, TVA documented the full scope of the life and death of Loyston.

In the 1930s, TVA brought rapid change to rural East Tennessee. TVA emphasized planned communities with modern conveniences while dismantling communities like Loyston in the name of progress. Visiting Norris and the public parks associated with the vast expanse of Norris Lake offers few glimpses of life in this region before TVA. The Lenoir Museum, located a short drive from the dam, displays artifacts documenting rural life and the earliest human inhabitants of the region. Family cemeteries above the waterline, a relocated gristmill and threshing barn, roads that disappear into the water, and named geographic points are the only tangible evidence of past inhabitants.[6] Like other removal projects of the period, the Norris Reservoir area was designed to return the landscape surrounding the lake to nature and otherwise have limited development and access points. Part environmental buffer and part snapshot of pre-Columbian geography, New Deal planners wanted projects such as Norris to transport visitors to a different time, but without the people. Evidence of past habitation was not part of their plan, and existing communities such as Loyston did not fit the mold. Further, TVA emphasized the narrative that the affected residents of Loyston would gain more from the benefits of Norris Dam than from keeping their community above water.

The removal process in the Norris Basin was well documented, and the lessons learned helped TVA create a model for later projects. As part of the Norris removal work, TVA produced dozens of reports on the sociological, economic, geographic, and political aspects of the region. The intention of these studies was not just to document what existed before TVA, but to create a baseline comparison for the improvements yet to come. TVA interviewed just over 3,800 families to document local needs and prepare for removal.

The voices of the displaced describe the town of Loyston and what was lost when it disappeared under the waterline. They speak from TVA's removal files for 313 individual families and six buildings, which account for the entirety of the town of Loyston. An examination of families who lived in Loyston offers insights into the complete loss of a community and how TVA altered the Norris Basin. Through its reservoir projects, TVA promoted a modern Appalachian identity which was much different from the culture that preceded it. This significant cultural break with the past, however, did not erase the history of lost communities like Loyston. In fact, the complete removal of such communities strengthened the memory of a "simpler and better" time. This type of romantic view of the life and lifestyle before TVA is informed by displays at the Museum of Appalachia, only a few miles from the Loyston Sea. Communities like Loyston may be physically inaccessible to those in the twenty-first century; however, the constructed memory of such places has become a permanent part of the history of TVA and the Appalachian South.

Many of the early works on the Tennessee Valley Authority ignored the theme of loss and instead focused on progress. Studies of TVA written by its former employees or published by the agency were largely celebratory or contained a triumphal message about how the agency overcame nearly insurmountable challenges to transform the region. For example, C. Herman Pritchett's *TVA: A Study in Public Administration* (1943) argued that the agency represented a symbol, a tool, and a promise for the future. Pritchett heralded TVA's engineering and administrative success, which could be replicated across the globe.[7] David E. Lilienthal's *TVA: Democracy on the March* (1944) extended this argument to align the agency with the Cold War mission to combat communism abroad. Lilienthal wrote that TVA represented a model of decentralization that gave economic power back to the people. Lilienthal's best-selling book, which was distributed for free to World War II soldiers, proclaimed that the agency had revitalized the region and inspired the people to take control of their resources.[8]

After World War II, scholars questioned TVA's methods and pointed to what was lost during the transformation of the region. Sociologist Philip Selznick also took aim at TVA's vision and administration. In *TVA and the Grass Roots* (1949), he criticized TVA for overpowering its rural constituents with bureaucracy and accused the agency of lacking a purpose beyond generating electricity. Selznick believed that TVA sided with large conservative agricultural interests instead of small family farmers, many of whom had been displaced by TVA. These large entities, he believed, were hostile to the poor Black and white farmers that TVA had pledged to protect. Instead of finding participatory democracy at the grassroots as Lilienthal had claimed, Selznick believed that Lilienthal has used his powerful tongue and pen to conceal the reality of TVA's cooptation in the region.[9]

In *The Tennessee, Volume II, The New River: Civil War to TVA* (1948) agrarian writer Donald Davidson explained that the loss of Appalachian culture to modernize the Tennessee Valley was not worth the industrial and social benefits gained. Davidson was one of the first critics of TVA's "reservoir clearance" program which prepared the terrain for the dams and reservoirs. In the absence of official numbers of individuals removed, he calculated that by 1946 TVA had removed at least seventy-two thousand people, which he estimated was half the size of Nashville or four times the number of people displaced during the Cherokee Removal. He explained that TVA's process for compensation was somewhat fair, but the agency did not take a leading role in helping resettle the displaced residents. Davidson asserted that perhaps half of those displaced were willing to leave, but the older residents were much more reluctant, and likely their "death was hastened by the removal."[10]

The process of removal and resettlement has been the focus of several studies. TVA employee M. Harry Satterfield wrote in 1938 that the agency did in fact make significant efforts to help displaced families find new homes. He explained that TVA caseworkers collaborated with other relief agencies to assist the families who needed assistance with resettlement. As to the question of where the displaced families went, Satterfield answered that the majority resettled as near as possible to their old homes. He admitted that resettled farm families often had less acreage than before, but a larger percentage owned their homes.[11]

Charles McCarthy, a TVA lawyer and father to author Cormac McCarthy, later wrote about his experiences in acquiring land for the Norris project. He explained that the agency's methods of acquiring lands were meant to be a fair process and to leave "the people who lived in the reservoir areas at least as well off as they were before TVA entered the picture." McCarthy did not elaborate on how to measure the latter claim, but he emphasized the importance of community relations, "which promotes respect and confidence rather than antagonism." In a 1950 essay on TVA's seventeenth birthday, McCarthy proclaimed: "The Tennessee Valley still has a long way to go, but the downward trend has been halted and reversed and its people are on the way back."[12]

TVA's declarations about "the people who lived in the reservoir areas" often carried an omniscient or paternalistic tone. Several scholars have pointed to TVA's original mission of regional social uplift as a distorting factor in policy making and community relations. Arthur E. Morgan, TVA's first board chairman, had a unique vision for what the agency could do for the region, but his ouster in 1938 ended widescale regional social planning and programs. Instead, TVA embraced cheap electric power distribution as a way to modernize the region and help those at the grassroots—who the agency believed could not or would not help themselves. TVA's adherence to this never fully evolved social commitment became a myth that hamstrung the agency's ability to work with the communities that it aimed to serve. One of TVA's last dam projects, the Tellico Dam, demonstrated the agency's commitment to its mythical social mission. With the Tellico project, TVA leaders believed so much in the agency's purpose to fulfill a social promise to the region that they ignored and ridiculed the concerns of Native American groups, environmental groups, and the Environmental Protection Agency. This thread of the agency minimizing local concerns in favor of larger objectives began with the first removal projects and became part of TVA's institutional culture.[13]

Luckily for researchers exploring the attitudes and intentions of the removal process, TVA made great efforts to document its early activities. The official records of TVA housed by the National Archives and Records Administration (NARA) at their southeast regional facility near Atlanta are voluminous.[14] TVA documented its removal work through a massive set of nearly twenty thousand files known as family-removal and population-readjustment case files, 1934–53. TVA hired local fieldworkers to conduct interviews with the residents affected by removal. In many cases, the fieldworkers who interviewed families facing removal and resettlement were often quick to judge and make inaccurate assumptions about the people they were trying to help. The resulting files for individual families (both owners and tenants) contained questionnaires, notes about visits, family profiles, related correspondence, and other material created during the removal process.[15] TVA employees used these files and other sources to create sociological reports which were heavy on data and on solutions for improvement. These reports began as confidential surveys, most of which would later be released to the public, which summarized the agency's methods for improving the people and communities affected by removal.

Beginning in the 1970s, scholars began analyzing TVA's removal records and early sociological reports. They also interviewed families and descendants who were directly affected by removal. Michael J. McDonald and John Muldowny's *TVA and the Dispossessed* (1982) was a landmark source on analyzing TVA removals. They provided a statistical snapshot of the socioeconomic life in the Norris Basin before, during, and after removal. This data-heavy book explored the displacement of thirty-five hundred families in the Norris Basin by TVA during the early 1930s. The authors demonstrated that TVA's removal process at Norris was experimental, haphazard, and not well coordinated. More importantly, the authors concluded that the majority of the removed families recognized the advantages of leaving their homeplace, but for most, relocation created a connection to older cultural values associated with a poorer, hard way of life. McDonald and Muldowny concluded that the "forgotten Americans" in the Norris Basin, who TVA attempted to help, lost more than they gained and resented being displaced. Their book discussed some of the cultural losses because of the building of Norris Dam, but the authors were more focused on TVA's removal processes and demonstrating the agency's lack of a unified and coherent policy.[16]

McDonald and Muldowny established that the removal of families from the Norris Basin fragmented the physical landscape as well as the memories of those affected. Their interviews with displaced residents some thirty years after removal revealed a strong penchant for romanticizing the past. McDonald and Muldowny's observations about how removed residents created new memories of pre-TVA life fit well with the later work of oral historian Alessandro Portelli. In *The Death of Luigi Trastulli and Other Stories* (1991), Portelli explained that oral histories, unlike written sources, change over time to create new memories. He explained that oral histories introduce "errors, inventions, and myths [which] lead us through and beyond facts to their meanings." The book, which compared cultural change in Harlan, Kentucky, and Terni, Italy, discussed the same reality that occurred in the Norris Basin in the 1930s: "a thriving traditional, rural culture was suddenly brought face-to-face with full-blown industrial development; there was hardly any gradual process of adaptation, or time for change and growth from within." The oral histories collected for *TVA and the Dispossessed* documented the memory of the rapid change in the Norris Basin and how those memories changed because there was no way for displaced families to return to the physical spaces lost to time or submerged by the shimmering water.[17]

The work of McDonald and Muldowny inspired other scholars to reevaluate TVA's reservoir removal program. In his 1995 essay in *The Journal of East Tennessee*

History, Michael Rogers explored the attitudes and expectations of a sample of 350 removed families from the Norris and Cherokee dam sites. His analysis of removal files demonstrated that residents had a mixture of resentment and excitement. Rogers argued that large numbers of interviewees welcomed TVA's promises of electricity and economy in exchange for their land and agrarian lifestyle. Of course, age played a significant factor in determining those who accepted TVA (usually younger families, between twenty-five and forty-five years old) and those who rejected TVA (usually older residents, over forty-five years old). Further, residents with more formal education, most often younger than forty-five, were more receptive to TVA. Rogers's study offered a more nuanced view of how affected residents coped with the coming of TVA. He also established that most of the pre-removal families living near the Cherokee site in 1940 were well below the poverty level, which supported McDonald and Muldowny's assertion that in the short-term TVA did not effectively help the region it was trying to help. But Rogers explained that many younger residents who prepared for removal remained optimistic about TVA and agreed that a significant break from the past was necessary to move forward.[18]

Assessing and Removing Loyston

In addition to representing a break from the past, the Norris Dam project was a significant achievement at a very dark period in American history. Electricity, flood control, and jobs made TVA a bright spot in Roosevelt's array of First New Deal programs. The agency took great interest in documenting the culture they were attempting to improve, especially with their early projects. The preparation of the Norris Basin involved removing families, relocating cemeteries, rerouting roads, and moving salvageable buildings. But Loyston was an example of an active riverbottom town that could not be recreated elsewhere, and its removal from the landscape created a complete loss of the physical community.[19]

Roosevelt and other New Dealers believed that the immediacy of the Great Depression demanded swift action. They successfully argued that the removal of people and places from the landscape to make way for lakes, dams, and river improvements in the Tennessee Valley was a necessary and fully justified loss. Such losses of local communities and networks were seen by many, including those directly affected, as a prerequisite to recovery. In fact, many of the farmers interviewed by TVA caseworkers expressed great support for the agency and recognized the opportunity to improve the local community as well as the entire nation.

In the short term, TVA brought jobs to the Norris Basin and in the long term Norris Dam meant a higher standard of living, modern conveniences, and new economic opportunities for the local population. Other residents in the Norris Basin, however, were less optimistic about federal outsiders and their plans to disrupt a culture that had been in place for many generations.

Human inhabitation of the bottomlands of the Clinch River stretched back several centuries. Prior to white European settlers, Native Americans such as the Cherokee and the Shawnee occupied the region. After the American Revolution, the state of North Carolina ignored previous treaties with the Cherokee and began issuing land grants to veterans for lands in what became the state of Tennessee. In April 1783, North Carolina issued a large grant of 200,000 acres to Richard Henderson, which opened up the Norris Basin to white settlement. By the early 1800s, several hundred families had settled in the region.[20]

The Loy family from North Carolina were one of the early families to settle in what was then Anderson County, just northeast of Knoxville. In 1833, a post office was established in the small settlement of Loy's Crossroads. The fertile bottomland supported farming, and nearby deposits of iron ore, lead, zinc, and marble attracted industry and mining. In 1836, brothers John and William Loy partnered with local resident Lewis Miller to build an iron furnace just a quarter-mile north of Loy's Crossroads. In 1856, this area become part of Union County, which was formed from portions of Anderson, Campbell, Claiborne, Grainger, and Knox counties. In 1894, the community changed its name to Loyston in honor of John Loy, who drowned in 1840.[21]

There was no railroad nearby, but Loyston was a hub of trading activity because it was situated at the convergence of roads that led to markets in Knoxville, Jacksboro, Maynardville, Tazewell, and Clinton. In the early twentieth century, Loyston was a typical East Tennessee farming community with two general stores, a gristmill, churches, a restaurant, a gas station, a barbershop, a blacksmith, schools, and a post office. Electricity had not yet made it to the area, but a Delco Lighting system served a few homes and stores with electricity. By the 1920s, the B. H. George Coach Company offered daily bus service to Knoxville, thirty miles to the southwest.[22]

By 1930, Loyston was one of the largest rural communities in Union County. TVA determined that at the time of removal there were seventy Loyston residents. Because of such a small number of residents, the agency and later scholars discounted the significance of Loyston, often referring to it as a village and not

The town of Loyston was a typical East Tennessee farming community. TVA
coordinated the clearing of the landscape and the removal of all of the buildings.
The site of the village of Loyston, ca. 1934, in Dorothy Barber, "Family Case Records—
Population Readjustment," 1944, 5, TVA Pamphlet Collection, MS-0631, box 2,
folder 2, Betsey B. Creekmore Special Collections and University Archives,
University of Tennessee, Knoxville.

a town. Closer examination of the 1930 census demonstrates that the number of residents in Loyston was slightly larger, but these sources indicate that the town was the central point of social and economic activity for hundreds of rural families. The 1930 census for Union County recorded 98 residents, representing 19 individual families with 14 unique family names, with the street address of Loyston Pike. Loyston was a central part of the northwest portion of Union County's District 4. The census rolls for the northwest part of Union County listed 941 residents which represented 194 individual families, many of whom were related or part of extended families with similar surnames.[23]

The demographics of Loyston residents mirrored other rural parts of East Tennessee. In the 1930 census, Loyston residents were all listed as white, most reported that they could read and write, 20 of the younger residents had formal schooling while only a small number of their parents and grandparents had attended school, and the average size of each family was 5 persons. The average age of residents was twenty-six years old, and the average age of at the time of marriage was twenty-one. The families in Loyston often included extended-family members, and overall each family had more younger members than older ones. Occupations of Loyston residents included merchant, laborer, farmer, schoolteacher, truck driver, and carpenter. For younger children, their work was farming or helping with family businesses.[24]

Loyston was the only town entirely within the purchase area for Norris Dam. To prepare for the Norris Reservoir, TVA purchased approximately 152,600 acres of ridge and valley lands in Union, Campbell, Claiborne, Anderson, and Grainger counties. The purchasing included land directly affected by the rising waters to the shoreline of the reservoir as well as buffer lands to protect the entire watershed area. TVA board chairman, Arthur Morgan, emphasized the importance of taking adjacent lands out of agricultural production. His fellow directors, especially Harcourt Morgan, disagreed, believing that such a policy hurt the small farmers who by the early 1930s already struggled with low farm prices, low yields, and few opportunities to add acreage. This policy of purchasing outlying areas was not continued with later projects. In addition, TVA avoided purchasing portions of farms affected by Norris Dam and instead purchased the entire property from the landowner.[25]

The social and cultural characteristics of the five counties in the Norris Basin mirrored TVA's conclusions about the residents of Loyston. TVA completed detailed reports of the five counties connected to the Norris project. There were small towns in the five counties, but the majority of the residents were rural. The

1930 census listed 19,736 families in the five counties. TVA estimated that 2,841 of those families, or 14 percent of them, were directly affected by land purchasing for Norris Dam. The agency found that most of the families were self-sufficient farmers with little yearly income, limited educational opportunities, and a standard of living lower than in other parts of Tennessee. A 1935 report explained: "Modern conveniences, such as electricity, telephone, running water in the house with bath and toilet, and efficient heating systems are almost entirely lacking in the homes of the area." Home ownership was a higher percentage than the statewide average, but there were still significant numbers of tenant farmers. The size of farms had decreased while farm values and farm population had increased. In other words, TVA declared that the five counties were "agriculturally overpopulated." TVA reported that the renewed cultivation of tobacco on steeper slopes had resulted in significant erosion and degradation of farmland, which further justified the agency's land-buffer policy.[26]

TVA's reports noted that the trend of population drain for the Norris Dam counties had been reversed. A 1933 survey explained: "A traveler passing through Union County in 1927 or 1928 would have noticed many apparently deserted farms. These East Tennessee counties, with their poor lands and rocky hills, were not able to compete with the attractions of Detroit and other cities for the attention of the younger generation. . . . It appears that a large number of those from East Tennessee were attracted to the automobile industry of Michigan." But, because of the Great Depression, the report continued, "This movement has now been reversed throughout the country, and today, if the same traveler returns to Union or the surrounding counties, he will find most of the young people back at home with their parents, wiser but poorer for having left the farm."[27] The challenge for younger farmers returning to the area was the lack of available farmland and few economic opportunities. TVA believed that the Norris project was a solution to farm overcrowding because the sudden activity to build the dam improved transportation routes, provided local employment, and made a tourist-based economy possible.[28]

An initial step in the removal process was to evaluate who was in the basin, what they owned, and where they might go. In the summer of 1934, analysts in TVA's economic research section of the Land Planning and Housing Division created an eight-page questionnaire. For many of the families removed from the Norris Basin, the lengthy questionnaire from the fall of 1934 is all that exists to document their pre-TVA lives. Only a portion of the files indicates what happened to the families after they left their homes.

Each questionnaire had four main components. First, it asked for demographic information about family members. This included questions about members of the household, including marital status, birthplaces, ages, educational level, church affiliation, magazine and newspaper subscriptions, books owned, physical defects or deaths, occupations, and any life insurance policies. The second page included a question about the nearest trade center and how often the families traded there. Finally, fieldworkers asked how many trips each family made to Knoxville each year. This information allowed TVA to establish some baselines and recognize patterns for the culture of the Norris Basin.

The second portion of the questionnaire was an economic assessment of property and personal items. The survey asked for details on rented and owned land, the type of farming, extent of crops and livestock, number of tenants, machinery, tools, furniture, and ownership of personal items like a car, radio, or sewing machine. Fieldworkers asked about personal expenditures and receipts for the past year, amounts of farm products such as gallons of milk or bushels of peaches, other sources of income, and family savings. TVA used this data to determine agricultural output and per capita income for each family. Most of the completed questionnaires included a printed receipt with final calculations of income and estimated net worth for each family.

A third portion of the questionnaire focused on removal and resettlement. Fieldworkers asked each family about what they desired in a new location and the resources they would need to relocate. Not surprisingly, most families wanted to continue to farm and desired a nicer home and more property, but other respondents preferred to rent land or stop farming entirely. The survey asked if any family members had specialized or professional skills such as teaching, carpentry, masonry, auto mechanic, or working as a merchant. In some cases, families had already secured new homes or living arrangements, which could be noted on the form. For those who expressed a need for assistance with relocation, TVA referred them to the University of Tennessee's Extension Division.

Finally, the last page of the questionnaire allowed the fieldworker to document concerns, observations, and challenges. Fieldworkers were able to evaluate how cooperative or hostile the interviewees were to the questions. The form included a scale to rank the respondent's attitude toward TVA, ranging from antagonistic to active booster. This last page contained blank lines for free-form responses to questions about whether a follow-up would be necessary or special problems existed. The questionnaire concluded with the question, "Give the gist of conversation with family." The final page of the questionnaires offered the wide range of responses and often provided the most insight into each family and their situation. By 1935, TVA shortened the questionnaire to only two pages, but it still recorded much of the same demographic and economic information about each family as well as fieldnotes. As a significant difference, interviews in 1934 using the lengthy form were much more about collecting information while the meetings with residents in 1935 had more urgency because the dam was scheduled to be completed in early 1936.

Rumors about TVA circulated through the Norris Basin as soon as the agency was created. As the family surveys demonstrated, a good portion of residents in the region subscribed to the *Knoxville Journal* and would have had access to information about TVA's plans for the Norris Basin. Before sending out fieldworkers to rural families who may or may not have heard about the Norris Dam project, TVA sponsored community meetings. These gatherings allowed TVA representatives to address local residents about the purposes of the agency and how the Norris project affected them. These meetings featured a range of responses. Many families understood the importance of the project to the area and in fact saw a great opportunity to relocate. Other more irritated residents voiced their opinions about TVA's land-buying policies and raised objections to family and cemetery removal. The last of these meetings in the Loyston area occurred at the Loyston School in October 1934 and drew hundreds of curious residents. This "last roundup" represented the final community gathering for Loyston residents in Loyston.[29]

In the fall of 1934, fieldworkers on behalf of TVA began meeting heads of households across the Norris Basin. TVA hired local residents, especially schoolteachers, to complete the fieldwork. They interviewed landowners and tenants to complete the removal questionnaire. In addition to collecting valuable data on each family, TVA used the lengthy questionnaire to make each family aware of the reality of removal. From the other perspective, many families were confused about what has happening to them and why. Interviews conducted by trusted locals allowed residents to respond and react to the new agency by talking with friends and neighbors. In addition, many of the questionnaires were completed by women in the household because their husbands were working. Through these difficult conversations, the fieldworkers on behalf of TVA expressed interest in and empathy for the families being dislocated. At the same time, fieldworkers added judgmental comments about families. In most cases, the fieldworkers also faced removal and often completed the form for their own household. Some interviews demonstrated complete ambivalence to TVA and removal, while other families were in great denial that they would ever have to leave. In a few instances, family members were angry and threatened violence or legal action against TVA.[30]

Because the fieldworkers were local, the questionnaires often contained preexisting assumptions about families. For the Loyston area, fieldworkers were quick to establish who was wealthy, prosperous, stable, struggling, poor, destitute, or even ignorant. The upkeep of houses was important, especially the exterior. Enos Miller's house included the nicest yard with flowers and shrubs, while many of tenant homes were dilapidated structures in need of repair. The assessment of personal items, especially home furnishings, was part of many completed questionnaires. A clean house or a modern kitchen was applauded, but "old and shaky and dirty" furniture was not. The appearances of the family members were often noted in the family files. During a September 1935 visit with the Miller family, a TVA caseworker explained that "Mrs. Miller and Lily, the eighteen year old daughter, were both dressed in rather loud sports dresses, and both were flashily rouged." A sampling of questionnaires for Loyston families recorded a wide range of attitudes and traits, which included friendly, clever, a heavy drinker, fine personality, unemployable, honest, grouchy, narrow-minded, chronic complainer, cooperative, not cultured, and capable of taking care of their own situation.[31]

The master list of family removal files maintained by TVA included files for 313 individual families and six buildings (two schools, a post office, a general store, a gristmill, and a sawmill) with Loyston as the main address. Nearly all of the families were from Union County, with only fifteen families from Campbell County. The majority of the families were landowners or tenants. There were also a few squatters who occupied untended structures or constructed their own shacks without permission of the property owner. The families were large, young, and faced a shortage of new land to cultivate. The older residents, many of whom had lived in the community for decades, clearly had much more to lose by leaving their homes and homeplaces. Their descendants and those new to the community were more open-minded about moving. J. A. Greenlee, a tenant who had rented ninety-one acres near Loyston for three years, explained that he did not care to move, but for the older people he was sorry because "They will never be satisfied after relocation and it will shorten their days."[32]

Racial diversity was not a part of the Norris Basin, especially in Loyston. The 1930 census pages for Union County that focused on Loyston listed no known people of color. TVA's interviews with Loyston residents confirmed that there were no African American families living near Loyston. TVA estimated that the entire Norris Basin removal area included fewer than a half-dozen African American families.[33] There were African American families in East Tennessee, often living in the rural margins or working in industrial jobs in cities like Knoxville or Kingsport. In an article focused on TVA's removal of African Americans, Melissa Walker used data from the 1930 census to estimate that 4 percent of East Tennessee's farmers were African American, compared to 15 percent in the rest of the state. She explained that African American farmers in East Tennessee were most often landowners and owned more land than African American farmers in other parts of the state; however, they were much less economically successful that white East Tennessee farmers. Later TVA projects involved the relocation of larger numbers of African American families and communities, especially in Middle Tennessee and Northern Alabama, but there is little evidence of African American families in the Norris Basin.[34]

Farming was the chief occupation of the rural populace, which made land very important. TVA's interviews documented the challenge of maintaining a livelihood based solely on farming. The lack of available farmland in the area resulted in the cultivation of rockier and hillier acres which yielded much less than the fertile bottomland. Farmers could not understand why TVA was eliminating the most prized acres in the basin. William Hutchinson, a farmer who owned 58 acres and rented another 10 acres near Loyston, explained, "The TVA had helped some people, the ones that have jobs, but it has hurt the men who owned good river farms and have to leave." Scarcity inflated land prices, which is why many respondents believed that TVA was not paying farmers enough for their property. Freeman Sharp, who lived in Loyston for 48 years and owned 52 acres, did not want to participate in the interview because he believed TVA was not paying enough for his farm. Hershel Nelson explained that TVA appraised his 43-acre farm at half the value. Similarly, George Witt, who had lived in Loyston for 71 years and owned 250 acres, wanted a fair price for his property. Witt observed that TVA treated some folks "worse than the Indians" when it came to land prices. The complaint about low compensation rates for land peppered the removal files from Loyston.[35]

The questionnaires also documented a variety of nonagricultural occupations in the Loyston area. Families reported jobs as store clerks, merchants, mechanics, preachers, mail carriers, miners, doctors, musicians, and schoolteachers. Most often these positions were in combination with some level of farming, but the income derived from these professions helped maintain economic stability for many families. For example, James Mitchell lived all fifty years of his life on a farm near Loyston and worked as a clerk in one of the stores in town. The onset of the

Great Depression resulted in unemployment in the area, but New Deal programs brought new jobs to the area. TVA employed many people to work at Norris Dam as carpenters and laborers. Other Loyston residents, such as Sherman Loy, worked on reservoir clearance to remove trees, structures, and other obstacles from the future lakebed.[36]

The Civilian Conservation Corps also had a presence in the area. In October 1933, the CCC established a camp near Loyston. The CCC hired younger local residents who had been unable to farm, including C. M. Claiborne and Aubrey Graves. Arthur Sinard, a tenant farmer from Loyston, found work as a cook in the camp. The CCC workers built trails, buildings, and roads within the new TVA property. The influx of CCC workers meant interaction with local residents. The relocation files include several cases of local residents selling moonshine to CCC workers. In October 1935, James P. Miller, a tenant farmer, lost his job in the CCC camp for selling whiskey to others in the camp. This incident resulted in Miller, his wife, and seven children immediately relocating to nearby Maynardville. Similarly, TVA's lengthy documentation for Andy Heatherly explained that he had been engaged in the whiskey traffic throughout the area, often selling it to neighbors or trading it for stolen government property.[37]

Other families in the Loyston area relied on federal relief to make ends meet. Fieldworkers recorded stark economic and living conditions for many families who needed help. There were numerous cases of tuberculosis, typhoid fever, and malaria mentioned in the files. The Cooper family had nine children ranging in ages from nineteen to one year old. When TVA visited in September 1934, the family had been renting a home three miles northwest of Loyston for the past nine months. Charles worked as a farm laborer, and his wife Lizzie washed and ironed clothes for the nearby CCC camp. They had been on federal relief and received food and clothes from neighbors. The fieldworker spoke of "Just about hard times. So many to eat and wear and can't buy books for the children. Not one of them in school." A large number of families reported owning no books except for a Bible, but the Cooper family did not have a Bible, so the fieldworker vowed to send them one. The next year, TVA completed a follow-up visit, and conditions for the Cooper family were much worse. Unable to secure stable work, they were squatters in a dilapidated house close to CCC Camp #7. One of daughters in the family had pneumonia, Charles was no longer employed, and a large rat inhabited the loft of their house. Mrs. Cooper explained they needed help from TVA to relocate as they had no place to go and no resources.[38]

Fieldworkers made frequent and sometimes unwarranted or at least highly sub-jective comments about the poorer families being ambivalent to their situations. For the Grissom family, who rented twenty-five acres near Loyston, fieldworker Rush L. Sharp explained: "Conditions were bad, the house looked as if it would collapse. 4 small ragged children, small crop, no worries it seemed, carefree, and ignorant." Similarly, Robert Kidwell and his small family rented a few acres three miles north of Loyston. TVA fieldworker Hazel Beeler noted during an August 1934 visit: "The family is very poor. They don't seem to care where they go or when they have to move."[39]

Other families in the Loyston area had signs of economic success. Kelly George and his two daughters lived on a small five-acre farm less than a mile north of Loyston. He worked as a carpenter for TVA, making $2,000 per year. The field-worker reported that the George family lived in an electrified, "up to date home, clean, pretty furniture." They owned two radios, an RCA record player, a sewing machine, a washer, and a Frigidaire. George drove a 1934 Ford V8 car which was listed as being worth $500. The family file explained that the family was "clever—courteous—well read."[40] Fieldworkers often connected a clean modern home with being cultured or more sophisticated. Further, TVA believed the more economi-cally stable families would not need any assistance in relocating, even though those families had more assets to manage, property to sell, and personal items to move.

In Loyston, family ties often indicated influence and economic stability. Five ex-tended families had at least ten different case files with the same last name and rep-resented nearly 30 percent of the entire Loyston population surveyed for removal by TVA. The families included Hill (eighteen), Irwin (ten), Loy (twenty), Sharp or Sharpe (fifteen), and Stooksbury (twenty-five). In addition, these same surnames appear throughout the removal files in surrounding communities. These five fami-lies had a significant influence on the development and vibrancy of Loyston. From an economic standpoint, the Loy, Hill, and Stooksbury families owned stores that provided residents with supplies and some employment opportunities. Each fam-ily also owned a large amount of property with homes, which they farmed them-selves or rented out to tenants. Within these dominant families there were close familial ties. For example, L. G. Hill reported that, in addition to a household of his wife, four sons, and five daughters, his sixty-three-year-old brother-in-law W. F. Stooksbury lived with them. Other families in the region also reported such overlap, including Isaac Anderson, who provided a home for his first cousin Alfred Stooksbury.[41]

The Stooksbury family was the focus of a 1972 essay by Michael J. McDonald and John Muldowny, which explained: "The Stooksburys were regarded as one of the leading families of the Loyston area. They were typical in their family ties, their life styles, and their attitudes of the thousands of farm families of the Loyston area and of east Tennessee." There were twenty-five Stooksbury families within a two-mile radius of Loyston, including C. R. "Cana" Stooksbury, who owned and operated a general store in Loyston. Most Stooksburys and their relatives owned their own land and were farmers.[42]

Using TVA removal records, McDonald and Muldowny explained that, between the Stooksbury families, eleven had a truck or car, most had sewing machines, two owned pianos, three had battery-powered radios, three had cream separators, one had a carbide lighting system, and one owned a Maytag washer. Despite the appearance of some modern conveniences, life was difficult for Loyston residents. The authors concluded that the growing Stooksbury families faced the reality of limited employment outside of the region, few chances to add new farmland, and a meager farm income derived only from what was not consumed by family members.[43]

McDonald and Muldowny viewed TVA as a positive step for modernizing the region, but they acknowledged that the agency was a mixed blessing for the Stooksburys and other Loyston residents. TVA offered displaced Loyston residents new opportunities and modern conveniences, but there were less tangible losses associated with removal. The authors explained: "the waters of Norris Reservoir covered things incalculable in merely quantitative terms—memories, fondly remembered landmarks, patterns and habits of rural and communal life."[44]

Relocating, Resettling, and Reimagining Loyston

During initial interviews with affected residents in the Norris Basin, fieldworkers asked each family if they were interested in relocation assistance. The answers varied. Some families connected their need to move with perceived progress at the dam site, misunderstood when removal was required, overestimated how much money they would receive for their land, or believed rumors about legal challenges against the agency that might postpone removal. Families who said no to relocation assistance might not have known what they were declining, which often led fieldworkers to note that certain families would not need help to move and resettle.

Washday at the Stooksbury homestead, near Loyston, Tennessee, 1933. "Washday at the Stooksbury Homestead," by Lewis Hine, 1933, Lewis Hine Photographs for the Tennessee Valley Authority, 1933, Records of the Tennessee Valley Authority, Record Group 142, National Archives, Atlanta.

Those who expressed an interest in relocation were referred to the University of Tennessee's Extension Division. In many cases, families held a deep sense of loyalty to the University of Tennessee because of the school's strong extension programs to rural farmers. For example, Phoebe Sharp, who had lived near Loyston for fifty years, explained to a fieldworker that she was "interested in university program but afraid of T.V.A." In May 1934, the UT Extension Division entered into a contract with TVA to aid in the relocation of Norris families. UT Extension agents compiled a list of available farms in East Tennessee, organized community events, and distributed information to county extension agents. Beginning in late 1934, extension agents worked with displaced families to locate a new home, move their belongings, and provide supplies during the first crucial months after the move.[45]

In early 1935, after the first rounds of interviews with affected residents were complete, TVA assessed the status and timeline for the relocation of affected families. TVA classified each of the families forced to move from the Norris Basin in one of three categories:

1. Completely independent families (location already secured or retiring with own means of support).
2. Families needing advisory service only (full-time farm owners, full-time tenant farmers, professional or vocational, or self-supporting through agriculture or industry).
3. Families needing both advisory and financial assistance (self-supporting after a period or submarginal).

The third category, which accounted for over five hundred families, or about 20 percent of those affected, was the most problematic for TVA. The agency did not have a clear relocation plan for these families, and TVA leaders believed that these families did not have the resources needed to relocate or were totally indifferent to the idea of moving.[46]

By late summer 1935, TVA focused on this third category of families. The more pressing issue was that as the dam neared completion families needed to vacate the river basin. On September 1, 1935, TVA created the Reservoir Family Removal Section of the Coordination Division to help remove and resettle the families who needed help. The new section employed sixteen social caseworkers who conducted family visits and worked with other agencies or organizations to help resettle affected families. TVA caseworker Marshall A. Wilson estimated that, of the five hundred families in the Norris Basin who needed resettlement assistance, one hundred families lived below the estimated level of the forthcoming reservoir.[47]

For the families who needed relocation assistance, TVA collected additional removal information such as summaries of later meetings with families or correspondence with the agency. Beginning in late 1935, TVA caseworkers scheduled visits with the just over a hundred Loyston residents who either needed assistance or were still in the process of vacating their property. As expected, some of these families faced significant challenges and had been unable to secure the resources needed to relocate. TVA frequently arranged for transportation of families and their belonging to new sites. Moving meant relocating farm implements, livestock, and valuable personal items. In a few cases, homes and other structures were moved in their entirety. In addition, during the initial interviews with families, TVA noted significant personal and irreplaceable items like quilts, antique furniture, clocks, musical instruments, and family Bibles which required special care during the move. In a few instances, especially with tenants who had to vacate but had no place to move to, TVA provided families with temporary tents and arranged for them to stay on nearby property until a new location was confirmed. The later removals facilitated by TVA were more time-consuming and sometimes difficult.

The Thomas family experienced a complex relocation. TVA caseworkers first visited the Thomas family in December 1935. Joe Thomas died in 1934 soon after he and his wife, Cinda, agreed to sell their land near Loyston to TVA. The caseworker explained that, after his passing, real estate agent Charlie Russell persuaded Mrs. Thomas to deed her already sold property to him in exchange for a farm in Claiborne County, near Tazewell. Cinda, who could not read or write, did not remember signing over the property to the agent and wanted to move to Fonde, Kentucky, to be with her older son and his family. The agent was unable to collect the money from TVA for the farm so he threatened a lawsuit against the Thomas family. In late December, TVA helped the family draft a lawsuit to file against Russell to claim the money from the sale of her property to TVA. Then, the agency contracted with a mover to help the family relocate to Kentucky. In mid-January 1936 the family moved to Fonde with the following items: two hogs, one load of corn, one hundred bushels of potatoes, one mule, one cow, two chicken coops, household furniture, a stove, canned goods, three beds, two plows, a harness set, and six hundred pounds of cured pork. The removal file ended with a successful relocation of the family but did not indicate whether Russell or Thomas collected the settlement money for the property.[48]

In a few instances, families who could not or did not want to move appealed to TVA. Oscar Oakes, a tenant farmer who lived just west of Loyston and reported eight people in the household, contacted the agency's Reservoir Removal Section directly. His November 3, 1935, letter explained: "I have traveled around all I could aford to hire and cant find any place and the man that owns this house says he is going to tear it down on Thursday 7th and leave us under the Shelter of the Blue Sky so if you can hep me I would Be very glad." By the end of the month, TVA had helped relocate him to a new tenant farm.[49]

A few Loyston residents wrote directly to President Roosevelt asking for help. In a January 13, 1936, letter to Roosevelt, Claude Graves wrote:

> I want to ask you if the TVA can put me out of a home. I have bin set out of a home for six weeks and havent got any home and I have a family of 6 and no where to take them a man works on the job by the name of Carmical run us out told me my house would be burned up the next day. . . . I have got my things piled up and no where to take them to I want you to write me at once if you can help me out any.
>
> Answer at once if you can help me out.
>
> [I] dont think it is your will for me to be set out and know where to take my little kids.

TVA received a copy of the letter and responded two weeks later. Apparently by late January, the Graves family had relocated to Kokomo, Indiana, so TVA considered the matter closed.[50]

Similarly, Maude Hutchinson wrote Roosevelt in October 1936 asking for help in resettling their family of eight to another rental farm. She was most concerned that none of her six children were able to go to school because TVA had torn down the Loyston school building. Hutchinson explained: "I believe you are a man that believes in children having an education. I also believe that you are a man that wants to help the poor. I'm sure you dont mean for us to be treated like this." Two weeks later, TVA Board Chairman Arthur Morgan responded on Roosevelt's behalf, saying that TVA had located a new farm for their family which had access to nearby schools.[51]

The majority of Loyston families facing removal were concerned over the formal and religious education of their children. The removal files include a consistent expectation that families have close access to schools and churches in their new location. When interviewed in August 1934, Mrs. E. Q. Hill explained that their family of ten wanted to be relocated close to good schools, churches, and a vibrant town. The caseworker noted that "the parents are trying to educate their children to be active citizens in any community. They are honest and industrious and are anxious to be relocated in a thriving community." Walter Craig, who was a mail carrier in Loyston and rented out a thirty-five-acre farm, wanted to move his family near a college. At the time, the family had one daughter at Carson-Newman College and two others at Horace Maynard High School in nearby Maynardville. The caseworker described the Craig family as "intellectual cultured and refined." During a September 1934 visit, a TVA caseworker noted that Irwin Plummer's wife was "A good Christian mother interested solely in the education and Godly rearing of her children."[52]

Another expectation for Loyston families facing removal was wanting to continue farming after relocation, either as landowners or as tenants. For example, Rhoda McCoy and her family had a successful fruit and vegetable farm just south of Loyston. She hoped to have a farm of the same size and type. Even extended families who owned and rented multiple farms were optimistic that the payout for their land would help them secure more property for farming. TVA estimated that more than 70 percent of all the families relocated in the Norris Basin expressed an interest in returning to farm work, while another 18 percent hoped to combine agriculture and industrial work. The majority of tenants wanted to continue as farmers, even if they did not have the opportunity to own their own land. Clearly, Loyston families were not ready to leave their farm lives behind even if they had to sacrifice their homeplaces to TVA.[53]

For the Norris project, TVA reported only a handful of relocation stories that involved lawyers or law enforcement to enact removal of families. In terms of Loyston families, there were many instances of noted resistance to the idea of removal, but no significant legal challenges of violence reported in the removal files. Many Loyston residents expressed dissatisfaction with moving. For example, Julia Carroll, who lived on a fifty-two-acre farm three miles southwest of Loyston, made it clear to a TVA caseworker that her family would never be satisfied anyplace else. On the other hand, some Loyston families supported what TVA was doing and recognized the benefits. Arlie Branum, who worked as a carpenter at Norris and rented a five-acre farm near Loyston, made it clear that TVA was good for the country. Further, Sillus Raley, a sharecropper with a wife and six children at home, expressed excitement about having cheap electricity so the family could own a radio.[54]

In December 1936, nine months after the dedication of Norris Dam, TVA officially concluded its relocation activities in the Norris Basin. The agency later declared that the Norris Basin families had been satisfactorily relocated, but admitted that such a broad statement was difficult to prove or disprove. In 1937, TVA did a study of 618 removed families (representing 25 percent) and reached the self-serving conclusion that relocation had benefited the majority of the displaced families from the Norris Basin. The next year, the University of Tennessee Extension Division administered a questionnaire to 50 removed families (32 landowners and 18 tenants). The results indicated that approximately 60 percent of the families preferred their new location. As for the area that TVA had purchased and developed, the agency explained that the Norris project has resulted in a number of local improvements. Some of the bright spots included improved county services, higher farm values, better transportation routes, increased trade with Knoxville, a recreation industry near the reservoir, more taxable property, and of course the modern, model, electrified town of Norris.[55]

So where did the displaced families of the Norris Basin go? TVA reported that displaced families did not go far—most moved about 16 miles from their original location, with landowners moving about twice as far as tenants. According to TVA, 62 percent of the families resettled in one of the five Norris Basin counties. Further, almost half of the families relocated in the same county where they started. In Union County, there was a net loss of 300 families.[56]

TVA considered a case closed once a family left its property, so often the family files end at the point of removal. There is limited information on resettlement of Loyston residents. In a few cases, however, former Loyston residents faced additional relocations. The Loyston removal files indicate that, similarly to the experience of John Rice Irwin's family, the Elkins family and the Sweat family relocated to the small community of Wheat in nearby Roane County. Wheat and a number of small farming communities were dissolved in 1942, and all of the residents were displaced to make way for the Clinton Engineer Works, later known as Oak Ridge.[57]

One of the more publicized displacements was former resident E. R. "Ras" Lindamood. In October 1931, a year and a half before the creation of TVA, the *Knoxville News-Sentinel* published a short piece about the eccentric farmer in Union County who allegedly had a fire burning in his fireplace for seventy years. According to the article, Lindamood's family came from Wythe County, Virginia, seventy years before and settled on a farm six-and-a-half miles northwest of Loyston. They claimed to bring live coals from Virginia which had been burning in the hearth ever since. The article painted Lindamood as an oddity who represented a vanishing mountain culture. In September 1934, a TVA fieldworker visited Lindamood to discuss removal from his 175-acre farm. The fieldworker explained that the house was very much like a barn, with saddles, bridles, and feed bags on the front porch. Lindamood kept detailed records of his farming and other expenses in ledger books. The questionnaire listed a loom, spinning wheels, and a reel as valuable items that needed special consideration for moving. There was no mention of a "perpetual fire" or hearth that needed moving. Lindamood remarked that TVA was "doing the wrong thing to destroy so many homes." He said he was not going to move and would instead move up to the ridge on his property and rebuild. The fieldworker explained that relocating Lindamood would be a special problem because "He has lived there all of his life and does not want to leave."[58]

In October 1934, the *Knoxville News-Sentinel* resumed their coverage of the perpetual fire story with a lengthy article containing images of the family in front of the hearth. The reporter, Lee Davis, referred to Lindamood as a "torch-bearer" for his fellow mountaineers. Lindamood, who sported a long flowing white beard, had no resentment for TVA: "It's one of these here things you've got to make the best of." He explained to Davis that "I was born in this room in the light of this fire 70 years ago." But he did admit that "I won't swear the fire has ever once gone out. I do know that the ashes in that fireplace seldom if ever have got cold in my lifetime." Lindamood wanted to take those coals with him to a new home where he would spend the rest of his days. He had started construction of a new home on his property at a higher elevation and was under the impression that TVA would allow him to do so.[59]

As with many families whose property was only partially affected by the lake elevation, TVA did not allow the Lindamood family to stay on part of their property. Instead, TVA offered to help the family locate a new home, but Lindamood resisted. In early 1935, Marshall A. Wilson, who worked in TVA's Reservoir Family Removal Section, recorded his interactions with the Lindamoods. He explained that "Rass Lindamood was an unusual and interesting person—a kind man. He had a remarkable memory of small, insignificant details. He wore a beard and his style of life was very old fashioned, although he was reasonably wealthy." Wilson suggested that the perpetual fire story had been exaggerated by the newspapers. During interviews with TVA, Lindamood "stated the fire had gone out many times, especially since matches became available," and denied that the fire had been consistently burning. By the fall of 1935, Lindamood had located a new home near Clinton. TVA reported that Lindamood moved on December 10, 1935, but it would have occurred sooner "had it not been for his obstinacy." There is nothing in Lindamood's removal file indicating that TVA assisted in relocation of his possessions, fireplace, or live coals. Later articles, including a newspaper account of Lindamood's visit to Knoxville in 1937, confirm that he did in fact transport live coals to his new home. He died in 1942 at age seventy-eight, and a few years the later the fire which may or may not have been decades old was also extinguished.[60]

The dissolution of the town of Loyston was largely complete by the end of 1935. Earlier that year, a group of families established New Loyston about four miles to the southeast of their original community. The focal point of the new settlement was the New Loyston Cemetery, where fourteen hundred graves from the Norris Basin were reinterred. One unique grave was a headstone made of iron from Loy's furnace, which marked the final resting place for John Loy, the town's namesake. Businesses from the original town, including Stooksbury's store, relocated to New Loyston. During the 1940s the town featured a movie theater, a garage, and several stores, but it never grew to the same size or influence as Loyston. Today, New Loyston is a small collection of buildings at the intersection of Tennessee state routes 61 and 170 (Hickory Valley Road) just south of Big Ridge State Park.[61]

Remembering Loyston began almost as soon as the town disappeared. In 1936, residents celebrated Decoration Day in late May at the New Loyston Cemetery. By the next year, the gathering became more formalized as a reunion of Loyston families displaced by Norris Dam. The 1937 gathering at the New Loyston Cemetery featured a memorial address by William L. Stooksbury, president of Knoxville Business College. By the 1940s, the event drew more than twelve hundred visitors to hear music, listen to speakers, decorate graves, and have a picnic lunch. The meal for the 1947 gathering included "piles of East Tennessee country ham, fried chicken and 40 different kinds of cakes, baked in the kitchens of New Loyston homes." In 1952, the *Knoxville Journal* published a lengthy article about the "Loyston Pilgrimage." That year on Sunday, May 18, approximately four thousand people flocked to New Loyston to remember the lost community. Like Decoration Day events at other TVA sites, the New Loyston Cemetery provided a link between the past and present by remembering the town's transplanted dead and decorating the graves. The event began at the Valley Grove Baptist Church with a traditional sermon. After lunch, Tennessee Representative Howard Baker (Sr.) delivered the "speech of the day." In the afternoon, attendees listed to mountain music and folks songs arranged by Knoxville business owner and politician Cas Walker. The gatherings continued until the 1980s, with Loyston reunions occurring in other places, including Norris Dam State Park, the Halls community, and the Fountain City Park.[62]

In 2008, Loyston was again in the news. Gwen Hubbard Sharp, an eighty-four-year-old retired schoolteacher who grew up in Loyston, donated a small playhouse to the Museum of Appalachia. When Sharp was five years old, a neighbor who was a carpenter built the playhouse for her. In November 1935, when the Sharp family was forced to move from their farm, they took the playhouse with them to New

Loyston. Sharp served as the caretaker of the structure, which she believed was the final remaining structure from the lost town of Loyston. When interviewed about the donation, Sharp explained that leaving Loyston was not sad for her but it was for the older people. She recalled, however, that when the buildings were torn down and the trees removed the landscape looked like "a war-torn country" and not the thriving community that it had been. John Rice Irwin, the founder of the Museum of Appalachia, who had a similar Loyston removal story, was excited to accept the unique donation. The playhouse was placed near a cabin close to the entrance to the Museum of Appalachia—only a few miles from Norris Dam and the Loyston Sea.[63]

▲▲

The design of the spaces for the Norris project reflected little of the people and places which once occupied the now tourist-friendly spaces. Agrarian writer Donald Davidson observed, "The nearer he [the motorist] came to Norris Dam, the more the countryside took on the appearance of an amiable wild park which told him, without words, how Tennessee ought to look if it were benevolently protected from man's foolishness." TVA worked with the CCC and the National Park Service to develop a park area for visitors. The original east park area, which is still largely intact and unchanged, included a lodge, a tea room, cabins, a camp-ground, hiking trails, and an amphitheater. As part of the design, the three federal agencies moved the Rice Grist Mill to a location just outside of the boundary of the park. The adjacent town of Norris was more of a statement from TVA of what the region might become. TVA landscape architect Tracy B. Auger designed the town, and Earle Draper, the agency's director of land planning and housing, supervised the construction. The well-manicured landscape featured modest elec-trified homes, which resembled the structures built at Colonial Williamsburg. Davidson commented that the town of Norris was a stark contrast to the nearby displaced communities and was not designed for the recently displaced. He ex-plained that "country folk could not live in a park, away from means of subsis-tence," and the small homes could not accommodate large extended families and visiting kinfolk. Instead the small homes and common areas were better suited for suburban dwellers, especially white TVA employees who worked in leader-ship and office positions. From TVA's perspective, the Norris project promoted efficiency, modernity, and community, which justified displacement and erasure of the predecessor culture.[64]

The legacies of Loyston are best understood as a contrast between the modern and more traditional ways which intersected in the mid-1930s throughout the Tennessee Valley. Norris and its nearby dam are stunning examples of engineering prowess and regional development through electric power and river control. The Norris project was TVA's first attempt to shape a modern Appalachian identity much different from the culture that preceded it. The town of Norris represents how the agency hoped to sculpt rural areas into modernized communities of the Appalachian South. Towns such as Loyston and the farm families in the Norris Basin represented a much different way of life even in the 1930s.

TVA's family removal files from Loyston document some of the losses of community erasure. The files demonstrate that Loyston was an important town for hundreds of mountain families. Loyston was listed as the most common response to the question about the family's chief trading center, with a high weekly frequency ranging from once a week to every day. The majority of residents surveyed depended on frequent visits to Loyston to sell their crops, buy supplies, go to church, or socialize. Family removal files from nearby locations such as Sharps Chapel and Andersonville also identify Loyston as a trading and community center.

The loss of culture and ties to family homesteads was real for many of the removed families, especially the older family members, but in many ways the erasure of towns like Loyston preserved it. For the removed residents and their descendants, Loyston represented a series of memories which changed over time. Those memories tended to focus on the more positive parts of life in the Norris Basin—nearby family and friends, the security of active traditions, and the ability to commune with their ancestors in family cemeteries. When the town of Loyston survived only as a set of memories, the more difficult parts of living there such as spring flooding, low prices for crops, lack of farmland, and isolation could be easily forgotten or misremembered. Over time, the memories of Loyston were passed down to later generations as fact, and those repeating the stories had no real connection to the town except through oral tradition. Thus, the town of Loyston became preserved into the present day, unlike other similar rural towns in East Tennessee which exist now only as a road sign near an empty crossroads.

The interconnected stories of Gwen Sharp and John Rice Irwin are evidence of displaced people caught between traditions. Their very identities changed when TVA arrived, and their memories of the past were significantly altered. Like many others residents displaced by TVA, they experienced a great deal of cultural and community loss. Their devotion to preserving Appalachian culture strengthened their memories of life in Loyston, even if those experiences occurred while they

The home of Harriet Hankins was located near the site of the planned town of Norris. TVA forced the family to move and razed their home to make way for the electrified homes in Norris. The home of Harriet Hankins in the area of the proposed town at Norris Dam by Lewis Hine, 1933, Lewis Hine Photographs for the Tennessee Valley Authority, 1933, Records of the Tennessee Valley Authority, Record Group 142, National Archives, Atlanta.

were children and not adults. Their parents faced a much different reality of relocating and either carrying on their traditional ways (like Ras Lindamood) or starting over, as many of their former Loyston friends and neighbors were doing. Sharp and Irwin connected their memories of the past through the donation of "the last known structure" from their hometown of Loyston to the Museum of Appalachia. Because of their efforts, today's visitors can see tangible exhibits of Appalachian life preserved as a permanent and static memory of lost towns like Loyston.

Today, a visit to Norris, the Museum of Appalachia, and a view of the Loyston Sea provides clarity on what was gained by the Norris Dam project and what was lost. Returning to the town is possible, but very difficult. The remains of Loyston sit beneath approximately ninety to one hundred feet of water, but in 1956 a severe drought allowed access to the former landscape. That January, reporter Carson Brewer and a news crew flew over the Loyston Sea to take pictures. Brewer "saw the foundations of the stores, the school building and the homes of what used to be the little town of Loyston." He also reported that cars were traveling on the once-submerged roads. Those cars carried archeologists, scavengers, and former residents trying to revisit where they once lived. More recently, scuba divers have been known to attempt this type of return to the landscape from the Loyston Point Campground. These adventurers have heard local stories about the ruins of a lost town at the bottom of the Loyston Sea just waiting to be rediscovered.[65]

3 The Gift of Good Land

Loss, Resettlement, and Stewardship through Everyday Nature in the Shenandoah National Park and on the New River

KATRINA M. POWELL AND
SAVANNAH PAIGE MURRAY

Like many other Americans during the Great Depression, Lula Haney wrote to President Franklin D. Roosevelt. Her 1936 letter asked him to help her family as they faced displacement from what would become Shenandoah National Park in the Blue Ridge Mountains of Virginia. She explained, "I always loved my 'mountain home' and never wanted to sell it." Haney provided President Roosevelt with some knowledge of "the location of this place," which she described as "100 acres here on top of the 'Blue Ridge' now the entrance of the 'Park' on Swift Run Gap."[1]

Haney's letter, written as her homeplace was being parceled away as part of the federal government's new plan for a national park on the nation's Eastern Seaboard, demonstrated the loss Haney faced as she and her family were displaced from their home. Letters like Haney's demonstrated "many of the ways that mountain residents resisted not only displacement" surrounding the creation of the park, "but also the ways that other people represented them." Between 1934 and 1938, many mountain families wrote to the federal government regarding their distress over losing their homes. These families were forced, via eminent domain, to sell their property at "fair market value." Other families, such as tenants or those who did not own homes or property, received no compensation. While Shenandoah National Park is often heralded as a successful accomplishment in American conservation, this 196,000-acre preserve came at the price of individual family as well as community losses.[2]

The loss of land, community, and livelihood in the area we now know as Shenandoah National Park has been well documented in a wide range of sources, from history and archaeology to folklore and storytelling. While the logistics of this resettlement have been detailed elsewhere, and loss of land and livelihood have been discussed in a variety of popular publications, scholars have yet to examine the loss associated with resident stewardship over the landscape. Many mountain residents were accustomed to farming, logging, and developing the land, all aspects of environmental stewardship that, once the park was created, residents were no longer able to continue. Once the park was developed, the government took over stewardship of the land.

The stewardship of local citizens in what was to become Shenandoah National Park was represented in letters closely aligned with Scott Hess's concept of "everyday nature."[3] In contrast, the park officials developed a notion of stewardship from the mainstream conservation movement at the time, which focused on elitist conceptions of what it meant to conserve the land, particularly in terms of maintaining the land as a recreational area for those with disposable income to visit the park. There was a conceptual divide between how residents and officials viewed stewardship. The displaced community and the National Park Service lacked a shared understanding of land stewardship, which resulted in several types of loss.

The historical context of the development of Shenandoah National Park provides an intellectual history of the stereotypes of mountain people and the roots of stewardship within the American conservation movement of the twentieth century. The popular conception of Appalachian residents as "backward," "ignorant," or "hillbillies" marked them as categorically opposed to the elite ideals of expertise and stewardship. Although many park officials could not conceive of mountain residents as land stewards, there is evidence that demonstrates the environmental consciousness of those removed, particularly their use of "everyday nature." This awareness inspired them to advocate for themselves as legitimate stewards of their surrounding environment. How park officials have worked over time to engage in new partnerships with mountain families is another layer of the Shenandoah removal experience. What happened at Shenandoah in the 1930s can be compared to the more contemporary removal controversy in the New River Valley in the 1960s and 1970s. This story of loss and gains demonstrates how residents, on the verge of being displaced for two proposed hydroelectric dams, used rhetorical constructions of everyday nature to make a case for their knowledge of and commitment to the stewardship of the land.

The National Park Service and Shenandoah National Park

When the National Park Service indicated that it wanted to establish a national park in the East, several Virginia business owners, including Skyland Resort owner

George Pollock, proposed a national park in Virginia. As business owners, they were convinced the park would provide economic development through tourism generally and for their businesses specifically. Like the Blue Ridge Parkway, the Shenandoah National Park was built with a highway so that tourists could drive their cars and see the vistas of the mountainous region. Park proponents glossed over the fact that there were nearly five hundred families living in the area and that in fact there was a socioeconomic range of land and business owners (subsistence farmers, large apple-orchard proprietors, gas-station owners, and timber and copper companies). Because the proponents did not consider the residents of the proposed park space, the National Park Service was unaware of the significant numbers of families living there. So after land was transferred from Virginia to the federal government, the process of removing families began.

Existing histories of the Shenandoah National Park focus on the group of local business leaders who proposed the mountainous Virginia area to the Department of the Interior in the late 1920s as an option for a national park in the eastern part of the country. Only a handful of scholarly sources acknowledge the process and challenges of family removal. Many landowners either sold their land willingly or donated their land in service of the park. African American families made up a small percentage of the five hundred landowners, and they left their property very early in the process. A few families required assistance in relocation and worked with local churches, the department of public welfare, or the Resettlement Administration to find alternative residences.[4]

Shenandoah, as a park founded in the already much-developed eastern part of the country, was different from many of the national parks because it was inhabited by people and did not fit perfectly into the notion of the wild, "natural" landscapes as conceived by the newly formed National Park Service.[5] The park's development was well underway by the time Franklin Roosevelt took office, but he was committed to land "improvement" as part of his New Deal agenda. The Civilian Conservation Corps (CCC) built Skyline Drive (connecting the Blue Ridge Parkway and the Shenandoah National Park), which became a positive example of how multiple agencies could complete New Deal projects and provide work during the Great Depression. Roosevelt was committed to soil conservation, dam construction, reforestation, regional planning, land improvement, and scenic preservation. Early in his presidency, he committed resources to improve entire regions of the country, especially in the South.[6]

The idea of improving the land is connected to the ways that conservation efforts were promoted during the early part of the twentieth century. As Sevren R.

Skyline Drive, built by the Civilian Conservation Corps, connected Shenandoah
National Park with the Blue Ridge Parkway. "Shenandoah National Park, Virginia,
Skyline Drive" by Arthur Rothstein, January 1942, Farm Security Administration,
Office of War Information Photograph Collection, Library of Congress Prints and
Photographs Division, Washington, DC.

Gourley explained, "Throughout the history of the National Park System, the ecological conservation movement has largely been supported by wealthier politically connected elites. . . . Conservationists also achieved early goals through the disparagement and marginalization of other cultures—paradigmatically evicting the poor to create playgrounds for the rich."[7] Indeed, Shenandoah National Park's founding was partially funded by John D. Rockefeller Jr., who, like many wealthy philanthropists at the time, held paternalistic (at best) views of the families living in the mountains. As a result, the participation of local communities in the stewardship of the land was blocked, creating a further sense of loss among surrounding communities.

The notion of wilderness as being unmarred by humans drove these views of improvement and conservation, both about the land and the people who lived there. Gourley argued, "Just and fair park resource stewardship cannot legitimately value the creation of a false wilderness over the concerns of cultural heirs of the displaced. These determinations take place within a broader debate about what constitutes the American identity—vague concepts of nature versus concrete elements in the heritage of American cultural pluralism. The National Park Service has an ethical obligation, rooted in equal representation, to reject management objectives that favor the privileged classes and to embrace park management for all Americans."[8] Gourley's argument about today's Park Service was based in the historical ways that elitist attitudes informed development of the park. Today, in fact, current administrators of the Shenandoah National Park—and other national parks—recognize this view and are engaged in a variety of community relationships and activities that recognize the importance of cultural history to the management of the park. This has not always been the case, however, as the sense of loss experienced by and continually expressed by communities affected by the creation of the park has been a critical part of the National Park Service's shift in community relations.[9]

Misunderstandings of Mountaineers and Stewardship

As a regional subgroup, Appalachian residents have been maligned, misunderstood, and disparaged for centuries. In *Appalachia on Our Mind* (1986), Henry D. Shapiro suggested that, in the decades following the Civil War, a burgeoning American middle-class consuming sensationalist local color literature about residents of Appalachia served as the intellectual basis for many common stereotypes of mountaineers. Thus, a narrative that Appalachian residents were isolated, backward, ignorant, and fatalistic dominated the public's perception.[10] Working from widely read travel narratives from the eighteenth century, Katherine Ledford pushed back the clock on these negative assumptions about mountaineers. In "A Landscape and a People Set Apart," Ledford argued that these vicious conceptions of a strange, underdeveloped, nearly feral population group originated even earlier than previously thought. Regardless of when these characterizations originated, they were deeply rooted and rhetorically powerful when the federal government began planning for family removals in the Shenandoah National Park.[11]

Throughout much of the late nineteenth and early twentieth centuries, scholars and popular writers cast Appalachian residents in a very negative light. For the residents of what would become Shenandoah National Park, perhaps none of these "serious" texts was more damaging than Mandel Sherman and Thomas R. Henry's *Hollow Folk* (1933), which appeared two years before the creation of the park. This study of "mountain people" in the Blue Ridge suggested that many industrious pioneers moved beyond the Appalachian Mountains into "the great valley of the Mississippi where today they are rated among our most progressive citizens." The authors suggested that the people who remained were "The 'Hollow Folk,'" who although being ironically "near to civilization," remain "strangely isolated" and have "undergone steady deterioration" as a result of their resistance to leave the mountains. Throughout *Hollow Folk,* Sherman and Henry provided a sensationalist, pseudoscientific analysis of people, culture, and daily life in the area that would become Shenandoah National Park. The authors explained that the names of people and places were fictitious, but they frequently chose similar names, such as referring to Corbin Hollow as "Colvin Hollow." *Hollow Folk* thus functioned rhetorically to cast the identity, culture, and lifestyle of the mountaineers in Shenandoah National Park in opposition to American progress, contributing to the hateful treatment and utter absence of collaboration with the National Park Service many residents were exposed to throughout the park's development.[12]

Misconceptions and stereotypes influenced how the National Park Service carried out the work of removal of mountain families in the area that would become Shenandoah National Park. Further, inaccurate characterizations of mountain life made it much easier for federal workers to ignore local culture, land stewardship, and dispersed communities in favor of progress and conservation. One of the misperceptions of families who lived within the park boundaries was that they did not understand the notion of conservation or that they engaged in farming practices that stressed the land. Researchers, reporters, judges, and social workers characterized mountain families as illiterate and uneducated in caring for the land.

Road Leading to Corbin Hollow in the Shenandoah National Park, 1935. "Road to Corbin Hollow, Shenandoah National Park, Virginia," by Arthur Rothstein, October 1935, Farm Security Administration, Office of War Information Photograph Collection, Library of Congress Prints and Photographs Division, Washington, DC.

Such rhetoric contributed to the decision by the state of Virginia to "condemn" the land in 1928 and donate it to the National Park Service in 1934.[13] However, many of the families living in the area loved the land, saw themselves as responsible for the land, and intimately knew the landscape as they traveled by foot or by horse across the rough terrain to visit neighbors, attend school, and use the post office. They maintained apple orchards and large gardens, and were not as isolated as park promoters suggested.[14]

Facing displacement, residents of what became the Shenandoah National Park, and similarly those along the New River later in the century, resisted and adjusted their sense of stewardship in the wake of a significant loss of land and community. The role of mountain stereotypes in these two cases of resettlement resistance also highlights the varied and "everyday" ways that communities face loss as it relates to land-use issues in Virginia and the country generally. Federal officials assumed a paternalistic view toward mountain families and therefore left residents behind during its development and ignored their requests to participate in the care for the land once the park became a federal entity. This lack of willingness to have residents participate further exacerbated what were already tensions building within communities, as families were resettled and federal workers prepared the land according to their plans.

Derek G. Ross suggested in his "Common Topics and Commonplaces of Environmental Rhetoric" (2013) that "stewardship" is a common term in environmental preservation in modern settings. In his survey of 125 visitors to the Glen Canyon Dam in 2007, Ross found that, for many visitors, responses relating to stewardship "put humankind in charge of the maintenance of the earth." Yet there was further nuance in the meaning of the term, ranging from "preserving or conserving resources, general cleanliness [of the park], or even wholesale destruction for the betterment of technological/financial gain." While Ross's survey data help us see that stewardship is still a common topic within contemporary environmental discourse, he concluded based on his own data that "more research" on the topic of stewardship "is needed."[15]

Environmental advocate and author Wendell Berry also discussed stewardship but in a spiritual context. In "The Gift of Good Land" (1979), Berry observed, "The divine mandate to use the world justly and charitably, then, defines every person's moral predicament as that of a steward." Further, "this predicament is hopeless and meaningless unless it produces an appropriate discipline: stewardship. And stewardship is hopeless and meaningless unless it involves long-term courage, preservation, devotion, and skill. This skill is not to be confused with any accomplishment or grace of spirit or intellect. It has to do with everyday properties in the practical use and care of created things."[16] For Berry, "The great study of stewardship, then, is 'to know / That which before us lies in daily life' and to be practiced and prepared 'in things that most concern.' The angel is talking about good work, which is to talk about skill. In the loss of skill we lose stewardship; in losing stewardship we lose fellowship; we become outcasts from the great neighborhood of Creation. It is possible—as our experience with *this* good land shows—to exile ourselves from Creation, and to ally ourselves with the principle of destruction—which is, ultimately, the principle of nonentity."[17] The removal of families from the land that became Shenandoah National Park affected multiple generations, who retained a deep distrust of the National Park Service.

In his interview data, Ross found similar connections between stewardship and religiosity, specifically Christianity. Quoting an interview with a fifty-nine-year-old man from Arizona, Ross wrote, "'I'm a God-fearing man, and I believe God put us here to take care of this earth.'" Ross offered his own analysis to help us understand this intriguing quote, suggesting that, "In this case, the respondent uses religion, specifically 'God,' to encapsulate an entire argument of stewardship" as stewardship "ties religion-based logic and emotional values to mandated environmental action." Likewise, the residents of Shenandoah National Park and the New River Valley perceived their responsibility in reverent, if not specifically religious terms, countering the assumptions about them as ambivalent to the land. Park officials did not recognize this reverent stewardship, perhaps because it was situated within the everyday and the ordinary, rather than the definition of stewardship as "special" or "exemplary." This view of land use emerged from the elite of the late nineteenth century who imagined the landscape as "pristine" for those with the leisure time and expendable income to enjoy a particular kind of conservation.[18]

As Ethan Carr explained, the creation of national parks in the early twentieth century opened up the "American countryside" to "middle class tourists as never before."[19] While the parks opened American vistas and scenic areas to some, this access to the environment was not equitable, as the majority of visitors coming to many of the parks, including Shenandoah, were coming to the park via car, a mark of socioeconomic status that was above average in the time of the creation of the park. The emphasis on automobile transportation in Shenandoah National Park is also apparent in the Skyline Drive that guides visitors into the park and connects to the Blue Ridge Parkway. The parkway and thus Skyline Drive function to link Shenandoah National Park and the Great Smoky Mountains National Park, thereby making the parks less accessible to visitors without cars. Though there are trailheads in the surrounding counties and some parking lots for those trailheads, the majority of visitors access the park via automobile.

Everyday Nature and Reverence for Place

Lula Haney's letter to President Roosevelt can be best understood through the theoretical term "everyday nature." In his 2010 essay "Imagining an Everyday Nature," Scott Hess questioned the romantic view of nature as "the place where we go, both imaginatively and physically, to escape" from modernity and the struggles, stressors, and trials of our daily lives. While many of us view nature in this romantic light, including many visitors to Shenandoah National Park, this view is not without consequences. Hess argued that, by distancing ourselves from nature conceptually, viewing it as a pastoral retreat, we actively skew "our environmental awareness and priorities in ways that blind us to the devastating ecological effects of our own everyday lives." For Hess, the modern conception of nature is crafted in "opposition to the social, the economic, and the everyday." While our mainstream conceptions of nature are not helpful for Hess, he offers everyday nature as a remedy to this disconnected and disillusioned version of the natural world.[20]

Everyday nature is rooted in understanding the interconnectedness of the natural world and our daily lives. Hess suggested that everyday nature includes understanding nature in its habitual "as well as heightened experience, work as well as leisure, human as well as nonhuman relationships." Everyday nature thus incorporates respect for and knowledge of the landscapes and natural environments we encounter in our everyday lives, as well as understanding nature "through our ordinary lives, work, actions, and relationships." Hess argued that "we can imagine nature without having to escape our own lives, work, and relationship," thereby "returning value and spirituality into our everyday lives and relationships as part of a wider process of re-sacramentalization." While Hess offers everyday nature as a contemporary remedy to our issues in environmental discourses and nature writing, the presence of this approach in residents' letters from the 1930s further highlights the rhetorical skill and cultural knowledge of these mountain citizens.[21]

Several residents' letters highlighted the ways that the landscape was often harsh, particularly for farming or during the long winter months. A connection to the land despite harsh conditions disputed the utopian notion of the pastoral, bucolic sense of nature. Several letters from residents in Shenandoah suggested a less than ideal situation and yet a desire to remain nonetheless. For instance, Otis Davis wrote to the Park Service to request "permission to plan the patches on

Ambros Shifflets place."[22] He explained that his land was not suitable to grow anything that year, and suggested planting on his neighbor's vacant property (which the Park Service owned at this point). As Terry Gifford argued, a post-pastoral or "right relationship with nature that is hopefully not utopian in the idealized sense" suggests an awareness of the land and farming practices that must work with the land.[23] Other letters spoke to residents' hope to use the land to maintain their lives, so that they would not have to "depend on the relief," suggesting their recognition that their connection to the land and proper use of the land would mean their autonomy.

Giffords's post-pastoral theory addresses this aspect of nature in our daily lives, and for the residents of Shenandoah the everyday difficult work of living in the mountains did not present an idyllic way of life, even if the landscape was presented as the idyllic setting for a national park.[24] Visiting the park as a tourist was indeed quite different from working the land for subsistence. These two conceptions of nature are clearly intertwined and served as rhetorical markers for the kinds of decisions made by state and federal legislators in the taking of property for the public good.

Challenging Displacement in the New River Valley

In the case of Shenandoah National Park in the 1930s, displacement occurred because park officials were unable to recognize residents' potential contribution to stewardship. In contrast, in the 1970s, a coalition of residents in Northwestern North Carolina and Southwest Virginia successfully rallied against corporate and federal efforts to further develop waterways in the New River Valley. Leaders of the coalition used the concept of everyday nature as a rhetorical tactic to successfully resist displacement and subsequent resettlement. In 1965, the Appalachian Power Company (APC) proposed the Blue Ridge Power Project, a plan that included two new hydroelectric dams on the New River within Grayson County, Virginia. In 1962, the APC conducted a feasibility study regarding the generation of hydroelectric power on the New River, particularly on an Upper New River tributary, Wilson Creek. On March 11, 1963, the Federal Power Commission (FPC) granted the APC a two-year permit for their study. Upon the conclusion of their study, the APC released a plan for proposed hydroelectric dams which would include a pumped-storage facility. The pumped-storage component of the dams would generate power during peak demand times by releasing water over the surface of the hydroelectric dam. During times of low power demand, water would be pumped from a lower reservoir back to the reservoir above the dam, so that, according to APC, the same water could be used to generate power two separate times.[25]

In addition to generating additional electricity for approximately twenty-five to thirty-five years to supply the growing energy demands of the United States, the proposed APC dams would also flood more than forty-two thousand acres of farmland within Ashe and Alleghany counties in North Carolina and in Grayson County, Virginia. When the Blue Ridge Power Project was first introduced, some local residents responded positively, thinking it might bring new industries and economic development to their communities. However, many local citizens opposed the dams, and an opposition movement to the APC and the Blue Ridge Power Project emerged soon after its initial announcement.[26] Residents objected, not only because of the massive economic losses that would be associated with the dams, as the APC would take lands via eminent domain, but also because of the interrelatedness of their identities and everyday lives in connection with the free-flowing river. This type of loss was evident in the following statement from one concerned citizen: "The New River was part of my growing up. The thought of it dammed, its lovely course swallowed up by a lake, the mountain coves and valleys drowned forever cuts like a knife. . . . If and when the New River vanishes, a part of my life will go with it."[27] As soon as news of the Blue Ridge Power Project spread, residents began to voice their resistance because, much like the residents of what would become Shenandoah National Park, citizens along the New River understood their daily lives, work, and communities and intimately connected to the surrounding landscape.

In January 1975, opponents of the dam project formally organized the National Committee for the New River (NCNR), a grassroots environmental organization composed of a vast array of individuals, including attorneys, schoolteachers, ballad singers, farmers, and politicians. NCNR members aimed to prevent the implementation of the APC's Blue Ridge Power Project, and further, sought to include the New River in the National Wild and Scenic Rivers System, the highest order of protection awarded to American waterways.[28] Within the first two years of the organization's existence, members of the NCNR attempted a variety of tactics to prevent the installation of the dams along the New River.

One of the NCNR's tactics included asking the governor of North Carolina to recognize the significance of the New River and to offer support for their opposition to the dams. For example, on Sunday, July 18, 1976, Governor James Holshouser Jr. granted "A Day of Prayer for the New River" in an official order, "with the hope that residents of the New River Valley in Ashe and Alleghany counties of North

Carolina" would be joined by "thousands of fellow North Carolinians in asking that God's Will be done along the New River." Holshouser's order included a prayer which embodies the interconnectedness of everyday life and the environment as associated with "everyday nature." The prayer not only centered upon the continuance of the "unique way of life which has been handed down for generations" among residents of the New River Valley, but also commented on the type of work these residents often do in their environment, stating that "these hard-working residents till fertile bottomland soil to feed the world's growing throng of starving." In addition to the type of work conducted in the New River Valley, this prayer also included descriptions of the residents' way of life in the region more broadly, as "these people enjoy their quiet, rural life among family farms, rustic churches and ancestral cemeteries within God's magnificent handiwork."[29] Holshouser's day of prayer announcement incorporated everyday nature by emphasizing the ways in which the landscape is *used,* rather than painting the New River Valley as a pristine wilderness. The prayer further demonstrated how closely connected to the environment local residents were not only in their work, but also in their homes, churches, and way of life.

In addition to calling on state leaders for support, NCNR dam opponents also spoke directly to federal leaders to communicate the intrinsic value of the New River, and how the river played an important role in their way of life. For example, while testifying before Congress about the proposed New River dams, Ashe County resident Sidney Gambill incorporated everyday nature into his statement by describing his county and the people who inhabit it. Gambill testified that, were the hydroelectric dams to be built, the United States "stands to lose its most venerable river; the people in the New River valley stand to lose a way of life. . . . They have been good to the good earth. They are more attuned to peace and quiet than to the hustle and bustle of industrialized society. They talk of politics, religion, home-spun philosophy, [and] how to improve their farming practices."[30]

In his testimony, Gambill portrayed himself and his neighbors as people whose lifestyle was well adjusted to the rural setting in Northwestern North Carolina and as people who are "good to the good earth" as stewards of the environment who are just as concerned with the development and success of their communities as they are with the yields and preservation of their farmlands. Both in the case of the New River dam controversy as well as the resistance to the implementation of Shenandoah National Park, invoking everyday nature articulated Appalachian identity and culture as well as mountain residents' intimate connection to the natural world. The case of the New River "dam fight" demonstrates that the issues of displacement are not limited to the first half of the twentieth century in the Appalachian South. Despite the differences in these two cases, the similarities in how residents articulated their understanding of everyday nature demonstrated mountain residents' rhetorical resistance to displacement and resettlement.

By the end of the second year of the NCNR, the organization's president, Edmund I. Adams, released a memo to all members informing them that they could finally "enjoy the satisfaction of having accomplished our prime objective— the saving of the New River." After more than a decade of wondering whether the dams would be implemented, thereby flooding their homes and farms, residents of Ashe, Alleghany, and Grayson counties finally received a definitive answer about the Blue Ridge Project. On September 25, 1976, Congress approved the bill to add the New River to the National Wild and Scenic Rivers System. This action officially prevented the construction of additional hydroelectric dams on the New River and guaranteed other environmental protections.[31]

On September 11, 1976, President Gerald Ford signed the bill into law which officially added 26.5 miles of the New River in North Carolina into the National Wild and Scenic Rivers System. To celebrate their long-awaited victory, members of the NCNR gathered along the banks of the New River at the Mollie Osborne Shoals in Grayson County, Virginia. NCNR President Adams described the event as one full of "good entertainment and merry-making on a serene river bank surrounded by mountains resplendent with fall colors." As a way to symbolize closure to the issue, NCNR members burned the Federal Power Commission license for the Blue Ridge Power Project, the hotly contested document which at many points within the "dam fight" functioned as the greatest hurdle to the group's success.[32] Invoking the connections between the river and residents' daily lives proved to be a powerful rhetorical tool to challenge and eventually defeat efforts to displace citizens.[33]

Mountain Residents and Stewardship through Everyday Nature

Perhaps the clearest example of everyday nature within a park resident's letter appears in the words of Walter Dean Taylor. Taylor owned sixty-two acres in what was to become Shenandoah National Park. After the state of Virginia condemned his land in 1935, he remained on his property until 1938 under a "special use permit." During this time, he wrote a series of six letters to park officials, requesting that they hire him to survey and catalog the "forest game and fish and flaurs." In one of these letters, Taylor asked for park officials to provide him with a camera and to employ him in making portraits "at the forest in all the Park and all the cliffs and falls and bieuty of lots of Placeses that has not as yet Bin taken" because many were not yet aware of those locations. In this same letter, Taylor attempted to demonstrate his own understanding of everyday nature, not only in his knowledge of some of the valley's most scenic spots, but also in his knowledge of "the different kinds of Vines and Berryes and weeds and flowers." He listed 127 variations of trees and plants, ranging from "64 kinds hickry," to "12 kinds ake" and even "2 kinds wild cherry." Throughout his letters, Taylor demonstrated his embrace of everyday nature as he saw the landscape around him in his daily life as intricately tied to his life's work. Rather than seeing the land that became the park as a place to escape, Taylor's knowledge of the region clearly demonstrated that his understanding of nature was intricately connected to his daily life.[34]

In addition to embracing everyday nature, Taylor also made a compelling case for his aptitude as an advocate and steward of the land that became the park. In his February 19, 1936, letter, Taylor stated that he "always take a Pride in saving [the] forest game and Birds and fish for if we dont Protect this we will soon have none." Taylor emphasized his immense knowledge of the landscape and his pride of it in order to emphasize his abilities as a steward of the land. Taylor further established himself as an effective steward as he reported on how others abused the environment. He wrote: "some serten Parties has Bin Fishing an white ake [White Oak River] and ather streams in [the] Park eria and have Bin using dinemite . . . and I though[t] you aught to no this." Similarly, in his October 7, 1937, letter he cataloged fruit, flowers, and game in the park and confirmed his willingness to document all he knew for the park. He wrote: "i will Be rite here nite and day to Protect all thes and I will take a Pride in taking Care af all."[35]

While Walter Dean Taylor's letters demonstrated his conception of everyday nature through his articulation of local knowledge about the region, his emphasis on the pride for protecting the park demonstrates that his understanding of everyday nature not only included being knowledgeable about his "everyday" landscape, but also feeling that, because of this everyday approach to nature, he was an ideal steward for this land. Taylor's letters explain how mountain residents understood their natural environment, not seeing the park as an escape, but as an everyday landscape that they knew intimately, one that they connected to their daily lives and work. Taylor's words also help us see that residents conceived of their ability to be stewards of the park landscape as not only a product of their everyday nature and local knowledge, but their pride in the place itself, all of which made Taylor and many of his neighbors eager to volunteer their services to the park as stewards.

Indeed, in their letters to park officials, several mountain residents requested ongoing participation with park officials to help maintain the land. Likewise, residents along the New River in North Carolina and Virginia advocated for the value of their unique knowledge of the land. In these two cases, and in many others, state and federal agencies made decisions about concepts of conservation, wilderness, and stewardship that excluded the people who lived there, thus overlooking their potential contributions.

In addition to their disparate understandings of nature, residents and National Park Service officials viewed the landscape differently. Rob Nixon's opposing terms, "vernacular" and "official" landscapes, articulated the divide between how the mountaineers and the government officials understood the environment and, thus, how best to care for it. Nixon suggested that a "vernacular landscape" is "shaped by the affective, historically textured maps that communities have devised over generations, maps replete with names and routes, maps alive to significant ecological and surface geological features" and is "integral to the socioenvironmental dynamics of a community."[36] For example, Taylor's letters emphasized that many residents of what would become Shenandoah National Park developed their own sort of "mental map" based on local knowledge of the surrounding environment.

The National Park Service approached the natural space as an official landscape, as depicted in their special-use permits, while Nixon argued that official landscapes were oblivious to the maps of vernacular landscapes. He wrote that "the land in a bureaucratic, externalizing, and extraction-driven manner . . . is often pitilessly instrumental."[37] The issuance of special-use permits demonstrated how little the National Park Service valued the vernacular landscapes of former residents and their communities. Rather than being respectful of the deep connections that many residents had for the land, Park Service employees seemed much more interested in "extracting" people and resources from the park, a management style that was instrumental at best, and patriarchal at worst. Nixon suggested that the implementation of an official landscape which is often "projected onto ecosystems inhabited by . . . 'dispensable citizens' . . . displaces and disperses those who had developed through their vernacular landscapes their own adaptable, if always imperfect and vulnerable, relation" to their surrounding landscape.[38]

The distinction between the vernacular and the official demonstrated the conflicting definitions of the landscape. Further, how to best care for protected natural spaces created tense interactions between mountain residents and Park Service officials throughout the development of the Shenandoah National Park. That the residents were ultimately displaced and not allowed to participate in the stewardship of the land was not only a loss for individuals, but also for the potential ways they might have positively shaped stewardship practices within the park. In discussing the history of federal land management, Sevren R. Gourley explained that the Park Service has "wide legal discretion in park resource management" and has historically favored ecological conservation over human history. He argued for a better balance between ecology and historic preservation in order to achieve ethical stewardship of federal lands.[39] While Gourley did not address the more recent efforts of the Park Service to do this, particularly through its cultural resource and educational interpretations divisions, he described the commitment of the federal government to be responsible stewards of the land.[40] How stewardship was defined and enacted affected the ways that surrounding communities have been treated with respect to their participation in stewardship of the land. Today, the National Park Service is making a more concerted effort through programming and interpretative content to acknowledge the importance of the vernacular landscape that many mountain residents still envision when they enter the park.

Contemporary Efforts for Resident Participation and Community Relations

Walter Dean Taylor's commitment to the land was bittersweet. His family was eventually moved by the Park Service and the Resettlement Administration to housing in Madison County, Virginia. Further, he was never hired by the Park Service, even on a part-time or volunteer basis. In the 1950s, former resident Richard Nicholson petitioned the federal government to let families move back to the park to live on easements, much like the practice in the Great Smoky Mountains National Park and along the Blue Ridge Parkway.[41] The Park Service denied the petition from Nicholson and other former residents multiple times. One way that families have been able to remain involved in the park's operations are through maintaining family cemeteries. Because Shenandoah was significantly populated before the land was taken, there are about one hundred family cemeteries in the park. Road access is not allowed in the wilderness-designated spaces, and therefore descendants have a difficult time visiting the cemeteries. Thus, the preservation of the natural landscape conflicts with the preservation of memorializing family remains.[42]

Ned Ellerbe, whose maternal grandmother was displaced from the park, maintains the Jenkins family cemetery. A few, like the Jenkins cemetery, are active, and Ellerbe has access, via government permission, to the fire road which leads to the cemetery where he performs routine maintenance. In a 2003 interview he said, "I feel like it's important to take care of my people. I make it look nice so that anybody can go up there and see their family, or see a little history."[43] In addition to maintaining the cemetery for his family's use, he recognizes the importance of his work for the cultural history of the park. This recognition of stewardship as including this cultural part of the park's history is a point of pride for Ellerbe. Only a very few non-park employees have a key to the fire-road gate, which demonstrates the trust that the National Park Service has for Ellerbe and others to do this work.

In addition to this cooperation with families having active cemeteries in the park, Park Service employees work with the community groups and leaders on a regular basis. This cooperation includes combating environmental challenges such as deer disease management, forest-fire prevention, hunting to control game populations, invasive species eradication, endangered species protection, and the effects of climate change. The superintendent of the park regularly attends county supervisor meetings to report on issues affecting the surrounding communities. These meetings are sometimes tense because of a long-standing distrust and bitterness from the descendants of those removed and other members of the local community. The complexities of community relations are part of the daily work of National Park Service employees to build local partnerships and manage the land. Indeed, this work has paid off as community relations continue to stengthen.

One aspect of these community relations includes a series of panels that the park participates in yearly. The Virginia Natural Resources Leadership Institute offers professionals working in conservation development (such as those in the Department of Transportation, the Nature Conservancy, and the Southern Environmental Law Center) a series of workshops to understand the complexities of working with the community when designating land for conservation. One panel, called the "History of Shenandoah National Park," includes panelists from the park, the community, and the scholarly community to discuss the long-term effects of the history and current relations. Claire Comer is a frequent panelist, a park ranger, and a descendent of removed residents. Comer researched and designed the Byrd Visitor Center's exhibit on the eviction of residents, working closely with the local group Children of Shenandoah, making the story accessible for the millions of visitors to the park each year. Another panelist is local schoolteacher Kim Dean, who participated in the "Teacher-Ranger-Teacher" program. She spent summers in the park learning how to incorporate historical aspects of the park into her curriculum. Dean, whose family was displaced but now owns land adjacent to the park, developed the educational content that is now on the park's website for all educators to access as they feature the park in their classes. Highlighting the cultural history of the park has positive effects for the surrounding communities as their connections to the park are made visible. Both Comer and Dean exemplify the everydayness of stewardship and the positive outcomes of communities and federal agencies working together.

Rhetorics of Memorialization and Healing the Past

Bill Henry, the founder of the Blue Ridge Heritage project, is another panelist for the Virginia Natural Resources Leadership Institute. This project is focused on constructing monuments to memorialize the families who lost their homes for the creation of the park. His group worked with the superintendent and other park officials, county boards of supervisors, and a committed group of volunteers to establish monuments in seven of the eight counties which have land within the park's boundaries. The Blue Ridge Heritage project includes members from the Children of Shenandoah, a group very active in the redress for the way the park was formed. Committed to telling the story of the park, they worked closely with Park Ranger Claire Comer as Shenandoah National Park employees designed the exhibit on cultural history. Today, the final Blue Ridge Heritage monument is planned in the last county, Albemarle. In a panel discussion in September 2018, Henry spoke about the park's role in supporting his group's efforts in creating monuments. These monuments are not located within the park but rather just outside the boundaries under the jurisdiction of local communities. Park employees attend the dedication ceremonies as a way of showing their acknowledgment of the past.

In addition to these efforts, park rangers routinely provide guided tours that point out the variety of cultural artifacts, including remnants of old homesites. The park, through funding from the Shenandoah National Park Trust, offers a variety of programs like Teacher-Ranger-Teacher that bring in archaeologists, historians, scientists, and educators who are researching the park's cultural history. In addition, the park recently released an innovative web-based interactive map, called "Exploring Shenandoah National Park History—One Tract at a Time." This project "provides the public with historic land tract boundaries 'linked' to information about the tract including land ownership, acreage, houses, structures and land use."[44]

These examples of "everyday memorialization" are part of today's educational and interpretive components of the park.[45] Inclusion of local communities in planning for the future of the park represents an important shift in how the Park Service approaches community relations. In each of these examples, the people who lived on the land and who are descendants of the displaced recognize the importance of the land to community identity and conservation. In this way, their words and actions directly counter the stereotypes used against families as decisions were made to remove them. While dissenting voices remain, many in the surrounding communities are interested in healing the past through participation in stewardship of the land, so that stewardship becomes a way to recover from loss.

▲▲

The instances of resistance to removal in both Shenandoah National Park and along the New River demonstrate that everyday nature informed how mountain residents understood and interacted with the landscape around them. In the case of Shenandoah National Park, the mountain residents who once resided on that land were displaced. The majority of displaced families settled in nearby areas, often on land adjacent to the park. Although these families were unable to stop the creation of the park and remain on their land, future generations have engaged with park officials in productive ways to honor the past of these lands.

Decades later and a few hundred miles south, residents in Grayson County, Virginia, and Ashe and Alleghany counties in North Carolina successfully defeated plans for more hydroelectric dams on the New River. The dams were never built, and communities were not displaced. The case of environmental activism along the New River demonstrates the rhetorical power of invoking everyday nature. As Scott Hess noted, everyday nature has great potential to help us establish a more secure and sustainable connection between nature and human nature because it allows us to recognize that "our environmental relationships are inseparable from social relationships."[46]

By internalizing nature deeply into their "sense of identity and culture," families displaced from the Shenandoah National Park and existing communities along the New River formed deep bonds with the surrounding landscape. They integrated their connection to the natural world into their daily life, work, and community activities. Everyday nature stemmed from a different view of nature, one in which nature is quite literally where we live, the place we call home, rather than a place for leisure or a pastoral retreat from urban life. While the connection between nature and home can make everyday nature a powerful rhetorical tool, it also makes displacement and loss, as in the case of so many residents in Shenandoah National Park, all the more painful and traumatic.

The complexities of eminent domain and forced removal contribute to the inevitable collisions between rhetorics of conservation and stewardship with cultural history and preservation. Many of the displaced families, through their deep identification with the land, saw nature and landscapes as including their daily lives. As concepts of wilderness shifted away from the false dichotomy between nature and humans, the Park Service has also shifted its practices in engaging communities and their histories. As decision makers continue to grapple with policy dictated by grand, abstract ideas, the Shenandoah removal and community renewal story should not be ignored. There is a great public responsibility to consider the everyday lives of people living in or near the parks, or in or near publicly used land of any kind.

In late 2018 and into early 2019, the federal government shut down for over a month. National parks were particularly affected by the closure. In several parks, thoughtless tourists abused the environment and overwhelmed the limited resources. Shenandoah suffered some "annoying" damage, but not as critical as that suffered at the Joshua Tree National Park. For thirty-five days, federal employees in the National Park Service were legally not allowed to report to work. Many local communities took up stewardship of the land. In Shenandoah National Park, the fundraising partner, Shenandoah National Park Trust, paid for the portable waste units to be emptied and cleaned and for refuse to be removed so that hikers and visitors could continue to enjoy the park.

In another example of working with the community, Shenandoah National Park collaborated with the Piedmont Environmental Council, US Fish and Wildlife Service, the Virginia Department of Game and Inland Fisheries, the non-profit Trout Unlimited, the Nimick Forbesway Foundation, and the Ohrstrom Foundation to construct a much-needed bridge at the Madison County trailhead entrance to the White Oak Canyon Trail. The new bridge is located on land belonging to the Graves family, adjacent to Shenandoah. Indeed, the Graves family had land taken when the park was founded. This long-standing relationship has taken decades to develop and, with the cooperation of these entities, a solution to parking and access was accomplished.

These and other community partnerships have become more critical, and the instance of the government shutdown highlights the importance of local networks.

Despite historical loss and the generational and cyclical effects of the loss of land, people's identities remain tied to the land. The history of the Shenandoah National Park is marked with an interest in protecting and preserving the land. Furthermore, the Park Service recognizes its racist attitudes during its early history and today is committed to racial equality both in its hiring practices and in providing access to all visitors.[47] Today there is a renewed commitment to local conservation and stewardship through partnerships which may be able to change the lengthy narrative of loss for those families and their descendants who were removed to make way for a shared natural public space for new generations to enjoy.

4 Contested Sacrifice

Loss and the Creation of Mammoth Cave National Park

ALYSSA D. WARRICK

On September 18, 1946, state and federal officials and hundreds of onlookers gathered at Mammoth Cave, Kentucky, to dedicate Mammoth Cave as the nation's twenty-sixth national park. In his address handing the property to the federal government, the Kentucky governor, Simeon Willis, honored those who had made the park possible, noting: "Many who helped are no longer with us. We dedicate this day to honor the memory of those who did not live to enjoy this day's triumph; to congratulate those still with us who struggled for the ideal; and to the millions who will come here from all over the world to provide entertainment, instruction, and inspiration."[1]

The governor honored the living and deceased members of the Mammoth Cave National Park Association, an organization of Louisville and Bowling Green, Kentucky, businessmen who banded together to create the national park. He did not mention one group who made the park possible—the five hundred 'or so families who once claimed as their homes the land that now made the park. The closest the governor came to acknowledging the families' loss was imparting a paean to the national park ideal: "Kentucky does not part with Mammoth Cave; it merely transfers to the custody of the nation a great national asset for the perpetual use of the great and generous people." The governor's address featured the first narrative of the park's creation and ignored that anyone had lived there at all, presenting Mammoth Cave as a near primeval world wonder, and the land above it as a nearly untouched wilderness. This "greenwashing" of the park's history was a new verse in an old song of dispossession, forced removal, and national park creation.[2]

Loss has been an ongoing theme at Mammoth Cave, especially during the establishment of the park. Mammoth Cave garnered attention as a tourist attraction in the nineteenth century, and the geography of the area and the prospect of extra income inspired cave exploration in South Central Kentucky. By the mid-1920s, the competitive nature of showing caves propelled a wealthier group of businessmen and civic leaders to push for Mammoth Cave's inclusion into the national park system. It was a difficult process to acquire Mammoth Cave and the surrounding caves, many of which today are known to connect together in the Flint–Mammoth Cave System, the longest cave system in the world at over four hundred miles of mapped and surveyed passages. The people who lived in cave country reacted to the park-making process, demonstrating opposition in courtrooms and on the environment itself. The question should be asked: What was gained, and what was lost in the creation of Mammoth Cave National Park?

Background of the Region

By 1750, white frontiersmen and the biological pioneers—diseases—had decimated the Shawnee and Cherokee people who had called the cave region home. Among the first written records about Mammoth Cave were surveys and deeds marking it as a saltpeter cave. Valentine Simons, the first deed holder of the cave, sold his interest to merchants Hyman Gratz of Philadelphia and Charles Wilkins of Lexington, who had contracted with E. I. du Pont to provide saltpeter to make gunpowder during the War of 1812. Enslaved African American men worked a twenty-four-hour mining operation at its peak. Gratz eventually purchased Wilkins's interest and operated the cave as a tourist attraction from afar, with a local man in charge of the meager lodgings and cave tours.[3]

In 1839, Dr. John Croghan of Louisville, Kentucky, purchased the cave and spent time developing the cave and surface amenities. Croghan even planned a hotel inside the cave, with visitors to be taken in via horse-drawn wagon, but this did not come to fruition. Croghan, like the Mammoth Cave owners before him, made his fortune at the cave on the backs of enslaved African Americans. Enslaved cave guides led wealthy visitors through cave passages, made subterranean discoveries, and contributed to the knowledge of the cave. Most notably, Stephen Bishop, one of the enslaved guides, created from memory a map of the cave for an 1844 guidebook. Upon Croghan's death in 1849, his will provided that his eleven nieces and nephews hold the cave in trust until the last one died, and then the cave was to be sold to the highest bidder. These nieces and nephews lived on the coasts, and thus served as largely absentee owners, with the exception of the husband of one trustee serving as a manager. Like many classical Appalachian narratives, these outsiders extracted a resource in the form of tourist dollars from the cave at the expense of locals in the Mammoth Cave region. While the cave offered employment to a rural population, in the late fall and winter visitation bottomed out.[4]

At the same time, some locals explored and developed other nearby caves as tourist attractions to compete with Mammoth Cave. Beginning around 1859, with the discovery of Diamond Caverns about seven miles from Mammoth Cave (and seven miles closer to the railroad station at Glasgow Junction, today known as Park City), local landowners started searching for caves on their property. Cave names indicate the attempts they made to confuse visitors and draw visitation away from Mammoth: Grand Caverns, Long Avenue Cave, Mammoth Onyx Cave, Crystal Cave, Great Onyx Cave, Colossal Cavern, and the New Entrance to Mammoth Cave all competed with each other at various times until the 1920s. The intense competition, known as the Kentucky Cave Wars, led to the death of local cave explorer Floyd Collins in February 1925. Collins's three-week ordeal of being trapped in Sand Cave made nationwide headlines and was one of the biggest human-interest stories of the interwar period.[5] With the last Croghan heiresses in their twilight years and the hypercompetitiveness between cave owners, businessmen in Louisville, Lexington, and Bowling Green organized the Mammoth Cave National Park Association (MCNPA) to create a national park out of Mammoth Cave and the surrounding area. Floyd Collins's death, the MCNPA argued, could have been prevented if Mammoth Cave had been a national park. Their effort coincided with a drive to create other national parks in the East.

In 1924, Secretary of the Interior Hubert Work created the Southern Appalachian National Park Committee (SANPC, later Commission) to study potential park sites in the East. Among sites like the Great Smoky Mountains, Grandfather Mountain, and the Shenandoah Mountains, the commission examined Mammoth Cave's possibility as a national park. Members of Congress and Secretary Work were not entirely willing to accept a cave that had been toured for over one hundred years and showed the scars of exploitation compared to the "untouched" western national parks. In May 1925, geologist Willis T. Lee and members of the SANPC visited the Mammoth Cave area to survey its potential as a national park.[6] The MCNPA entertained the National Park Commission and accompanied them on visits to caves. Kentucky Congressman Maurice H. Thatcher, who sponsored a Mammoth Cave National Park bill in the House of Representatives, confided to Louisville & Nashville Railroad (L&N) real estate agent and MCNPA secretary

George Zubrod that the commission had been "unfriendly to the project" initially.[7] The visit changed their minds.

In their report, the Southern Appalachian National Park Commission agreed that Mammoth Cave should become a national park. The SANPC declared that, in addition to the score of show caves opened for touring, "There is good evidence that many more caverns yet to be discovered exist in this immediate territory and it seems likely that most if not all of this entire group of caverns eventually will be found to be connected by passageways forming a great underground labyrinth of remarkable geological and recreational interest perhaps unparalleled elsewhere."[8] Additionally, the commission believed that the approved park projects at Shenandoah, Great Smoky Mountains, and Mammoth Cave should begin purchasing options on land so that they could donate it in fee simple.[9]

Even with the SANPC giving the approval for a Mammoth Cave National Park, many others interested in the project expressed doubts. Secretary Work did not make a favorable report on Mammoth Cave.[10] Following his superior, influential National Park Service director Stephen T. Mather remained silent on the matter. Some members of Congress did not feel the park would be big enough.[11] A growing voice in nature preservation, Robert Sterling Yard of the National Parks Association, could not envision a cave as a park at all. Writing to John C. Merriam of the Carnegie Institution, Yard lamented, "I can't get used to calling a cave a park, for it's exactly what it isn't."[12] The dark underground passages contrasted with the soaring mountains, colorful canyons, and the giant sequoia and redwood trees found in national parks in the West. To Yard, national parks must meet a certain standard; Mammoth Cave did not qualify. Furthermore, a national park at Mammoth Cave "invites tragic national loss" of high standards and could open the door to a plethora of unworthy projects.[13]

Despite these misgivings, in the spring of 1926, Congressman Thatcher had good news to report to the Mammoth Cave National Park Association. Although the bill had been through "most serious difficulties," including "departmental and legislative hurdles," Thatcher informed the association that the bill had finally passed the House and Senate.[14] On May 25, 1926, President Calvin Coolidge signed the Mammoth Cave National Park into law. Robert Sterling Yard was livid. In Kentucky, the *Louisville Courier-Journal* cheered the victory for the national park but reminded readers that the work was not yet complete: "Mr. Thatcher has done his part. . . . Kentucky must do the rest."[15]

The proposed Mammoth Cave National Park was comprised of 70,618 acres of land "including all the caves" in Edmonson, Hart, and Barren counties and surrounded three different ridges running north and south that spread like fingers.[16] Mammoth Cave Ridge held the underground passages of Mammoth Cave; Flint Ridge, to the east, contained Great Onyx Cave and the Crystal Cave. West from Mammoth Cave Ridge was Joppa Ridge. Just north along the ridges, the Green River bisected the area north and south. In addition to the caves, ridges, and river, the acreage also consisted of between five and hundred and eight hundred families and landowners.[17] The Mammoth Cave National Park idea had a host of prominent backers, including the governor of Kentucky, the state legislature, and a number of county-level officials in cave country. The main players involved in the park's creation were the Mammoth Cave National Park Association, a private organization of public-spirited men; the Kentucky National Park Commission (KNPC), created by the state to aid land acquisition; and eventually the National Park Service.

Purchasing Mammoth Cave

Before the ink dried on President Calvin Coolidge's signature on the bill authorizing Mammoth Cave National Park, the Mammoth Cave National Park Association was collecting options to purchase land. To be sure, most landowners voluntarily sold their land, especially when faced with tight economic times, but a small, vocal, and active minority fought the creation of the park almost every step of the way.[18] Opposition came from three main sources: cave owners, landowners and tenants, and a local newspaper editor.

Cave owners stood to lose their source of income, and took their fights to court. At the time of the park's legislative passage, four main caves were significant players in the Cave Wars. These were Mammoth Cave, still operated by the trustees; the New Entrance to Mammoth Cave, developed by Ohio mining engineer George Morrison; Great Onyx Cave, a small cave owned by the local Cox family; and Floyd Collins's Crystal Cave, soon to be under the management of a nearby dentist, Dr. Harry Thomas.

A number of landowners in the park area were in favor of the idea of the national park, but not at the expense of their lands. While some of them fought condemnation in the courts, others tried to increase the value of their lands or stay in their homes, and still others used extralegal means of protest. Still, owners received some payment. Tenants or renters would not be compensated for losing a home or land, and would have to move without as many financial resources as owners would have.[19] Some renters held out as long as they could to protest the park's creation.

Perry Meloan, the editor of the local newspaper, the *Edmonson County News*, gave a voice to the opposition in a number of editorials against the park. A bulldog in the park fight, Meloan kept a watchful eye on the MCNPA and the KNPC for potential corruption and kept local residents up to date on the park's progress.

The most important tract of land to acquire was Mammoth Cave itself. The challenge would be finding a way to acquire the cave within the restrictions of Dr. John Croghan's will. His 1849 will passed possession of the cave to his nieces and nephews and, upon the passing of their heirs, required that Mammoth Cave be advertised for sale.[20] When the legislation passed through Congress, the final heiress, Serena Livingston Croghan Rodgers, was ninety-two years old. Her much younger cousins, Mary Jesup Sitgreaves, Violet Blair Janin, and William E. Wyatt, served as trustees of the Mammoth Cave estate. On August 28, 1926, Rodgers died, leaving Sitgreaves, Janin, and Wyatt in control of Mammoth Cave's future.[21]

Rodgers's death opened the possibility for a quick sale to the Mammoth Cave National Park Association, which would be a significant step forward in making the park a reality. It could also mean a rival or competitor like George Morrison of the New Entrance would swoop in and buy the cave from underneath the association and prevent the park from happening. The trustees had opposed earlier efforts to make Mammoth Cave a national park, and there was little evidence to suggest they would willingly sell to the association. Max B. Nahm, one of the chief park promoters, was doubtful of a sale and believed "the only thing that will eventually be down [*sic*] with her will be to condemn the Cave."[22] As a private fundraising and purchasing entity, however, the Mammoth Cave National Park Association did not have the power to condemn property. Besides, they still needed to raise money to purchase properties for which they had options.

A public fundraising crusade kick-started major land-buying efforts. Early in 1928, Republican Governor Flem Sampson declared "Mammoth Cave National Park Week in all Kentucky" to push for fundraising. Churches, schools, civic organizations, and businesses contributed or pledged money to the subscription fund for the MCNPA.[23] The *Louisville Courier-Journal*, the largest newspaper in the state, published donors names for all to see as an incentive to donate. Governor Sampson made a tour throughout the state and addressed citizens from Louisville on WHAS radio. For Sampson, one of the biggest appeals of the national park was that it would "eventually and automatically bring about the construction of a veritable network of improved highways in Kentucky," linking them together with the "outside world."[24] The campaign proved somewhat successful, bringing in approximately $800,000 from nearly 17,000 donors of all ages.[25] Others merely pledged money; collecting those pledges grew increasingly difficult when after two years of fundraising the Mammoth Cave estate was still in private hands and the national park seemed no closer to existence.

In January 1928, Mammoth Cave trustee Violet Blair Janin indicated to the cave manager that if the association took an option for $500,000 "she would probably give it."[26] The real estate agent for the L&N, George Zubrod, doubted that the cave and lands were worth that much. He was confident that, "with the right to condemn," the key piece of property could be purchased for less than the $350,000 they had originally offered.[27]

The association wanted powers of eminent domain for its own use in the park's creation. The articles of incorporation for the MCNPA did not include the power of condemnation; that power could only be granted by the state.[28] While the association asked the legislature for this power at the following session, the state general assembly held back.[29] Instead, Louisville attorney and MCNPA leader Blakey Helm began drafting a bill that would provide for a state organization to acquire land for the park using eminent domain.[30] Introduced in the Democratic-controlled state legislature, the Bartlett-Strange bill appropriated $30,000 over two years to a six-member bipartisan commission. The Kentucky National Park Commission had the power to purchase and "condemn land, caves, and cave rights." Mammoth Cave–area state representative Beverly M. Vincent hoped to amend the bill so that the commission would not be able to condemn "personal property," but his amendment failed.[31] Now, two organizations would be in charge of acquiring lands and caves: the publicly controlled commission and the privately run association. As some leaders in the park movement saw it, the association and the commission would be a carrot-and-stick model to get the lands and caves for the park.

If they worked well together, the Mammoth Cave National Park would be the first of the three eastern parks authorized in 1926, ahead of Great Smoky Mountains and Shenandoah. That looked to be the case in April 1928 when the commission offered $300,000 to the Mammoth Cave estate trustees with the threat of condemnation should they reject the offer.[32] These kinds of intimidation tactics occasionally worked on small landowners, but cave owners had exactly the resources the MCNPA wanted, and they were willing to take a chance with their county neighbors on condemnation juries. Cave purchases followed a similar pattern. The park promoters offered what they believed was a fair amount, and cave owners countered with a much higher price. When negotiations failed, the MCNPA turned to the KNPC to condemn the land. Despite what agent George Zubrod had predicted, the trustees turned it down and demanded no less than one million dollars for the world wonder.[33] The next month, the KNPC, with the help of the state's attorney general, James W. Cammack, filed suit in Edmonson County to condemn the eighteen hundred acres of land and the cave.[34]

It was important to the state entities that the park project appeared as a local concern. This localized aspect could also assuage fears that residents were losing their land and assure them that they were instead giving to the nation. In addition to the state attorney general's office bringing the suit on behalf of the KNPC, the Edmonson County attorney also participated in the proceedings, as well as another local attorney, John B. Rodes, hired especially for the condemnation trial.[35] This gave the whole affair the look of a local interest against the outsider trustees who had been managing cave affairs from afar. That notion disregarded the fact that the husband of trustee Violet Blair Janin, Albert C. Janin, had been at Mammoth Cave since the turn of the century.[36] By the end of the summer of 1928, however, Albert Janin was dead, which left the trustees with no immediate handle on the situation.

The trustees were not interested in giving up their inheritance. As nonresidents of Kentucky, the trustees were granted a longer time for their attorneys to answer the condemnation suit, which meant more time to plan their opposition to the state and local attorneys' case.[37] While plotting its defense, the commission moved along on the case.

Edmonson County Court–appointed commissioners began fixing the value of the Mammoth Cave estate for the proceedings. Taking into account the worth of standing timber, the land, and the cave with all the improvements, the commissioners valued the property at $496,000.[38] This was more than the MCNPA had offered, but also significantly less than the $1 million the heirs had demanded.

Neither the trustees nor the MCNPA and KNPC members were satisfied with the result. The Kentucky National Park Commission filed a "bill of exceptions" to the valuation, claiming it to be too high. The most valuable part of the property was the cave, they argued, and it was worth only about $250,000. The trustees countered by rejecting the court's authority altogether and filed a motion to transfer the condemnation suit to federal court. They argued that, since the issue was a disagreement between residents and officials of several states, federal court was the proper jurisdiction. When the county judge overruled their motion, they appealed to a higher court, further delaying the national park effort.[39]

After Albert Janin died in June 1928, Violet Janin and her cousin Mary Jesup Sitgreaves had less enthusiasm for the cave affairs. Aging and finding travel more difficult, and with the potential for a negative result in the condemnation suit, they decided to sell their interest in Mammoth Cave to the MCNPA. On December 31, 1928, the association purchased the women's two-thirds interest in the Mammoth Cave property, which included the cave and more than twenty-two hundred acres, for $50,000 less than the county valuation.[40]

Acquiring Adjacent Caves

By 1929, the assurance of acquiring the Mammoth Cave property signaled an important turning point in the park effort. Once the association had two-thirds control, members expected that the remaining one-third could be condemned at a much more reasonable rate to their budget. More importantly, the purchase all but guaranteed the park project's success. Now all they needed was the money to buy the rest of the land and caves. Promoter Max B. Nahm congratulated real estate agent and MCNPA Secretary George Zubrod on the deal and encouraged using the sale as leverage: "With [Mammoth Cave] in hand, we can go to the people and win. We can secure a million I trust from the State Legislature—for they can all see now that we have crossed over with the realm of success."[41] After two years of businessmen and state officials talking about a national park, the giving public could envision it as a reality.

Their supposition proved correct. The knowledge that Mammoth Cave would soon be in federal control helped to increase fundraising and acquisitions. In February 1929, Edmonson County attorney and judge for the Kentucky Court of Appeals, M. M. Logan, pledged to sell to the MCNPA some eight thousand acres of property north of the Green River within the park boundary. The following year, Governor Flem Sampson pushed for an *ad valorem* tax predicted to raise more than $1.5 million in revenue for the Kentucky National Park Commission's land purchases.[42] The purchase of Mammoth Cave brought a windfall of successes, so much that the association announced their control of more than half of the land necessary for the National Park Service to begin development of the area. In the local newspaper, the MCNPA claimed to have "possession or control of more than 13,000 acres, including Mammoth Cave, New Entrance to Mammoth Cave, and Colossal Cavern. We are negotiating for the purchase of the other important caves and of more land."[43] The association projected confidence and surety, even at the expense of honesty.

To be sure, the association was making progress through its partnerships. If the KNPC could condemn the remaining one-third of the old Mammoth Cave property, and if the L&N donated their Colossal Cavern lands to the MCNPA, the association would have an even better case to make for money and purchases. But the New Entrance to Mammoth Cave, opened by George Morrison just over ten years prior, was still under private control and operation. Morrison's organization, the Mammoth Cave Development Company also operated the New Entrance Hotel, a competitor to the Mammoth Cave Hotel.

Complete control of the old Mammoth Cave made the association members anxious to purchase rival caves. In September 1929, the Mammoth Cave National Park Association took control of their two-thirds share of the Mammoth Cave estate. The following year the KNPC condemned the remaining one-third.[44] The association set out on a course to purchase New Entrance one way or another. Along the way, the promoters would also try to buy the remaining competing caves, Great Onyx Cave and the Crystal Cave, east of the Mammoth Cave property. At their monthly meeting in October 1931, park advocates stressed the urgent need to purchase New Entrance. Gaining control of the rival cave "would place the association in a very strong position in its efforts to purchase the other one-third of Mammoth Cave, as well as all other required caves and lands." Plus, state officials were skeptical that Congress would accept the lands for the park without the New Entrance, given that it was connected to the old Mammoth Cave.[45]

The commission and the association began working closely to get the New Entrance. Their cooperation was made much easier when the state legislature passed a bill changing the way the governor appointed members to the KNPC. Originally the governor could appoint anyone. In the new 1930 bill, the governor was limited in his appointments in that they could only come from a list provided by the association. The association could provide up to eighteen names; the governor would then choose nine. Five of those chosen were also members of the MCNPA, giving the association control of the commission. The legislature also significantly increased funding to the KNPC, appropriating the group $1.5 million for land purchases.[46] The association, with full powers of condemnation and a budget through the commission, was ready to buy land and complete the park.

Here the MCNPA and KNPC acted as the carrot and stick. The association offered Morrison $70,000 for the New Entrance. The commission threatened condemnation. Spurning the association's offer, George Morrison took the KNPC to court. In April 1930, Morrison's Mammoth Cave Development Company sued the Park Commission in federal court, questioning the constitutionality of the KNPC's power of eminent domain. The Mammoth Cave estate trustees had made a similar claim, but it was after the condemnation proceedings had already begun. Morrison was making a preemptive strike on the commission. The court granted a restraining order against the KNPC while considering the suit, so the state organization could not immediately implement condemnation charges. Morrison thus had more time to develop and strategize his fight against the park effort. The courts upheld the condemnation powers of the Kentucky National Park Commission, however, and Morrison's prospects for remaining in cave country decreased.[47]

Courts clearing the way for condemnation meant the state was ready to use any means necessary to acquire the New Entrance. Kentucky Attorney General Cammack believed the commission should start "at once" to get the New Entrance under state control, but an outright purchase might not be possible. In a December 1931 meeting of the Kentucky National Park Commission, an attorney for the New Entrance explained that the investors in the cave had no interest in the national park effort and were unwilling to make a deal for less than $290,000.[48] But as the Great Depression decreased tourist travel and sapped Morrison's ability to spend money in developing the cave, he was compelled to sell his life's work.

On December 28, 1931, the KNPC voted to purchase everything covered in the New Entrance deed, including the New Entrance Hotel, furnishings, exhibits, land, and cave rights; Morrison accepted the deal in early January 1932. The Mammoth Cave National Park Association held the Mammoth Cave estate, and the state commission now owned the New Entrance. Park promoters looked forward to the national park as a certainty. Attorney General James Cammack thought this would "eliminate most of the opposition in the park area."[49] Together, the groups claimed to own more than twenty-one thousand acres and had been promised one thousand more from the Colossal Cavern Company. With high optimism, MCNPA Chairman Huston Quin predicted the National Park Service would take over the area by the end of the summer.[50] Only two of the major caves remained in private control: Great Onyx Cave and Crystal Cave on neighboring Flint Ridge, just east of the Mammoth Cave estate.

In 1926, when the Mammoth Cave National Park Association began buying land, the members believed they would encounter little opposition. Before the park legislation even passed, land agents had been taking options for purchases. Once the funds began rolling in, a blank map of parklands slowly began coloring in with purchases. The onset of the Great Depression gave the park promoters pause, but in some ways they used it to their advantage. Alongside a news report of farmers in the town of England, Arkansas, raiding the local mercantile to feed their families and real estate listings for farms, the KNPC advertised that they were "in position to pay cash for land" within the established park boundary.[51] The juxtaposition to landowners could not be clearer: sell your land or risk starvation.

Cave owners were in a different position; they had a bargaining chip. The Mammoth Cave estate trustees and George Morrison were outsiders. Local cave owners Dr. Harry Thomas of Crystal Cave and L. P. Edwards, Lucy Cox, and her husband, Perry Cox, of Great Onyx Cave had long-established ties and influence in the area. Although they were rival cave owners, Thomas and the Edwards-Cox family found themselves on the same side of the park issue. They stood to lose deep investments and their livelihoods at showing caves. The attempts to purchase Crystal Cave and Great Onyx Cave demonstrate the fierce local opposition to the state commission and the Louisville-based association.

The acquisition of Crystal Cave for the national park initially looked to be an easy task. In April 1926, the Collins family still held the title to their late Floyd's Crystal Cave as well as the Collins farm. Speaking on behalf of his father, Lee, Homer Collins informed real estate agent and MCNPA Executive Secretary George Zubrod that "for enough money" Lee Collins would give an option for the cave and lands. The youngest of the Collins family cautioned Zubrod that, while the family did not wish to "do anything against the national park plans," the Collinses would not extend an option for purchase beyond six months.[52] The association at that time was most focused on fundraising and acquiring the Mammoth Cave estate, however, and not worried about losing a chance at Crystal Cave.

Unbeknownst to them, a rival cave owner had set his sights on Floyd's cave. In August, Marshall Collins informed Zubrod that another party was "ready to buy" and that, if the MCNPA wanted the cave, the deal would "haft [sic] to be all cash ... we had rather sell to you and keep the middle man out."[53] Zubrod turned down the chance to purchase Crystal Cave from the Collins family, but he could not understand why other parties would buy the land within the proposed park boundaries for speculative purposes. After all, to reach their goal of a national park, the association would buy lands "either from the present owners at a fair price or," he threatened, "[we] will ask the Federal Court to tell us what a fair and reasonable price [is], later on."[54]

The "middle man" was Harry Thomas, a dentist and owner of the Mammoth Onyx Cave and Hidden River Cave in the town of Horse Cave, Kentucky. Thomas hoped to use Crystal Cave as leverage to make his hometown a gateway community to the park, and thus bring more traffic by his caves.[55] Thomas appeared before a meeting of the MCNPA to offer his option on Crystal Cave for $10,000 at the same price to the association, but only if they also purchased an extra 676.5 acres of his land along Dixie Highway in Horse Cave.[56] If that plan failed, however, Thomas could exploit Crystal Cave. On November 12, 1926, Thomas purchased

Crystal Cave from Lee Collins for $10,000.[57] As late as 1927, Zubrod believed Dr. Thomas to be "a friend of our National Park movement" who would sell "if the national park proposition went through," but Thomas was already showing Crystal Cave—and Floyd Collins—for his own financial ends with seemingly no hint of giving it up.[58]

In June 1927, Dr. Thomas exhumed Floyd Collins's body from the cave grounds near the ticket office and placed the casket inside Crystal Cave's main room, the Grand Canyon, along with a tombstone declaring the late caver to be the "Greatest Cave Explorer Ever Known."[59] Visitors to the subterranean chamber could peek at the body, "if anybody wants to look at it," according to Carrie Thomas, the dentist's wife.[60] Floyd Collins's brothers sued Dr. Thomas for disturbing the burial, and although a county clerk found nothing in the deed related to the status of the body, a court found in 1929 that Dr. Thomas had legally obtained clear title to both the cave and Floyd's corpse.[61]

Placing Collins's remains on display in Crystal Cave might have signaled to the park promoters that Thomas never intended to give up his growing cave empire. Evidently it did not, as the Kentucky National Park Commission hoped for the "immediate purchase" of the cave in June 1928, even before the association had acquired any part of the Mammoth Cave estate.[62] In addition to producing revenue (with apparently the chance of extra money from corpse viewing), purchasing the cave for the "very, very reasonable" price of $10,000 might drive down the values of caves and lands where owners asked between $100,000 and $150,000. A purchase could also increase subscriptions for the MCNPA by demonstrating progress in the movement.[63] Dr. Thomas dangled a purchase agreement to the Mammoth Cave National Park Association, going so far as sending deed information to association secretary and real estate agent George Zubrod so he could make property abstracts.[64]

In July 1928, the purchase of Crystal Cave seemed imminent. Zubrod waited for Attorney General Cammack to approve the abstract and for a sum of $10,000 and money to pay the abstractors.[65] The association, however, had "no funds for this purpose" and hoped the KNPC would underwrite the expense of paying the abstractors and Thomas.[66] Using the impending purchase and the condemnation work of the state commission as proof of progress, the association implored its subscribers to send in money to meet their pledges so that the association could "be prepared for opportune purchases and court judgments."[67] Looming in the background was Thomas's demand that the park promoters also take the Dixie Highway acreage, which was well outside the proposed park boundary. Internal memos suggest that Zubrod believed that the association should not accept such land, and that, if it were to do so, it "would have to get Congress to change the boundaries for the land for the gateway to the park."[68] Furthermore, Thomas also wanted "an impossible thing"—to operate Mammoth Cave ostensibly on behalf of the National Park Association, who had never managed a cave and, as of the summer of 1928, did not own any part of Mammoth Cave.[69]

The attorney general's office approved the abstracts for purchase, but the extra obligations in Thomas's offer were too much for the association to undertake.[70] Some members of the commission believed that Thomas was anxious to close the deal for Crystal Cave, and that he would be willing to relinquish his demands.[71] On August 13, 1928, association president Huston Quin informed Thomas that they would take the $10,000 option on Crystal Cave, but that they could not "bind" themselves to buying property not in the proposed park boundary. The association was open to Thomas continuing to manage and profit from Crystal Cave through 1929, "provided the property is not to be deeded to the United States Government."[72] The final decision was up to Thomas, but problems between the association and the commission may have pushed his hand.

The executive secretary for the KNPC, George Newman, had been in contact with the association secretary, George Zubrod, regarding the touch-and-go nature of the deal. Five days after the association's offer, Commissioner Newman informed his association counterpart that Thomas turned down the offer, so the commission "will be forced to condemn."[73] Zubrod countered that immediate implementation of condemnation proceedings was too "hasty." The dentist had not responded to Quin's letter and, even if Thomas had doubts, Zubrod was confident he and the other MCNPA executives (that is, fellow businessmen) could persuade Thomas to sell; sending cave-country land agents to Thomas's office to put on the pressure would only backfire. "Dr. Thomas is just as fair and square a man as you can find in that neighborhood," Secretary Zubrod assured Newman, "but when he has so many people jumping on him, it naturally riles him."[74] Zubrod was adamant that the KNPC stay out of the entire negotiations as he focused on acquiring Crystal Cave.

Just as Crystal Cave may have been in reach, the Executive Committee of the Mammoth Cave National Park Association had to focus elsewhere. The Edmonson County commissioners valued the Mammoth Cave estate, putting the most important piece of the national park puzzle in flux.[75] At their August 23, 1928, meeting the MCNPA executives expressed their concerns that no condemnation proceedings be filed against Crystal Cave by the commission and that George Zubrod give up the deal to concentrate on fighting the prices quoted for the Mammoth Cave estate that they believed were inflated by local commission-ers.[76] The offer to Thomas was essentially abandoned, but a glimmer of hope re-mained when Zubrod visited with him that October. Thomas indicated that he and his wife would sign the deed to Crystal Cave when the association produced an agreement for him to manage the Mammoth Cave when it came into the asso-ciation's control.[77] Thomas thought he had the park promoters exactly where he wanted them—in control of his caves in Horse Cave, plus three of the four caves in the national park boundary, essentially complete control of the major caves in the area, with the likelihood for more.

Race in Cave Country

Land purchases were the talk of the Mammoth Cave community, and like in many small communities, news and rumors spread in equal measure. Thomas's loose lips proved to be the undoing of the deal. Matt Bransford, an African American guide at Mammoth Cave, and owner of a hotel on Flint Ridge for African American visitors to cave country, wrote anonymously to the association to inform them of some of Thomas's plans.[78] He claimed that Thomas was bragging to everyone in "this Territory" about his arrangement with the Park Association and that "there won't be a Negro left in this District."[79] Imploring the Louisville businessmen to act, Bransford passionately argued for the rights of the African American com-munity that had worked for and supported the cave businesses over the years and, for the time being, still called the Mammoth Cave region home: "[We] have paid for our homes & we love them. We don't feel like being drove out by one man & we feel that there is enough Red Blooded Kentuckians left yet to defend and we are going to advertise and ask the people of [Kentucky] not to support a thing of this kind. We having gave liberally to the National Park and are in favor of it, but if there is going to be a National Park made out of Mammoth Cave, Ky. it Should be Run by a gentleman."[80]

Zubrod, now the association's official communications link with Thomas, in-formed the aspiring cave magnate that he did not believe the rumors, but "if you intend 'to run all the Negroes away' when you get 'control of the caves,' please do not start doing it now." The park promoters still had to acquire land from the African American families who lived and worked at Mammoth Cave and preferred to maintain good relations with them, at least for the time being.[81]

The African American community and economically disadvantaged white residents in the Mammoth Cave region found themselves at the mercy of their state government for a national project. In essence, the Mammoth Cave National Park Association was not out to preserve the caves and the land from use so much as they wanted to make the area "safe" for middle-class tourism. These residents, many of whom worked in the cave economy in South Central Kentucky as solicitors and guides, were part of the problem, and had to go.

Many of the African American residents in cave country had worked or did work for the Mammoth Cave estate and had nurtured their small but significant community. In 1866, Mat Bransford, one of the formerly enslaved cave guides, became one of the first Black landowners in cave country when he used his wages from guiding to put a down payment of $150 on a piece of land east of Mammoth Cave on Flint Ridge. Nicholas Bransford, another formerly enslaved guide, donated land to create a schoolhouse for African American children in the neighborhood, including his grandchildren. Black residents founded their own institutions by custom, such as the Pleasant Union Baptist Church, or by law, such as the Mammoth Cave Colored School. Matt Bransford (grandson of Mat Bransford) and his wife Zemmie's operation of overnight accommodations created opportunities for the touring African American public.[82] These institutions and the tight-knit community were now at risk of destruction to make way for the national park.

The Crystal Cave purchase never happened, thwarting Thomas's plans. Extant records are silent as to whether the association withdrew the offer to focus on the purchase of the two-thirds interest or if Thomas gave up the pursuit of managing Mammoth Cave and cancelled the arrangement. The Mammoth Cave National Park Association was never going to gain control of Crystal Cave without a fight. The Park Association could turn complete attention to Flint Ridge, however, only when they had control over both the Mammoth Cave estate and the New Entrance to Mammoth Cave. This lack of attention created a new sense of competition from Thomas that would remain a thorn in the side of the park promoters and officials even beyond his death in 1948.

Great Onyx Cave

The park promoters' effort to purchase Great Onyx Cave followed a similar pattern. Just before President Coolidge signed the bill authorizing Mammoth Cave National Park, a land agent collecting options met with the Great Onyx owner, L. P. Edwards. The agent informed Zubrod that Preacher Edwards "was anxious to sell and get out of the cave business" following the death of his wife.[83] That same week a

Cave City banker met with Edwards as well; by the end of the week the cave owner changed his mind about selling.[84] With the momentary setback, the MCNPA turned their attention to the Mammoth Cave estate. In 1929, when the association could look at other caves, a local attorney representing Edwards in a contentious lawsuit confidentially informed them that Edwards might ask $250,000 for Great Onyx.[85] That was far above what the association was willing to pay, especially considering what was at stake. Local attorney John B. Rodes cautioned commission president Huston Quin that Flint Ridge especially was "a territory, where . . . the people might become 'cave conscious.'"[86] When people knew what they had under their land, they could use that knowledge to their advantage in bargaining with the association or the commission. A lawsuit over cave passages in that section had great significance for the park project and beyond, and as it turned out, Edwards was at the center of it.[87]

In April 1928, Edwards was sued in court by his neighbor, Fielding Payton "Pate" Lee, who sought from Edwards $60,000 in damages for withholding possession of Great Onyx Cave from him. Lee also sued for damages for "rent, profit, and admittance fees" from Edwards's exhibiting parts of Great Onyx Cave which ran under Lee's land.[88] The suit was an official grievance between the neighbors, who had in the past disputed property boundaries on the surface. This underground fight that played out in court had consequences beyond Flint Ridge. Lee's suit was based on information from cave explorer and disputed discoverer of Great Onyx, Edmund Turner. Lee knew that Edwards had purchased cave rights from another neighbor, Frank Davis, and that his own property lay between Edwards's and Davis's. But apart from Turner's information, Lee had no official confirmation of passages under his farm. This, of course, made it difficult for the court to resolve and so, in December 1928, Edmonson County Judge Porter Sims ordered a survey of the cave at Lee's expense. To protect Edwards's business interests, Judge Sims instructed that the survey be disclosed to no one outside the court.[89] Sensing the possibility that Edwards would eventually have to settle with Lee, Edwards's attorney secretly contacted an MCNPA official regarding what it might take to purchase Great Onyx Cave, while publicly fighting for his client.[90]

The Great Onyx Cave condemnation case proved to be a pivotal moment in the struggle to create the national park. First, the jury's large award, though far short of what Great Onyx owners hoped for, was too excessive for the land buyers. The cave, which was a small fraction of the length of Mammoth Cave, albeit one uncommonly rich in limestone formations, was valued almost as much as Mammoth. To the Great Onyx jury, the size of the cave was not as important as what was inside. This set the tone for future condemnation decisions. Second, the condemnation case was the first involving a local landowner against the Louisville-based promoters. Even if Preacher Edwards and his family were unpopular, as Secretary Zubrod believed, the county jury sided with the family they knew; if the park advocates wanted the park badly enough, they should be willing to pay a fair price for lands and caves—"fair" meaning what a jury of an Edmonson Countian's peers deemed just. Third, the case highlighted the rising opposition to the park movement, led by the editor of the *Edmonson County News,* Perry Meloan. Over the coming years, Meloan focused his scrutiny on the park organizations, the L&N, the state government, and the federal government in the Mammoth Cave National Park project. Meloan also gave a voice to the landowners who did not wield the influence of a show cave under their lands.

Local Opposition

In the early years of the park project, the *Edmonson County News* was mostly an impartial source, reporting on land deals and fundraising efforts. The 1928 creation of the Kentucky National Park Commission brought the newspaper's first caution to readers of the park area. The commission's broad powers, especially the power of eminent domain, set off alarm bells for the editor. Meloan took comfort in that former state senator A. A. Demunbrun, an Edmonson Countian "well informed on cave area conditions," was on the board for assessing land values.[91] Demunbrun, whose family roots ran deep in cave country, had over the years been a teacher, a timber agent, and a merchant with extensive local knowledge as to the cave and land situation.[92] L&N real estate agent and Mammoth Cave National Park Association Executive Secretary George E. Zubrod was also on the board. Zubrod's Louisville connections with the railroad and MCNPA made him suspect to Meloan. Indeed, with almost every step of progress towards making a park, Perry Meloan found what he believed to be corruption.

Meloan's target was the outside influences in the area. The 1928 Bartlett-Strange Act, which created the KNPC, funded the project for only two years. When the legislature renewed the KNPC in 1930, they made a critical change in matters of gubernatorial appointments that had a significant effect on the relationship between the park groups, and between those groups and locals in the Mammoth Cave area. Under the new system, the association would nominate eighteen people for the governor to choose nine members.[93] When the association unsurprisingly controlled the KNPC during its busiest period of purchasing and condemnation (1930–32) without a single member from Edmonson County, which had the largest amount of land involved in the park project, Meloan railed against the too-close relationship between the privately run association and the publicly created commission.[94]

Meloan made a personal mission to oppose the national park "projeckers," as he called them, on behalf of the impoverished residents.[95] As Meloan saw it, those who did not own caves and depended primarily on subsistence farming and timber hauling, (that is, the majority of Edmonson Countians in the park area) were being taken advantage of by powerful interests. The L&N, which he referred to as "Miss Ellen N.," the mother of the Park Association and grandmother of the commission, had the state's authority to condemn land and "harass" the owners.[96] Meloan also raised questions as to the fiscal responsibility and forthrightness of the association. Accusing the officials of "great secrecy" as to the group's expenses, the newspaper may have echoed resentment of local readers living within the proposed boundary.[97] Meloan contrasted the association's alleged wastefulness with hardscrabble farmers in the Dickey's Mill neighborhood making a two-day trip to Munfordville to sell railroad ties "to buy a little food for their starving families."[98] Given that Meloan's newspaper regularly gave notice of Red Cross relief drives "for the poor," government programs for drought and flood relief, the editor was probably not exaggerating.[99]

Meloan's editorials charging that there was an incestuous relationship between the commission and the association were effective. In 1932, state senator Tom Ferguson from Edmonson County shepherded a bill through the legislature giving the governor "unqualified power" to appoint a new seven-member commission to four-year terms, rather than two years as previously.[100] The *Edmonson County News* noted that the "only opposition to the bill" came from Louisville, where members were close with the L&N executives on the association and commission.[101] While the *Edmonson County News* cheered the new commission and the subsequent appointment of A. A. Demunbrun to that body, the park-supporting *Louisville Courier-Journal* looked skeptically at the change. The state's largest newspaper hoped the new commission would not "swing to the extreme of satisfying land owners in price, to the dissatisfaction of the other Kentuckians who are putting up the money," and that the new KNPC would get along with the association "on the same basis of friendly cooperation" that acquired Mammoth Cave, New Entrance, and around twenty-one thousand acres in land.[102] For the time being, the newspaper was optimistic about the commission.

Meloan criticized the Association for using Mammoth Cave as "a private club where fifty 'high-brows,' nine-tenths of them residents of Louisville," had a free, personal playground, paid for by church congregations, schoolchildren, and the state, at the same time that "thousands of Kentuckians are hungry." He charged them with using their public project as a "smoke screen" to "give the L.&N. Railroad Company complete control of the Hotel and Cave."[103] As Meloan saw it, "a National Park will never be established as long as the Club-Associationers are in control" because the MCNPA operated Mammoth Cave and kept the profits. Meanwhile, the supporters who had given money to create the park were left behind. When the association picked former commission president Huston Quin as the new MCNPA president to replace Max Nahm, who had been named the new commission president, Meloan saw the move as proof positive of the problems still ahead.[104]

Natural Resource Destruction and Development

If Perry Meloan did not necessarily get all the facts straight in his editorials, he nevertheless gave voice to the opposition. Other Edmonson Countians fought the park promoters as well. Landowners and tenants expressed their opposition in many ways beyond the pages of the *Edmonson County News*. Meloan reported on and criticized the park progress while also highlighting the work of locals who opposed the effort. They did not see the banner of progress claimed by proponents, and may have represented only a minority of those who lived within the park boundary. What they lacked in traditional forms of economic and political power, opponents on the local level turned to their natural and built environments to stake claims to power. Opponents took their frustration out on the very environment the park promoters hoped to protect. Traditional land uses and emerging possibilities from new knowledge about the land in cave country became one way of fighting the park effort.

Timber was an important source of income for many hardscrabble farmers. From 1859 when the L&N laid tracks through nearby Glasgow Junction, and 1886 when a spur line, the Mammoth Cave Railroad connected the wonder to the world. Cutting railroad ties became a way for farmers to make money. A number of tie yards and agents throughout Edmonson County attested to the significance of the local timber industry. Riverbottoms around Green River and Nolin River provided rich agricultural possibilities, but for those on the hilltops and ridges, cutting ties could mean the difference between having food on the table or starving through the winter.[105] When the park promoters began purchasing land they issued a notice to area landowners not to cut and sell their timber, asserting that "standing timber . . . will be as valuable to you or more so, than you can realize out of it at this time."[106] Land agents counted timber in valuating land prices, so those who cut their trees only hurt themselves in the long run. In the short run, families needed food and shelter. Park advocates feared that even timber at the Mammoth Cave estate was being clear-cut for the profits of individual workers, or else by timber thieves.[107]

After gaining control of the Mammoth Cave property, the association banned the cutting of trees on the estate. They made an exception for official purposes, such as for minor repairs around the Mammoth Cave Hotel.[108] Dead timber could not be harvested for rail ties, either, leading to increased devastation from a forest fire in April 1930.[109] Suspecting that the fire was intentionally set by a local timberman, the association took out an ad in the always-critical *Edmonson County News,* instructing readers that "any person cutting timber on these lands will be prosecuted."[110] Rumors about timber cutting at the estate circulated to Louisville, where association secretary George E. Zubrod flatly denied any authorized cutting, charging only "spasmodic raids by unauthorized persons" as the source of tree felling.[111]

The appeals to landowners in the area and the threat of prosecution did not deter residents from cutting their timber. An attorney working for the association informed Zubrod that landowners were "murdering" the trees on their land. Those who could not cut their own timber sold it to those who could. "We were around part of the Doyle sisters' property," the attorney related, "and it is being simply stripped."[112] A drought in the summer of 1930 increased the willingness of residents to cut their timber. With their crops dying, and a population "suffering," Edmonson Countians gathered at a mass meeting where they elected a committee whose intention was to meet with members of the association and commission for a break on the "timber embargo." In a resolution, the citizens explained that they were "facing dire distress," were hungry, and "without work as a result of the embargo and the drought."[113] The association did not relent, but residents continued cutting trees to the extent that by 1934 when the first landscape architect of the National Park Service came to cave country he found a land almost devoid of first-growth forest, with "the remainder . . . going rapidly as some railroad ties are being cut from every tree large enough to make a single tie."[114] Cutting their trees gave owners a chance to get the most from their land, they believed, before a corrupt association cheated them out of it.

Purchasing land from long-established families presented a problem. Members of the Southern Appalachian National Park Commission outlined the issue in a

June 1926 letter to the Mammoth Cave National Park supporters before major land-buying programs started:

> The problem of acquiring lands within the proposed park areas will necessarily have to do occasionally with the handling of isolated settlers who have homes surrounded by small tracts of land and who may resist any action on the part of the Government to remove them from such property. It is the opinion of the Commission that a few such old homesteads well within the park area may be acquired from the owners with the provision that the owners be allowed to reside thereon during their lifetime or until satisfactory arrangements can be mutually agreed upon their removal from the park area.[115]

In 1927, A. A. Demunbrun, the former timber buyer, teacher, and merchant local to Edmonson County, campaigned for the state senate in part on a program that, after getting "a good price for their land," park area landowners should be able to remain on the park land until the park's establishment.[116] Demunbrun lost the election, but not before some owners were able to make arrangements with the Mammoth Cave National Park Association buyers that permitted them to retain possession "and cultivate it" through 1929.[117] This became an incentive for both the MCNPA and landowners; the association had a promise for land, and the owners were able to use the land as they previously had until the park promoters needed to turn the land over to the federal government. Park Association president Huston Quin even instructed land-agent Gillis Vincent that he could tell landowners that they could remain on the land "rent-free," paying only the property taxes and thereby saving the association money.[118] However, with a number of deals arranged through these "gentlemen's agreements," the park promoters found themselves with a number of squatters.[119]

Squatters remained on the land for many reasons. Some were tenants, rather than the landowners, and had their homes sold out from underneath them. Others believed that they had nowhere else to go. Certain squatters hoped to reap the benefits of the land while the park promoters were busy with their cave condemnation suits. In 1927, oil fever swept Edmonson County. Bowling Green, Kentucky, oil speculator Margaret Hobson's workers successfully drilled a well north of the Green River near Mammoth Cave.[120] In an *Edmonson County News* column, "Nimrod" wrote against the inclusion of Flint Ridge into a park because the land—and people—would be better served with oil wells. "To H— with the National Park, some are planning to give free leases in order to start rigs to work."[121]

The MCNPA saw a threat to their project: if oil proved more successful they would either have to pay exorbitant prices for the land or possibly fail to purchase it and have to adjust park boundaries through an impatient Congress.[122] Exploiting valuable minerals from the land was a greater danger to the project than farming or grazing. If oil was under land, drillers could bankrupt the association for high land values or hold out a sale and leave the park with patches of privately owned land.

The closer the promoters believed the park was to fruition, the more willing they were to allow sellers to remain on the land. The commission even sought to rent vacant property to people other than the original landowners.[123] As long as the renters stayed away from the operations of Mammoth Cave and New Entrance and did not interfere with land sales, promoters like Quin eased their ire against people on the land.

For the first six years of park creation, the opposition to the park was local, concentrated, and personal. Most of Perry Meloan's *Edmonson County News* editorials were not against the national park idea per se as much as they were against the Louisville-based L&N-backed Mammoth Cave National Park Association. The collusion between them and the public organization, the Kentucky National Park Commission, was corruption of the worst kind. Meloan found cronyism and graft instead of progress and economic development in cave country. Park advocates continued to believe support for the park to be widespread, even in the local area, and that any opposition was due to selfish concerns about prices for land instead of a public concern for the state's economic health.[124] By the end of 1932, the park movement stalled momentarily amid the changes in the commission, unfriendly local condemnation juries, and owners' refusals to sell their land in the deepening Depression. The same spirit of reform that brought changes to the KNPC swept Franklin D. Roosevelt into the White House and breathed new life—and a new line of local opposition—to the national park project.

Federal Aid and Opposition

In the first hundred days of President Franklin D. Roosevelt's administration, the Civilian Conservation Corps (CCC) began transforming the landscape of the nation and its politics.[125] One of the first camps was at the proposed Mammoth Cave National Park area. There was enough work on the property that CCC officials added three more camps in short time, including one camp of African American CCC recruits.[126] The CCC's role at Mammoth Cave was vital to its conversion to a national park. The recruits literally transformed the surface and subsurface landscapes, planting trees and building roads and trails, and proved an important partner for the National Park Service. In some ways the camps were a boon to the surrounding community, but anti-park locals found the groups intrusive and a threat.

In May 1933, officials announced the selection of Mammoth Cave as the site of one of four CCC camps statewide.[127] Since the National Park Service was restricted from taking any possession of land until 45,000 acres were acquired for the project, the CCC became the first federal presence in the park area. The CCC's goals of fire prevention, erosion control, planting trees, and eliminating wildfire-fueling underbrush in forests matched well with the surface environment of cave country. A naturalist dispatched to the Mammoth Cave area found scars from forest fires and cleared riverbottom lands eroded away, and on the hilltops the all-too-familiar effects of timber harvesting: bare, steep slopes cut by deep erosion gullies.[128] Park area residents seemed welcoming to the reforestation goals, enough for the first superintendent of the camp to express to the Kentucky National Park Commission his "appreciation for the cooperation which had been shown him by local people."[129] The warm introduction to a federal agency seemed to portend good things for the future national park by creating a mutually beneficial situation on the ground for locals and park officials alike.

The CCC earned praise because it provided assistance to the local communities. In its efforts clearing brush and getting rid of dead trees, the CCC donated surplus wood to the Red Cross and county relief agencies.[130] The Park Commission even used firewood as a bargaining chip in the creation of roads through privately held land. An elderly African American resident allowed the CCC to use a corner of her property to build a road in return for a winter's supply of wood.[131] The commission found the CCC's presence extremely helpful for making amends with a community bristling with opposition to their management of the park effort. The KNPC thus passed resolutions granting the CCC allowance to either use or tear down and salvage any vacant buildings on commission lands.[132] Like their counterparts working in Shenandoah National Park and Great Smoky Mountains National Park, the CCC workers built a "natural" environment in part by destroying the lived-in, human landscape of homes and barns left behind by former residents.[133]

More importantly for park boosters concerned with getting more land for the project, the CCC opened the door for federal funding for the land-buying process. In November 1933, rumors from M. M. Logan, then a US senator in Washington, reached the Kentucky National Park Commission that up to $300,000 might become available to purchase emergency conservation work lands to reforest.[134] Although the enabling legislation for the parks passed by a Republican Congress

During the 1930s, there were several CCC camps at Mammoth Cave, including an African American camp. The CCC's role at Mammoth Cave was vital to its conversion to a national park. Group of CCC enrollees sawing wood in forest clean-up, ca. 1935, Civilian Conservation Corps in Mammoth Cave National Park, Mammoth Cave National Park CCC Archival Photograph Collection, Mammoth Cave National Park.

forbade the federal government from purchasing lands for park purposes, Roosevelt's Executive Order 6542 funding emergency conservation work in the eastern national parks provided a backdoor solution to that problem. The following year, the project gained enough land to add two more camps at Mammoth Cave for a total of nine hundred enrollees building infrastructure and conserving lands for the national park.[135]

The CCC work pushed Senator Logan and Congressman Glover Cary to draft a bill for the National Park Service to begin the takeover of lands near Mammoth Cave. The Park Service had been growing more and more impatient at the lack of progress on the proposed park. The Great Smoky Mountains National Park, which required the purchase of much more land than Mammoth Cave, was ready for establishment in 1934.[136] If Mammoth Cave were to become a full-fledged national park, the federal government should take possession and control away from the ineffective state and private park proponents. Park Service Director Arno Cammerer testified in favor of the bill before the House Committee on Public Lands that the takeover was necessary for conservation and law enforcement purposes. He explained: "some of those people down in that section are setting fire to the woods as a matter of spite, with local politics interfering, that the people ought to get off the ground and have their houses razed as soon as they have got the money, and the local commission cannot get them off."[137]

Members of the House Committee, especially Representative Dennis Chavez of New Mexico, expressed some doubts regarding a provision in the bill allowing the Department of the Interior to use powers of eminent domain to acquire lands. Cammerer stressed to the committee that the state's efforts to condemn lands often resulted in local juries providing an "outrageous price" for the landowners.[138] Still, the image of struggling farmers and poverty-stricken families being kicked off of land they owned struck a particular resonance with Chavez. Federal condemnation of lands for a national park seemed an unusual solution. The National Park Service director noted, "it is also very unusual in our experience for any State government to come to the Federal Government and say, 'Please enact a law to take our land.'"[139] The Kentucky General Assembly had more than just said it—they passed an appropriation granting $250,000 and the power of eminent domain to the federal government to obtain lands, caves, and cave rights.[140]

Representative George Durgan, a Democrat from Indiana, agreed with the director because he "knew a little bit about the people in there. They are all second cousins or third cousins, most of them, and connected in some way with the landowners."[141] The slight against the rural folk of South Central Kentucky was insulting, but it was hard for park boosters to ignore the condemnation, jury members' surnames being among those of many of the larger and long-established families in Edmonson County in particular. On May 15, 1934, President Roosevelt signed the Logan-Cary Act to accept thirty thousand acres of lands for national park purposes at Mammoth Cave and to empower the federal government with eminent domain to complete the national park project.[142] They were just sixteen thousand acres away from Park Service development, but local opposition to the park was about to become more intense.

The main opposition came from those losing their land and the only homes they had known. In early April 1934, Park Service Director Arno Cammerer instructed that homes in the park area be "immediately vacated" and razed; he included the opportunity for owners themselves to take the lumber and salvage it, which would also save the park the effort of disposing of it.[143] Some residents took advantage of keeping the boards and timbers that had been their homes. Many, however, refused to leave. Officials on the ground noted more than twenty tracts of land already purchased for the park that remained occupied, adding that "strenuous efforts will be made to have those tracts evacuated."[144] The Logan-Cary Act gave Park Service officials a method of executing those orders in federal court, as opposed to the local-friendly county courts.[145]

Enforcing Removal

Robert P. Holland was the first National Park Service superintendent at Mammoth Cave. A bespectacled West Point graduate, Holland had one mission: to turn the land around Mammoth Cave into a national park, and do it as quickly as possible. Any obstacle to that goal would be dealt with by any and all means necessary; one of his assistants recalled that this included methods "outside the law."[146] Holland recruited two CCC workers, Vernon Wells and Joseph Ridge, to be deputies to work with the park ranger for law enforcement and to assist him in his mission. Wells and Ridge, along with Holland, became targets of opposition due to their jobs in the park. Holland's take-no-prisoners attitude ran through almost every-thing he did at Mammoth Cave, which stoked more opposition to the park and to the National Park Service.

In the summer of 1934, Holland, Wells, and Ridge went to enforce an evic-tion notice. The tenant, identified in the records only as "Mr. Richards," did not own the home he and his family were living in and refused to leave the property. Holland ordered his deputies to tear down the structure with the family still inside.

Only then did the family comply with the notice. Word quickly got around the neighborhood about the Park Service's enforcement tactics.

While some people left willingly after the incident, other residents stood ready to confront the officials. An elderly widower threatened "there would be a gunfight" if park officials tried to move him. His daughter, who lived in nearby Horse Cave, hoped he would move in with her. While he was visiting his daughter, the Park Service trio swooped in with "a crew of 3C boys and a bulldozer." Wells recalled that, after the man returned home to "a pile of rubble," they stayed away from his land out of fear for their own safety in case he tried to retaliate.[147]

Holland and company did not just target tenants and the elderly. One of the most critical victories for the park group came at the expense of a fairly well-to-do landowner. Eldred Parsley had been a thorn in the side to both the MCNPA and the KNPC for a number of reasons. Although he had moved to Brownsville and sold his land within the park boundary, Parsley kept a tenant on the property. Knowing that Parsley went to court on Mondays, Holland ordered sixty CCC workers with Wells and Ridge to tear down the structures on Parsley's former farm. A neighbor heard the commotion and went to Brownsville to alert Parsley. When he returned and encountered Robert Holland, the superintendent informed the former resident that, if Parsley went back to Brownsville and got a restraining order from the local courts against tearing down the house and barn, Holland and his men would obey it. While the farmer did just that, Holland ordered the CCC workers to finish the job.[148] The message to any other owners was clear. Robert Holland did not care how influential a landowner might be on the local level. He was determined to make the national park a reality.

Tearing down homes was part of the process to make a park, but Holland overstepped his authority in many ways. In the spring of 1935, for instance, Holland and Ridge discovered that two farmers in the Green River Valley were continuing to plant and harvest crops. The park men dumped the plows into the Green River.[149] Dellard Parsley (first cousin of Eldred Parsley) and Bill Webb filed a lawsuit to claim damages from the loss of their plows. Parsley also claimed that he had an arrangement to keep farming the land until it was a national park. For Webb, the situation was quite serious, as he claimed that he had lost "the only plow he owned."[150] The incident mobilized opponents of the park. In reporting the warrants for Holland and Ridge in the *Edmonson County News*, Meloan compared them to "White Caps, Kluxers, night riders, and other outlaw organizations," except that those groups operated "under cover of darkness," not "on Sunday when the Christian people of the community were worshipping God in the simple

Eldred Parsley sold his property to make way for Mammoth Cave National Park, but he objected to the National Park Service removing the structures from the property. In early 1937, park superintendent Robert P. Holland ordered CCC workers to tear down the structures on Parsley's property. House on Eldred Parsley Place, January 4, 1937, Civilian Conservation Corps in Mammoth Cave National Park, Mammoth Cave National Park CCC Archival Photograph Collection, Mammoth Cave National Park.

edifices attended by them and their ancestors for a century or more."¹⁵¹ Nothing, Meloan suggested, was sacred to these "plowdrowners."

The response was swift. Local law enforcement hauled Holland and Ridge into an unfriendly court. Since the park superintendent was technically on the payroll of the KNPC, and the attorney general's office was the chief counsel for the commission, the *Edmonson County News* noted, it placed the top lawman's office in the unusual position of "defend[ing] parties charged with violating the laws of the State."¹⁵² In a civil suit, Holland and Ridge reimbursed Dellard Parsley twenty-five dollars for his plow (which was recovered), and forty-six dollars to Bill Webb for his plow (which was not recovered) and work days lost.¹⁵³ In a criminal court that November, Holland and Ridge each paid a twenty-five-dollar fine to Edmonson County. The men's actions stunned even some of the park promoters. State Senator Beverly Vincent sent a petition to Park Service Director Cammerer requesting Holland be removed from the Mammoth Cave area "because of his temperment [*sic*] and lack of understanding of the people of Edmonson County."¹⁵⁴ Despite the opposition, the Park Service kept Holland at Mammoth Cave for the time being.

In the fall of 1935, local opposition to Holland's methods hit a boiling point. On Monday, October 28, Wells and Ridge encountered three men hunting squirrels on park lands. Hunting had been outlawed since 1933 on commission-owned lands, but enforcement had been a problem.¹⁵⁵ When the unarmed park rangers approached the men "with the intention of asking them not to hunt," one of the men fired at Vernon Wells, striking him in the left shoulder and arm.¹⁵⁶ According to the account in Perry Meloan's *Edmonson County News,* Joseph Ridge jumped into the Green River until the men left, and then returned to get Wells to safety.¹⁵⁷ Ridge had actually jumped in to get a rowboat to get his partner across the river to the nearest CCC camp.¹⁵⁸ When Ranger Wells was taken to the hospital at Glasgow, Kentucky, doctors removed "seven buckshot [from] his shoulder and upper arm."¹⁵⁹ This was the most serious incident of local opposition.

Most protests against the park targeted the environment rather than people. Among the skills taught by the CCC was firefighting. Enrollee George Childress recalled that residents whose land had been condemned would sometimes be so upset "they'd set a fire on top of one hill . . . and that was one way they had of trying to get even with Uncle Sam for buying that and putting them out of there."¹⁶⁰ In January 1935, Mammoth Cave Hotel manager W. W. Thompson reported that nearly 400 acres had been burned in the past year, most of that coming in a single fire that had consumed 250 acres.¹⁶¹ The CCC built a series of fire towers and created a system for reporting locations of fires. Recruits cut underbrush and learned fire-prevention techniques, including how to identify dead trees and cut them down, provided they were not a home for wildlife.[162]

Ever suspicious of the CCC workers, editor Meloan often charged them with deliberately setting fires to earn more money. He explained that fighting fires was just one of their "multiferous [*sic*] duties, including the destruction and 'drowning' of farm machinery."[163] An enrollee from the only African American CCC camp wrote Meloan to correct him on both counts, that they were not setting the fires and that they did not earn extra money for fighting more fires. This caused Meloan to double down in his attacks against the CCC for taking jobs from Edmonson Countians, and accused African American CCC workers specifically for setting fires late at night so they could have the next day off.[164] Meloan had no use for the CCC workers, Black or white, and neither did Edmonson County, he argued. "For more than one hundred years," he claimed, "Edmonson County got along without the presences of Forest Rangers," and did not have forest fires "of any consequence." The problem was obviously the "full fledged and duly authorized contingent" of "plowdrowners."[165]

Arson was a tool for those disaffected by management decisions beyond land condemnation. For some, it was the last straw for what they saw as an unfair system. In August 1936, Superintendent Holland reported that the house of a Mammoth Cave ferry operator had been destroyed in a fire. The house was burned the night before a new ferry operator was to move in; the recently discharged operator, L. P. Dossey, was the obvious suspect.[166]

L. P. Dossey had had a long history with the park proponents and demonstrated some of the dire straits in which many residents found themselves. As early as 1927, Dossey sought help from real estate agent George E. Zubrod. The MCNPA land agents had taken an option on his land along Green River, but Dossey had to pay back loans which were due just before planting season. If Zubrod would not buy his farm and Dossey lost possession to his creditor, "I have nowhere to go, nor no money with which to buy a home for myself and motherless children."[167] Of course, Zubrod had no money with which to purchase Dossey's farm even if he wanted to assist the struggling farmer. In 1928, when the association was purchasing lands, Dossey offered his farm "at an attractive price," on account of his being "a great park enthusiast," and pleaded for the privilege of farming the land until it was turned over to the federal government.[168] Not long after the association finally purchased his land at auction in February 1929, they hired him to operate the Mammoth Cave ferry on the Green River.[169] After a number of "small infractions of park regulations," park officials fired him. Even if he had been charged, an Edmonson County jury might have had mercy on the local man.[170]

Holland's assistants had proved their worth. On September 1, 1936, Vernon Wells and Joseph Ridge were commissioned National Park Service rangers, which Holland later claimed helped bring about an "immediate reduction of forest fires and vandalism."[171] The park antagonists Holland referred to as the "do as we damn well please" residents, who faced the potential of federal courts that might be less friendly than their neighbors in Brownsville, mostly gave up their "abuse to the park."[172] By 1937, Superintendent Holland believed the fires to be under control. Five years later, the park superintendent reported that, in terms of fire protection, the relationship between the park and local people had completely changed due to the ranger force working with the locals to make them "fire conscious."[173]

The CCC made dramatic changes to the surface environment. Workers from the four camps removed more than two hundred miles of fence wire, removed and salvaged more than three thousand "undesirable structures," built more than six hundred temporary check dams to control erosion, planted nearly a million trees, and built park infrastructure like tourist cabins, park residences, roads, hiking trails, pump houses, campgrounds, and picnic areas.[174] W. W. Thompson, the hotel manager at Mammoth Cave, praised the work as "restoring the area to its natural beauty."[175] Like their counterparts at the Great Smoky Mountains National Park, Shenandoah National Park, and across the country, the CCC built the park essentially from the ground up. To the former residents, "restoring natural beauty" meant an erasure of their lives and any evidence of their occupation in the area.

Finalizing the Park

With the fires under control, park promoters turned back to land acquisition. As late as 1937, the owners of two of the chief rivals to Mammoth Cave, Great Onyx and Crystal Cave, had successfully fought being condemned or purchased. In 1932, shortly after a jury fixed Great Onyx's value at $398,000, park advocate Max Nahm and US Senator M. M. Logan discussed the possibility of excluding those caves from the park boundaries. Nahm wrote to Park Service Director Arno Cammerer to justify the plan, noting that, with New Entrance, Colossal, and Mammoth Cave, "we now have all the caves that we could ever show and more."[176] Even if the park promoters owned Great Onyx, Nahm added, it "would not add a cent to our revenue."[177] If Congress was willing to change the park boundaries, it might be possible to exclude Crystal and Great Onyx caves.

In 1934, the Logan-Cary Act gave the Department of the Interior (DOI) powers of eminent domain for park purposes. By the time the National Park Service had enough acreage for the park in 1936 to actually begin developing it as a federal entity, the DOI had taken up a number of condemnation cases for the acquisition of lands.[178] Federal officials were unsure whether to pursue condemnation charges against Crystal or Great Onyx caves. In August 1937, US Senator M. M. Logan instead pushed a bill through Congress that authorized the secretary of the interior to exclude those specific properties at his discretion.[179] The bill did not *require* the caves to be excluded, so if DOI condemned the caves it would still be legal to accept them. In mid-September, Cammerer instructed attorneys for the Park Service to dismiss any condemnation proceedings. The fact that a previous jury had fixed a price on Great Onyx worked against them, he believed. Even though Crystal Cave was never condemned or valuated by an official body, Cammerer wanted to dismiss condemnation until they had funds available for purchase.[180] The Cox family and Dr. Thomas's family continued to operate Great Onyx and Crystal caves as inholdings within the park until 1961.

On July 1, 1941, the National Park Service officially declared Mammoth Cave as the nation's twenty-sixth national park. Two months later, the Park Service "formally assumed complete administration" of the park by taking over the guide service. Superintendent R. Taylor Hoskins noted it was likely the first time the Park Service had ever taken over a site "which was already a going concern, and without any changes in personnel."[181] The guides employed at Mammoth Cave had a combined service record of nearly 365 years.[182] It would have been more, however, if not for some key retirements a few years prior. When Matt Bransford, grandson of Mat Bransford (an enslaved African American guide leased by Dr. Croghan), retired in 1937 after thirty-two years of guiding, he proclaimed: "All of my life my ambition has been centered around two things. One is my church and the other is Mammoth Cave. I have studied the cave. I have lived with it. It has been my life's work and I am proud of it."[183]

Although a celebratory newspaper article about the Bransfords predicted "there will always be a Bransford in the cave," Louis Bransford, also a grandson of Mat Bransford, was the last African American guide at Mammoth Cave National Park for a generation when he retired in 1938. When Jerry Bransford became a guide at Mammoth Cave National Park in 2004, he was the first Bransford to guide since his great-uncle Louis retired. The guide force who first wore the National Park Service uniform at Mammoth Cave National Park, then, was the first all-white force since perhaps the immediate post–War of 1812 period. Federal control of

The original cave guides at Mammoth Cave were African American and often took visitors on less-explored routes. By the late 1930s, most of the guides were white and followed strict protocols for visitors as part of the preparation for the national park designation. Cave guide and four men on stairs of Historic Entrance to Mammoth Cave, ca. 1939, Mammoth Cave National Park Nitrate Negative Collection, Mammoth Cave National Park.

Mammoth Cave meant white control of the cave at all levels—ownership, knowledge, and land-use decisions for the entire national park area.[184]

▲▲

Displacement to make way for the creation of Mammoth Cave National Park resulted in significant changes to the local economy, the natural environment, land-use patterns, and community networks. These changes brought an end to many facets of the local Appalachian culture. When officials dedicated the park in 1946, they celebrated what they believed the nation had gained. However, homes, barns, fourteen schools, and buildings of more than five hundred families had been torn down, leaving only a few lonely chimneys as reminders of what had been. Three white churches were allowed to remain standing, and more than seventy-five cemeteries were evidence of communities that once called the area home. The small but significant African American community on Flint Ridge that was erased from guiding was also erased from the landscape, as no standing structures exist to mark their one-time presence. Almost all the caves in the area were united under the control of the Park Service to be preserved for the enjoyment of future generations, and the main routes inside Mammoth Cave and New Entrance included sturdy trails courtesy of the CCC.

The Mammoth Cave experience changed as well. Visitors no longer saw the cave based only on their guides' torches or lanterns, but soon viewed the cave using electric lights fixed on the same points of interest. The fixed routes meant that everyone visited the same places; there was no chance to explore or tip the guide to see something off the established route, as had been the case in the nineteenth and early twentieth centuries. Later management decisions aimed at protecting the cave's ecosystem and environment included ending the Echo River boat tour in the cave, and the end of a practice known as "torch-throwing," whereby cave guides would light up dark places in the cave by flinging an oil-soaked bit of cloth that had been set on fire.

The "national park" designation also meant changes in the exploration of Mammoth Cave. Under Park Service control, exploration of Mammoth Cave by the guides was now off limits.[185] Cave exploration presented a lot of risks, but also there was so much of Mammoth Cave to show to visitors that it seemed unnecessary. The caves not included in the park, particularly Crystal Cave, would ironically become more important sites of exploration than the national park in the wake of this decision. Even then, exploration was less about finding new tour routes and more about resource knowledge and conservation.[186]

Despite the loss of land and homes, those who opposed the park had some success. Efforts to halt the park significantly delayed the park's establishment and forced Congress to change the park's boundaries, saving some fifteen thousand acres in private hands beyond Great Onyx and Crystal caves. Some of the gains of the pre-park landowners have benefited visitors to the cave. The former owners succeeded in getting Park Service officials to ban entrance fees to the park, so that they would have access to the cemeteries where loved ones are buried. This decision has kept Mammoth Cave an affordable option for a family vacation. Visitors who wish to go inside the cave are required to purchase tour tickets, but the ticket prices are lower than privately operated caves in the area, including Diamond Caverns, which is still in operation. The boosters of Mammoth Cave were correct in that it would lead to economic gains: over half a million annual visitors to Mammoth Cave National Park contribute over $60 million to the local economy.[187]

Economists can assess financial gains, but it can be harder to calculate loss, especially given the amount of other changes that have taken place in the United States and Kentucky cave country since the Great Depression. Gone are the days when "Red Buck" Esters's booming voice "like a mountain lion" announced his presence through the hollers, carrying a railroad tie under each arm. As tourists are more likely to travel to Mammoth Cave via Interstate 65 and county highways, the tie to local business has all but disappeared. The schoolyards that once featured the running feet of future Mammoth Cave guides like Henry Bransford, Bob Lively, and Lewis Cutliff have been silenced, along with other one-room schoolhouses. Communities like Temple Hill and Maple Springs are now known for being backcountry campsites with hiking trails rather than as the homes of the Davises, the Merediths, the Houchinses, or the Blantons.[188]

Loss affected everyone, but some Mammoth Cave neighbors experienced it differently. All of the pre-park families had to pack their belongings and leave their homes and the communities they had known, but there was a greater sense of uncertainty for the African American families displaced from the area. As Joy Lyons explained, the loss of communal ties meant "there was no longer a white neighbor like Martin Shackleford or Josh Wilson willing to sell them some land, co-sign a note or, if necessary, show them where to sign or make their mark on legal documents." Indeed, displaced African American families were more likely than white residents to move to urban areas; perhaps it was easier to rent homes in cities than to buy land in rural communities.[189]

Along with the loss of communal ties was a loss of trust of the federal government. Hunting in what were once neighbors' fields and using fish traps in the Green River now became poaching in a national park, as did collecting ginseng from the forests. Coming back from doing business at the county seat to a home that had been torn down by CCC crews made it difficult to believe the park was really for anyone's benefit, other than the likes of the political and business elites who gleefully cheered the governor's remarks to dedicate Mammoth Cave National Park.[190]

5 Layers of Loss

*Removal, Segregation, and Reconversion
at Oak Ridge, Tennessee*

RUSSELL OLWELL

When sociologist Lindsey Freeman was young, her grandfather took the family on a trip to find the "Ghost of Wheat," described as "Oak Ridge's most famous phantom . . . named after one of the farming communities that was confiscated, evacuated and eviscerated to make room for the Manhattan Project in the early 1940s." This ghost was thought to be the afterlife haunting of a farmer named John Hendrix, whose land was taken for the project, and could appear as a man dressed in overalls or as a ball of light. While Freeman did not find the ghost herself, the image remains a compelling one for all who grew up in the region. Freeman concludes, "The Ghost of Wheat is part of my nervous system, as well as the nervous system of Oak Ridge, unruly, a bit paranoid, sometimes matter, sometimes spirit."[1] The ghost can be seen as representing one of the losses endured by residents of the region—one whose memory persists in folklore and oral history.

Freeman's description of the Wheat community as a ghostly presence in the region is apt. The loss of such communities hangs over and around the margins of the history of Oak Ridge, Tennessee, an unresolved issue to this day, both in the city and in its historiography. As long-time resident Dorathy Moneymaker wrote in *We'll Call It Wheat* (1979): "When a new place is to be built, the first thing that must be done is to be rid of the old place, even though all buildings are removed the impression already made on the people who lived in the old place cannot be erased. These people go to live at another place, but they are still what they were. They become a part of their new community and add to that community those characteristics 'left over' from the place that is gone."[2]

When people talk about loss of the rural communities that preceded Oak Ridge, they often quote the above passage, which reflects a rather countercultural view of the Manhattan Project. Rather than celebrating scientific, technological, and educational progress for the region, Moneymaker focuses on the loss of the communities that were a prerequisite for the development of Oak Ridge. Like Thomas Kuhn's notion of scientific changes from one paradigm to another, there is an incommensurability about this change because what was lost in Wheat cannot be compared to the gains that came from the development of Oak Ridge.[3]

While only one physical place can occupy a piece of territory at one moment in time, loss can form into layers. In the place currently known as Oak Ridge there exist several different layers of places that have been lost or are in danger of being lost. There are four aspects of loss at the site: the removal of farmers from Wheat and other predecessor communities of Oak Ridge, the segregation of African Americans at the newly created Oak Ridge, degradation of the environment due to contamination from the plants, and the slow loss of Oak Ridge's Cold War mission.

The first layer of loss is the settler communities that came before Oak Ridge, which were rural farming villages with schools, churches, and small businesses. These communities included Wheat, Edgemoor, Elza, East Fork, Robertsville (New Hope), Bethel, and Scarboro. In the early 1940s, the federal government took control of these once occupied spaces and built facilities which would be used to produce fuel for atomic bombs. The residents of Wheat and other nearby communities suffered a swift and tragic set of losses, in which their land, community, and identity were transformed by the federal government and used for secret purposes. This was not a straightforward loss but was complicated by the fact that residents were never told why their land was taken and never got to see their land and communities again. Rather than a straightforward mourning per psychiatrist Dr. Elisabeth Kubler-Ross, this was (and is) a complex grief, in which federal policy prolonged the feelings of loss and helplessness that some residents experienced, particularly those who had dwelled for a long time in the area, and whose ancestors and family were buried there.

A second layer of loss is the experience of African Americans in the Oak Ridge region. While recruited to come to the area with the promise of good wages and a better life, they found themselves and their families trapped in an environment more restrictive than earlier communities. In fact, Oak Ridge provided its African American residents fewer civil rights and liberties than they expected. Oak Ridge's new status as a federally run city meant the implementation of restrictive policies for African Americans and their families. This shift, too, is incommensurable, as African American migrants gained in wages and stability of employment while suffering through dismal housing and community conditions.

As a third layer, environmental degradation, not publicly discussed during the early decades of the city, became an important issue by the 1960s and 1970s. As the Cold War ended, a more accurate accounting of the full costs of the project, in terms of environmental and human damage, was being assembled by scientists and researchers. Documentation of chemical and radiation releases from Oak Ridge, understood even by scientists in the 1940s, became more available to the public and cast a shadow backwards on the 1940s and 1950s. Similarly, as information became more available about the effects of the project, residents of the site began to talk more publicly about their experiences, leading to new oral histories of long-term residents. Many of those who spoke out discussed the significance of the removals and the founding of the city on them and their families, giving historians new evidence about the development of the region.

The final layer of loss is the slow ending of Oak Ridge's identity as a Cold War city. The souring of relations between the Soviet Union and United States in the wake of World War II made Oak Ridge relevant beyond the surrender of Japan. By the late 1940s, Oak Ridge was not slated for closure and abandonment but for a long-term role in nuclear weapons production and research. As long as nuclear rivalry persisted, the economic and political future of the city was virtually guaranteed, producing both white- and blue-collar prosperity.

The city of Oak Ridge, built on the site of farming communities and incorporating at least some of its residents, became an endangered place with the end of the Cold War. The community mobilized to preserve as much of the facility as practicable and to fashion a new identity around atomic tourism. However, in the post–Cold War period, even as Oak Ridge became part of a new atomic national park, there was a sense of loss of the economic vitality of the region, which had long stood out in its Tennessee surroundings. The mourning of the loss of a favored status in the region, as well as a loss of meaning from the end of the military mission of the site, are still unfolding today. The work of Lindsay Freeman focuses on the concept of "atomic nostalgia," in which residents of the region feel a sense of loss as the atomic past recedes, replaced by an uncertain future.[4]

These layers of loss intersect in ways that have been productive for historians. As the residents of Oak Ridge rethink the historic legacy of their town and residents better document their past through oral history, the public is more focused on the predecessor communities that existed before Oak Ridge. The history of African Americans in Oak Ridge and in the region prior to Oak Ridge has also been well documented in recent years. Oak Ridge has grappled with what its creation has meant to the region and the nation, bringing the cost of its creation for those who lived in this area before into sharper focus. While works such as James Overholt's *These Are Our Voices* (1987) featured essays on the Wheat and Elza communities, essays on the displacement caused by the project comprise less than 10 percent of the work, leaving the focus squarely on the urban and scientific development of the region.[5] The latter's history has been given greater prominence than at any time up until now. With the rapid passing of the generation that grew up in the area in the mid-twentieth century, capturing these voices through oral history and other means becomes even more important, as these stories are in danger of not being preserved due to death and the advancing age of those who lived through these changes. This type of loss is yet another layer in the story.

Historiography of Loss in Oak Ridge

The history of loss can be a blind spot for historians, even those who purport to be filling in the blanks in previously written histories. I certainly include my own historical work about Oak Ridge in this statement. This is particularly true when writing about the history of a monumental project such as the Manhattan Engineer District (MED). The massive effort to create atomic weapons during the Second World War casts a historical shadow over all that follows—even when the historian's intent is to counteract this effect. Even while trying to write a critical history of the project, and trying to bring in voices of people marginalized in official histories, it can be easy for historians to be swept away in the narrative of achievement and progress that surrounds these events.

I began my historical research on Oak Ridge in the 1990s. I intended to write a history of the scientists who were working on the project but who did not enjoy the marquee status of a J. Robert Oppenheimer. As I read further, I realized that Oak Ridge was a city of nearly 100,000 during World War II, with an array of workers and support personnel all toiling on the project. This became the focus of my book, *At Work in the Atomic City: A Labor and Social History of Oak Ridge, Tennessee* (2014), which sought to tell aspects of the project neglected in the official histories and popular mythology. Now, fifteen years later, I recognize that there is much more to uncover and understand.[6]

People who set out to write critical histories of the Manhattan Project can fall into its mythologies without meaning to do so. The papers from key actors and leaders, such as director of the Manhattan Project Leslie Groves Jr., feed the narrative that the project was an inevitable and progressive unfolding of scientific and technological knowledge into the social and political world. In my book about the Manhattan Project and Oak Ridge, the subjects of loss and regret came up very little. In my chapter on the people coming to Oak Ridge to work in the plants, I neglected the story of the displaced people who lost their communities for the creation of Oak Ridge. The narrative of Oak Ridge and the winning of World War II was so powerful that it obliterated the memory of what and who had occupied the space before.[7]

This theme can be seen in curricular material for teachers available from Oak Ridge's American Museum of Science and Energy. In the teacher information section of the museum's website, designed to help teachers prepare for a field trip, the information about predecessor communities to Oak Ridge is sparse. The content fits with the traditional understanding of the region in the Manhattan Project narrative: "The final quarter of 1942 saw the acquisition of the roughly 90 square mile parcel in the ridges west of Knoxville, the removal of relatively few families on the marginal farmland, and extensive site preparation to provide the transportation, communication and utility needs of the town and production plants that would occupy the previously underdeveloped area."[8]

The above sentence accurately summarizes the official version of the taking of the land that would become Oak Ridge. First, there is no subject of the sentence—instead, the land is simply "acquired," leaving out the actions of the federal government to take this land from residents. Second, the size of the action is downplayed throughout—farms are taken from "relatively few" families, and this land is "marginal." While both of these statements have some truth to them, the effects on the people whose land was taken was life changing, even if it was a relatively small number compared to those who moved to the area for the Manhattan Project. Whatever the economic viability of that farmland, the US government was going to seize it, making the argument that it was "marginal" irrelevant. Finally, throughout the twentieth century, reformers and government officials pronounced Appalachia as "underdeveloped," but without a balanced assessment of the development and its problems. While Oak Ridge was certainly developed by the MED, its nuclear production has had health and environmental effects far more sweeping than would have been caused by farming.

Like other parts of East Tennessee the area that became Oak Ridge consisted of small farming communities. Oak Ridge, ca. 1939, U.S. Department of Energy.

Historical rethinking does not always emerge from the study of primary sources or interviewing participants. Often it takes new scholars entering the field, or new life experiences of the historian, to change the thinking about a powerful narrative of progress. Thus, other historians have highlighted the loss inherent in the project. Peter Hales's *Atomic Spaces: Living on the Manhattan Project* (1997) drew on court cases and other documentary evidence, particularly photos, to highlight and document the losses of those whose land was seized by the courts to make way for the Manhattan Project. Hales was perhaps the first scholar to highlight the photographs and removal files which have been available at the National Archives in Atlanta for decades.[9]

Lindsay Freeman's recent work has most opened up the discourse about the history of Oak Ridge. *Longing for the Bomb: Oak Ridge and Atomic Nostalgia* (2015) brought a new lens, both theoretically and historically, to the study of the Manhattan Project. Having grown up in the area, Freeman explores the range of feelings and myths produced and manipulated during the atomic age. She therefore creates space for research and writing that no longer sees the Manhattan Project as a vast, inevitable undertaking, but as a human endeavor, which produced a range of mixed reactions and results.[10]

Freeman's chapter on relocation, "The Atomic Prophecy," examines the experience of those who lived in a series of predecessor communities. John Hendrix is credited, both in the scholarly literature and within Oak Ridge culture, with predicting the development of great factories, the extension of railroads, and the tearing up of the area by earthmoving equipment at the turn of the twentieth century. Freeman pointed out that, rather than dwell on the issues of displacement and loss, much of the historical discourse centered upon a prophecy of Hendrix, first cited in 1946, taking the spotlight from the damage inflicted on the existing communities to the strangeness of one man's vision.[11]

Drew Swanson's recent book on Appalachian history, *Beyond the Mountains: Commodifying Appalachian Environments* (2019), reconceptualizes Oak Ridge not as a unique facet of the history of the southern mountains, but as part of a larger story of federal involvement in the region. He writes, "Oak Ridge represented this important mid-century Appalachian phenomenon. It symbolized the power of government bureaucracies and federal spending to reshape the southern mountains. Government money, planners, and employees forced rapid change on substantial swaths of Appalachia, sometimes in response to the needs of local people and sometimes in opposition to their desires." Following on the heels of TVA, and as a predecessor to the Appalachian Regional Commission, Oak Ridge brought East Tennessee from the periphery to the center of events. Summing up this trend over the decade, Swanson wrote of Oak Ridge and other federal endeavors in the area, "Rather than existing as an anomalously isolated region, portions of the southern mountains had been drawn into the central purposes of the state."[12]

Loss and Removals in the Oak Ridge Region

The federal government's removals of the communities that became Oak Ridge took place to the west of Knoxville, Tennessee, in a predominantly rural area, divided between Roane and Anderson counties. The government classified only 15 percent of the population in both counties as "urban." The federal government claimed fifty-six thousand acres of land in 1942–43, more than TVA acquired during this time. Residents were given as little as two weeks to relinquish their property and move, with no planning as to where they were to resettle, and little assistance offered in the process. The vast majority of the people removed were farmers, with some small business owners, educators, and religious leaders included in the population.[13]

The differences in gender and race were not as salient as the different treatment of those who owned land and those who rented. Landowners received some compensation to purchase a new farm or new home, but sharecroppers, tenant farmers, or those working on a farm for wages received no compensation and needed to enter the wage workforce of the area. Hales's study demonstrated that the creation of Oak Ridge forced between twelve hundred and two thousand nonlandowning tenants to leave the area. Hales notes that this removal group never got their day in court, because landowners lacked the resources to openly challenge federal actions. Instead, they simply disappeared as their homes and workplaces were taken by the federal government.[14]

Unlike other federal removal projects in the region, the government did little to nothing to help displaced Oak Ridge families resettle. This meant that many families simply moved on to neighboring areas, hoping to continue their family's tradition of farming. In some cases, families started businesses in other areas, or worked for wages in one of the emerging wartime industries of the area. Many young men volunteered for or were drafted into the military, taking them far outside the region altogether. This stream of refugees joined those already on the move from the South and from other regions who were moving as part of wartime recruitment efforts.

The US government justified the removals because of the need for land for the newly created Manhattan Engineer District. The area around Knoxville was seen as both in proximity to resources (TVA electricity), accessible by transit networks such as railroads, relatively sparsely populated, and sheltered by the geography of the region from prying eyes. While the MED was certainly justified in its choice of Oak Ridge for its new plants and city, project propaganda inaccurately portrayed the region as backward, economically marginal, and sparsely populated.

The existing communities in the area, while overwhelmingly rural, had higher mean population density than the United States did at the time and numerous long-standing cultural and economic centers. The communities in places such as Wheat included businesses, schools, and churches with deep roots, which were entirely wiped away by the government action. Even simple gestures, such as allowing former residents access to cemeteries, were resisted by the federal government for decades. Peter Hales captured the evidence about the sites in his book *Atomic Spaces,* drawing on photographs used in the appendix to a government report on the region pre-removal that showed an industrious farming region, with traditional clapboard farmhouses dating back to the nineteenth century, surrounded by large barns and outbuildings. Picture after picture showed fields of rye, hay, and tobacco, their custodians standing in their midst, harvesting, sampling, or posing with examples of the crops. The composite image presented a prosperous region, rich in community values and traditions—a cohesive traditional American community, full of the symbols of a nostalgic American rural past."[15]

Families were given little time to leave their property and were given less compensation than would be needed to find new accommodations in the area. The sheer extent of the seizure, and the more than three thousand people involved meant that those who wished to continue farming would have few options, and those who were sharecroppers or tenant farmers would be pushed into wage work in war industries.

While some farmers protested the seizure of their land in court and to local politicians, the entire episode was effectively quashed by the War Department, the local media, and politicians. In the overwhelming atmosphere of wartime secrecy and "patriotic consensus," the sacrifices made by the families of those living in the Wheat community and others seized were subsumed in the greater wartime sacrifices required to support troops overseas. As a result, protest was muted and localized, and the national media did not report on the origins or the building of the secret city. Further, by the time of the Oak Ridge removals, residents of East

Tennessee had great familiarity with federal relocation efforts, first for the Smoky Mountains National Park and later for TVA projects. This history of forced relocation made it easier for the Army Corps to take what was needed from local farmers and to pay them a nominal fee for their land.

African American Gains and Losses in Oak Ridge

When I researched the labor and social histories of Oak Ridge, I looked for stories that had long been ignored in favor of the development of big science and big technology. But while I read and conducted oral histories, or dug through documents and newspapers, certain types of stories seemed to be more prevalent, and some types of stories caught much more of my attention than others. For example, I organized much of my thinking around the idea that Oak Ridge was a place that people moved to, and then created a community out of what they found there. Women moved from farms to the city and its plants. African American workers moved from the Deep South to work at Oak Ridge. They recognized their situation in Oak Ridge as unjust, but still maintained that the opportunity allowed far greater advancement than would have been possible in their former homes.[16] Recruited with only vague promises of higher wages and better working conditions, the sheer hopelessness of their situation in the South drew them to employment in Oak Ridge.[17]

In my research on Oak Ridge, I dug into material on the changes that the area underwent in terms of racial composition. I certainly noted that the area was a vital, active farming community, where people had lived for generations. This could be best described as a checkerboard—African American and white families, certainly not politically or socially equal—living adjacent to one another as they had for generations. The reasons for the rural area's coexistence of African American and white residents was not an accident, but part of the region's long history. Slavery was part of the early settlement of the area, and the earliest burial plots of African Americans are located on nearby former plantations. The 1940s census for Roane County showed multiple examples of African American and white farmers living in close proximity, with many in both groups living on farms that their families owned.[18]

The massive federal intervention that created Oak Ridge changed this racial composition beyond recognition. Rather than viewing Oak Ridge's change as a unique piece of military and technological history, Oak Ridge's creation can best be seen as part of the transformation of many wartime communities in the United

States, in which the exigencies of wartime production bumped up against a federal policy of racial segregation in housing. Works such as *The Color of Law: A Forgotten History of How Our Government Segregated America* (2017) by Richard Rothstein, as well as work on the history of public housing and housing policy in America, made it clear that Oak Ridge's segregation and vastly unequal housing by race was neither an accident nor the product of idiosyncratic decisions. Instead, it was part of a broader policy effort that used federal housing policy as a tool to create separate and unequal housing conditions by race.[19]

The city of Oak Ridge was an urban, fully segregated residential and industrial community in a way that the rural communities it replaced were not. While not a model of racial equality, rural East Tennessee in the pre–World War II era was a region where African American and white residents lived in proximity and interacted regularly. While in no way separate from the issues of racial discrimination in the United States in the twentieth century, and the scene of race riots in 1919, East Tennessee at this time featured African American neighborhoods, businesses, and labor unions. The city of Oak Ridge was a different story. The federal government created a racially divided and unequal residential experience in the city. African American workers were limited to hutments for their housing, with men and women living in separate areas, even when married. These hutments were the most primitive housing available in the atomic city, consisting of a small shack with an oil stove for its only heat.[20]

Early in the city's history, many Black and white workers lived in less-than-ideal housing. Many white families were consigned to vast trailer areas, but over time options improved. For African Americans, housing conditions remained dismal even after the end of World War II. As white Oak Ridgers, like other white Americans, were moving from temporary wartime housing to more stable rental housing or even homeownership, federal policy kept African Americans from these opportunities as a matter of policy. Only muckraking accounts by African American newspapers, especially the *Chicago Defender,* moved the federal government to close the hutment area and provide slightly better housing to Black workers. African Americans also held the least desirable jobs in the facilities, focused on maintenance and cleanup, and their children received the least access to educational resources.[21] Oak Ridge schools were segregated until *Brown v. Board of Education of Topeka,* and the nearby community of Clinton suffered several racist attacks in 1956, covered in the national media.

Rothstein's work described parallel communities, with the example of the Western Addition in San Francisco. Rothstein made clear that public housing

African Americans formed their own community in Oak Ridge, which was segregated from its establishment in the early 1940s until the mid-1950s. Recreation at Oak Ridge, ca. 1940s, U.S. Department of Energy.

policy in America regulated the market to move African Americans into the lowest grade of housing possible, which maintained a system that kept African Americans and their families in this housing and limited any opportunity to attain better housing, even when individuals could afford to do so.[22] Thomas Sugrue argued in *The Origins of the Urban Crisis: Race and Inequality of Postwar Detroit* (2005) that public housing in America was often the site of racial conflict and struggle, with the federal government policing the boundaries between African American migrants and white residents. For its first decade, during the war years, all dwellings in Oak Ridge were federally owned public housing and were kept racially segregated by federal edict.[23]

Ultimately, the story of the generation of African American workers and families who came to Oak Ridge resists easy narratives of gain and loss. But certainly, the history of racial policy in the wartime and postwar years is a story of missed opportunity. Had federal housing and employment policy treated African American workers and their families fairly, the story of the next decades would have been far different, and produced a far more favorable trajectory for African Americans than the story historians can trace up to the present.

Rethinking Loss in Oak Ridge: Oral History and Memory

Stories of the people displaced by the Manhattan Project and TVA did not resonate with me in the same way, and I failed to connect the dots of this story in more than a minimal way. In hindsight, I fell into a traditional narrative of Oak Ridge, that the city had improved life for residents in terms of education, workplace, and community. When I conducted research in the 1990s, residents were still quite reticent about sharing their Oak Ridge experiences. Despite substantial outreach, I found only a handful of Oak Ridge residents willing to talk, due to the culture of silence that enveloped the site that began in World War II and continued through the Cold War.

Since that time, the oral history evidence for Oak Ridge has expanded and been made more widely available. Building on the stories captured in Overholt's *These Are Our Voices,* these oral histories give details of the losses sustained by people who lost their farms and communities to the Manhattan Project. Now, through efforts of local historians and institutions, there is far greater availability of voices to give a different perspective on the events of the 1940s. These oral histories from this period rebut the standard Manhattan Project narrative, but one would have to listen and connect the dots in order to recognize what people lost in the transition from the Wheat community to Oak Ridge.

There have been many moments in the history of Oak Ridge, a city that has itself been in danger of being closed and forgotten with the end of its Cold War mission, when its prehistory and predecessor communities have been the focus. In the historical work done at the site, the passing of decades has meant that there can be more focus on what was lost when Oak Ridge was built. During the Cold War, much of the discourse about Oak Ridge and work done there was bound by community norms of secrecy. With the end of the Cold War, and the shift of discourse to understanding the environmental legacy of the project, the conversation became more open.

Most notably, community members and historians have gathered oral histories of residents of Oak Ridge and its predecessor communities. The interviewees were more willing to talk about their experiences because of their advanced age and their fear that the memory of what occurred at Oak Ridge would be lost. The sense that this "greatest generation" was passing away without telling their stories generated interest nationwide. In Oak Ridge, the public library became a repository for oral histories, many of which are now accessible online. Nearly three decades ago, when I was conducting oral history interviews, there was much less interest by potential interviewees to document their past and share their stories with others. Luckily for the next generation of scholars, people became more willing to talk and thus enriching the historical record.[24]

While many of these oral histories focused on traditional Oak Ridge topics— such as the creation of the city, the building of the bomb, and organizing community services—people began talking more openly about other topics. The Wheat community and the aspects of life that people displaced from such areas lost, including access to the cemeteries where their families had been buried, made for a common thread. In the process of building Oak Ridge, the whole system of burial and remembrance in the region was disrupted. Even today, many of the graveyards in the area are a matter of guesswork.[25] Despite this attention, the main narrative of Oak Ridge as the city that was justifiably created to help win World War II dominates exhibits and official histories, ignoring the importance of the predecessor communities.

The oral history work done in Oak Ridge in the late 1990s fills in some of the blanks about loss in the community caused by the land seizures. The Oak Ridge Public Library manages an oral history collection and provides online access to the recordings and transcripts. These sources allow historians to begin to reconstruct the history of the communities that were wiped out. In an interview of people raised in Bethel Valley, one respondent told the interviewer about the removal process:

> Well, it was a scary time because we couldn't find anywhere to move to. We were one of the last families that moved out. We had one old cow that we just turned her loose and we would go up and down this valley late in the afternoon and we'd find her. We rode the mules and would find her. We had one old mule if you fell off of her, you walked home because she stood still until you'd get up from under her feet and she left you. We moved out here when I was in the seventh grade. I went half a year at Wheat and then I went to Harriman. Finished my school at Harriman. Then I went some to Roane State but I didn't graduate.[26]

Part of the problem with this type of oral history evidence for professional historians is that it is not always linear. People are being interviewed at a time in life when they may struggle to remember details long ago and, in many ways, a world away. One often repeated narrative in the history of Oak Ridge is how much the development of the city improved education in the region by bringing a more cosmopolitan school system to the area. For people living in the region, however, institutions such as the Wheat school were well positioned to develop the students who lived in these areas. More simply, rural families did not always benefit from an educational system that was geared toward the children of scientists and engineers.

In other oral histories, evidence about loss is more direct but does not fit into the conventional narrative that Oak Ridge was a source of community development. James Brennan, who had a long skilled trades career in Oak Ridge, reflected on the experiences of his father, who lost his farm during the creation of the city. Thus, Brennan, who gained decades of livelihood from the city, captured what it meant to have his family's land taken from his father, who never recovered his footing as a farmer.

MR. BRENNAN: Anyhow, as time went on, then, my parents kept me pretty well up to date on the happenings and how changes were going on and where it was and the lot.

MR. MCDANIEL: Now when did they have to move?

MR. BRENNAN: They had to move out in November—or December.

MR. MCDANIEL: Of '42.

MR. BRENNAN: Of '42. And they gave them ten days. And we must of had 40 head of cattle and maybe that many hogs. . . .

MR. MCDANIEL: Well, do you remember how much they paid him?

MR. BRENNAN: They were only going to pay him $7,000.00 to begin with, and he took it to federal court.

MR. MCDANIEL: Did he?

MR. BRENNAN: And they just about double what he had been offered to start with. But he still. . . .

MR. MCDANIEL: It still wasn't enough, was it?

MR. BRENNAN: No, sir. And his money was held up and he never did ever own any farmland anymore.

MR. MCDANIEL: Is that right?

MR. BRENNAN: No, he wanted to get a farm, but he never was able to have a farmland anymore. . . .

MR. MCDANIEL: He just felt like they'd done him wrong.

MR. BRENNAN: Well, they really had. I don't know what the fear of the people who was living there was like, but for some reason they wanted all those people out.[27]

Brennan's comments reflected the loss sustained by families when the land was taken, the confusion and immediacy of the time, and the long-term consequences. Even within a single family, the development of Oak Ridge had great positives and could entail great losses. The way that the government seized the land did not provide a means for these farmers to continue to pursue their livelihood and was seen by Brennan as a lifelong wrong, even if the economic possibilities in the area increased for the next generation.

In another oral history session, several residents reflected on both the area lost as well as on how contemporaries portrayed it in print. In the interview below, several former residents talked about the Wheat community and the way people have written about it.

MRS. HOLMBERG: [W]hile I have the floor I would like to read something about what writers said of this valley. . . . Daniel Lang's book called Early Tales of the Atomic Age.[28] He said, "Scarboro, Wheat, and Robertsville are names of vanished places where the hill folk of this region went in for what amounted to non-profit farming, some tobacco plants, a couple of hogs, some poultry, perhaps a head or two of cattle, and a little moonshine making." He went on to say, "The Army Engineers and Contractors arrived on the scene in 1942, and went to work on the scrappy, unattractive, particularly routeless terrain, and quails roamed the place, and the guards picked off skunks with their rifles." Not a very nice picture of the area.

The creation of Oak Ridge transformed rural farming communities into an industrial center of scientific research with environmental consequences. Pictured is the K-25 Gaseous Diffusion Plant, which at the time was the largest building in the world, located near the site of an antebellum plantation which had a large slave community. The building was demolished in 2013 and today there is a K-25 Interpretative Center on the site to help visitors understand the complex history of the region. Aerial view of Oak Ridge, ca. 1950s, U.S. Department of Energy.

MRS. ZUCKER: Well, I think it is beautiful land.

MRS. WINTENBERG: Let me tell you about our farm. Our farm, my father always grew. It was 180 acres. Let's see, it came from the Olivers. My grandmother, or great-grandmother, Amelia, I'm getting lost here. We've been looking up so much of my genealogy and it has gone so far back and back. There was a lot of land from the Olivers, but apparently, as different ones took it, a grandfather and then maybe even on down. My father didn't sell any. But it had been like a 1,260 acre tract of land. But when my dad got it, it was around 180, up and down the Turnpike. My father enjoyed farming. In fact, an uncle told me in long years after my father was gone, but what my dad had that no one else seemed to have in the family, was contentment. I said, "What do you mean 'contentment'?" He said, "He loved farming; he loved you kids; he loved his wife." Of course he had had two or three wives, so maybe he didn't know what he was talking about. (Laughter)[29]

Former residents lost both their land and their community, and also saw those portrayed in ways they found inaccurate in the contemporary writings and histories that followed. Many similar descriptions found in Lang's work were repeated in historical works on Oak Ridge, in both official histories and academic or popular writings. In the historical memory of Oak Ridge, a clever turn of phrase, such as the quails and skunks above, or a striking story of eccentricity such as the omnipresent John Hendrix, can reappear over and over, while the history of many other people remains invisible or in the background.

Returning to Wheat and Other Lost Communities

The story of Wheat and other communities does not have a happy ending or closure. Removed families were never allowed to return to their original property to purchase or rent. The most that the federal government has been willing to do is allow more visiting and touring of the area, as well as resident access to cemeteries. During and for the decade after World War II, no one was allowed to own property in Oak Ridge. Since 1959, residents were allowed to purchase homes in residential zones, but this did not extend to the right to buy the previously seized farms that dotted the area.

More recently, residents of Wheat and other removed communities participated in extensive oral history and community documentation projects. While the results of these efforts certainly show the bias of people who grew up in an area and spent their childhoods playing outside on its land and in its waterways, their stories are not any more romantic than the general discourse about Oak Ridge, whose birth as a city has been romanticized in its own right. As Lindsay Freeman pointed out in *Longing for the Bomb,* festivals, tours, museums, a train tour, and other cultural artifacts have been developed to preserve the history of Oak Ridge as an atomic city. There is little evidence of cultural activity to present the other narratives of pre–World War II Oak Ridge.[30] It remains to be seen how this historic presentation of Oak Ridge will affect the community. It could bring the community together around the sharing of historical stories, or it could be another layer of loss, in which the community sees its history reflected in ways that it finds inauthentic.

The difference of relation to the land between the Wheat community and what became Oak Ridge is extreme. While no utopia, the farming communities that preceded Oak Ridge were firmly connected to the land. Residents who grew up in the area later remembered the natural world as the source of much of their childhood memories. These rural communities existed as part of a vibrant ecosystem that included forests, streams, and other natural features that formed part of the cultural life of the region.

Oak Ridge itself was, by contrast, a vast industrial enterprise that transformed this natural environment, ultimately making parts of it uninhabitable. The construction of the atomic materials plants, the development of chemical and electromagnetic processes of uranium production, and the ultimate disposal of chemical and radioactive waste irrevocably altered the natural landscape. From the beginning of the Manhattan Engineer District, there was little long-term planning for the waste products created as part of this process. As a result, workers dumped or stored waste materials and radioactive substances, which seeped into the air, the water, and the ground.[31] While Oak Ridge did not suffer any massive, one-time radiation releases such as those that took place at the Hanford, Washington, nuclear site, the city and its residents experience long-running problems with environmental contamination. To illustrate, Oak Ridge was featured in a section of Makhijani, Hu, and Yih's *Nuclear Wastelands* (1995), which addressed communities degraded by nuclear material worldwide.[32]

Makhijani and his coauthors attempted to quantify the damage done to humans and the environment by the atomic weapons program at Oak Ridge but found such a lack of clear evidence that only very rough estimates of damage could be made: "The immense range of release estimate for the X-10 reactor and associated chemical processing illustrates the nature of uncertainties confronting serious analyses of what actually happened in terms of doses and health effects as a result of nuclear weapons production. The main problems relate to secrecy, inadequate documentation, and the difficulties of reconstructing day-to-day events that took place for decades."[33]

What is known about nuclear and chemical contamination of the Oak Ridge site is almost mind-boggling in scope. Reviewing official studies and released information, Makhijani and his coauthors conclude that there are more than six hundred sites requiring remediation in Oak Ridge, and that the US Department of Energy and its contractors have identified over six hundred contaminated sites for investigation and remediation. Radioactive substances were released to the air, water, and the soil at the site, over the decades, though not on the scale of Chernobyl or other massive sudden releases.[34]

Oral History of Environmental Loss

While much of the environmental issues of Oak Ridge were hidden behind a wall of classification by the federal government, as issues emerged into the public realm through use of the Freedom of Information Act and legislative hearings, participants also began to be more forthcoming in oral histories. Their testimony indicates that the Atomic Energy Commission and its successor agency, the US Department of Energy, were quite knowledgeable about potential environmental and human ramifications of their activities, both at the time and in the decades that followed.

Spencer Gross, who worked for a citizen's environmental advisory board in Oak Ridge, indicated the problems with mercury in Oak Ridge were due to a combination of factors, including the long-term issues of demolishing buildings that were both heavily contaminated and falling down at the Oak Ridge site. He told an oral historian:

GROSS: . . . the other thing that's going to happen is there's a number of buildings that need to be torn down at Y-12. They're reasonably sure there's a lot of lost mercury under those buildings . . . and so when they tear the buildings down, it will release that mercury. They're fearful they could flood, not flood, but get back into the creek again. They're building, I think, they're about ready to start construction on the mercury treatment plant there. . . . At the headwaters of East Fork Poplar Creek to capture that mercury so that when they start tearing the buildings down, they will be able to get most of it.[35]

Here, the losses for Oak Ridge pile up. The end of the atomic era leads to the abandonment of program buildings, which then decay, and become part of the larger ecological problems of the community as the waste attached to the buildings moves into the environment. Unlike the Cold War period, in recent years these losses have become more publicly known and visible, and residents can now have a fuller account of the effects of atomic weapons research and production on their community and their environment.

In a 2013 interview with Clayton Gist, an Oak Ridge Associated Universities researcher, he described the investigation of mercury contamination in the city:

And through the process of handling all this mercury, these numbers are a little foggy now, with time that passed, but there was something like a half a million tons of mer-c[ury]—a half a million pounds of mercury was unaccounted for. And part of it, they think, was just bookkeeping. That they would get these, what they called mercury flasks that were 70 pounds apiece. And sometimes they weren't completely full. And the way they inventoried was by counting the flasks. And so a lot of it was lost due to bookkeeping. There's some that was lost through spillage. And some of it was lost though vaporization. That loss through spillage, it went down into a sump in Y-12 in the, as I remember, that was the Alpha 4 building.[36]

This disputed volume of mercury continued its journey from here, as Gist explained: "And then that went into a piping system that ended up spilling out into East Fork Poplar Creek. And that went—that drained into what was called New Hope Pond in those days, which doesn't exist anymore. And then from New Hope Pond, it ran down in the creek and passed through town." This mercury continued its dispersal as it found its way into the soil, and then this soil was used for a variety of local building programs, "and they used a lot of that contaminated soil on the sewer line. So we had these blotches of contaminated soil clear across the city. . . . But there were a lot, probably some of our highest concentrations and largest contaminated areas, were on the Civic Center."[37]

This revelation takes us full circle, as the Oak Ridge Public Library, the home of these oral histories, is adjacent to the Civic Center, and a researcher sitting in the library reading this account would be reading about their own connection to Oak Ridge's environmental problems. There is truly no place to hide from environmental damage and loss in Oak Ridge, as even places built to house the records and memory of the city are built on soil poisoned by its industrial plants.

The Incommensurable Gains and Losses at Oak Ridge

What was lost and gained in the relocation of families from communities such as Wheat is impossible to historically assess. It is, in many ways, an incommensurable comparison, as people gave up a way of life that they would not be able to regain. As the amount of land taken was so massive and displaced so many in such a rapid manner, families could not find other farmland in the area to resume their activities. People's attachment to their land and community was more than just economic. The areas had community activities, schools, stores, and churches, all of which bound people together. These were swept away by the arrival of the MED, and what came in its place may not have been "better" for the people who had lived there. While the official histories are scornful and dismissive of the lives people led in places such as Wheat, they had institutions and traditions they were proud of and that served their needs.

In my own career as a program developer and grant writer, I came to understand more about loss and grief from my experience in public housing than I ever did from archival or oral history accounts of land seizure during the Manhattan Project. I helped in the efforts of the Ypsilanti Public Housing Commission to secure federal, state, and local funds to tear down World War II stock housing in southeast Michigan and replace it with new townhomes (reserved for low-income residents). Each time I toured the Parkridge Homes community, a neighborhood of dilapidated structures which lasted long past their prime, I was reminded of Oak Ridge. I was committed to the residents having a better place to live and raise their families. At the groundbreaking ceremony for the rebuilding project in August 2016, I was struck by the attachment of the residents to their community. Residents of Parkridge wept openly for the loss of their homes, as these structures, however poorly maintained, were places that held meaning for them, and had contained the history of their families and their neighborhood for generations. In the rush to tear down and rebuild, I had missed the need of people to grieve and remember the positive aspects of what had been there before. In this moment, I recognized my own blindness as a person and as a historian, falling into a narrative that I should have known to question, and, as a result, missing a lot of the story that I should have been telling.

The removal of the residents of Wheat and other communities has never penetrated the consciousness of Americans in the same way as the story of Oak Ridge as an atomic city that helped win World War II. While one would guess that Oak Ridge would recede from historical memory, the opposite is true. Nonfiction and fictional books have amplified the history of the city, most recently the story of the young women who came to work in the plants.[38] A new national park dedicated to the atomic age has come into being with a continuation of the focus on people moving to the area to win the war and the building of the atomic plants and the city that supported these efforts.[39]

The new curriculum for the park has a section on displacement of existing communities. The exhibit puts the removal events within the context of World War II, explaining, "You have been told that the government needs the land for a project that will help end the war. Everyone wants to end the war and bring their boys back home. Everyone in the community has been affected by the war and many people have husbands, sons, brothers, and fathers that are away fighting. Your entire town is displaced." Then the curriculum asks students to write a letter based on this situation: "Imagine that you will have to find a place to stay for you and your family while you look for a new residence. Compose a letter to a relative explaining what is happening to you and your family. What plans will you have to make? Where will you live? How will you move? What emotions is your family experiencing?"[40]

While this is a step in the direction of greater understanding for families who were displaced, it still tells students, directly, how to answer the question: everyone in America would be in favor of this project, which seeks to end the war. While the family may experience negative emotions leaving their farm, it is clear that their sacrifice is only part of a greater, more important sacrifice that the war requires. The narratives of Oak Ridge that started with the beginning of the project in 1942 are still being repeated, despite new knowledge we have of the effects of the project on those it displaced.

6 When Minds Wander Back

Memory and Loss on the Road to Nowhere

MATTHEW CHISHOLM

One of the best examples of a misnomer in Western North Carolina is the attachment of the label of "Great Smoky Mountains Expressway" to US Route 74, which runs from Waynesville to just west of Bryson City. What is curious about this nomenclature is that the road never enters the Great Smoky Mountains National Park, and that it directs would-be tourists to a town whose dreams of being a "Park Gateway" were shattered decades ago. As the road runs west out of Bryson City, it links up with North Carolina Highway 28, the northwest segment of the Mountain Waters Scenic Roadway that roughly borders the southern edge of Fontana Lake for its entirety. Both of these roads offer motorists the stunning beauty of the rugged landscape. Travelers are taken up and down through old mountain communities and coves such as Almond, Panther Creek, and Welch Cove toward the Tennessee and North Carolina border, where Fontana Lake dumps her still waters 480 feet down into the Little Tennessee River.

There is something about this area that feels like the epicenter of the soul of Appalachia, but it also has a ghostly presence that has descended on the landscape. There are of course businesses, homes, farms, and churches all along these stretches of highway, but they all pale in comparison to the behemoth of Fontana Lake that is frequently drained down and out of view. This part of Western North Carolina seems haunted, containing the souls of buried communities, sunk in time and memory beneath a weighty sense of loss, that only reveal echoes of a rich history that bloomed and died when the waters of Fontana Lake inundated the deep coves and branches.

In early fall 2019, I drove with my daughter to see the Fontana Dam and Fontana Village. I had not been to Bryson City and the surrounding area in quite some time, and though I had heard rumors of growth and sustainability, I wanted to see the town and outlying communities with fresh eyes. My daughter was particularly excited about hot chocolate and watching the Great Smoky Mountain Railroad depart for its "Great Pumpkin" ride to a pumpkin patch ($56 for an adult!), but I wanted to see how the landscape had changed and get a hint at how the residents in this mountain community were faring.

During summer 2018, the federal government gave Swain County the remaining $35 million of an initial $52 million settlement in exchange for never completing the "Road to Nowhere." The money, however, was not immediately dispersed to the Swain County commissioners to do as they pleased with it. All $52 million was held in trust in Raleigh at the North Carolina Treasurer's Office, and Swain County officials can only draw on the interest produced by the account to pay for its many infrastructure projects. In short, Swain County is still starving for cash, and despite the uptick in downtown development catering to tourists, this area is still well behind the rest of the state in providing for its own citizens. In 2019, Swain County voters approved a $0.25 sales tax to help support the county school system. In the coming year, Swain County officials will begin to draw upwards of a $1 million a year in interest to further develop their community beyond downtown Bryson City.[1]

The first time I drove past the billboard that read "Welcome to the Road to No-Where: A Broken Promise 1943–?, No More Wilderness," I was in my early twenties exploring the rumors of an abandoned tunnel that served as a majestic gateway into the heart of the southern part of the Great Smoky Mountains. But instead the road was never completed, and the tunnel is literally the terminus point of a road to nowhere. The cryptic message on the billboard stirred up my curiosity about whether some power had robbed this area of Appalachia of something essential. In hindsight, and after reading about the removal of the area's inhabitants, I realized a sense of loss permeating the area like a dark fog.

During my fall 2019 trip to Bryson City, I drove the same road, Lakeshore Drive, that led out to the tunnel. I wondered whether the billboard would still be there since all of the settlement money had been received, but it was still standing near the entrance to the Great Smoky Mountains National Park. Even more surprising, it had been replaced by a brand-new, shiny, glistening, and colorful version of the old one. It is tempting to register the end of the Road to Nowhere controversy with

This billboard, located on Lakeshore Drive near Bryson County, North Carolina, represents local frustration with the federal government's inability to complete a road on the north shore of Fontana Lake. Despite a 2018 settlement between the federal government and Swain County for $52 million, local residents have upgraded the sign to reflect the ongoing sense of loss and betrayal with the "Road to Nowhere." 1. Opposition sign posted on private property at the entrance to the road looking NW, by David Haas, 1996, Historic American Buildings Survey/Historic American Record/Historic American Landscapes Survey, Library of Congress Prints and Photographs Division, Washington, DC.

the final dispersal of money, but the billboard represents that an ongoing sense of hurt, loss, and government betrayal persists.

I concluded my fall 2019 visit with a closer look at the dam and resort. My three-year-old and I scurried to the edge of the dam to look into the nearly vertical spillways that plummet hundreds of feet into an enclosed abyss at the end of the valley floor. The effect of looking into those enormous cylinders of concrete was both terrifying and a bit nauseating, but the magnitude of this engineering project was impressive. The adjacent Fontana Village is a sprawling resort and marina that caters to out-of-town tourists seeking a mountain bike excursion, a round of disc golf, or a quiet walk among the dense foliage of the mountains. An enormous lodge complete with poolside cabana rooms dominates the facility, but despite such recent updates, the original Fontana Village is intact. With only a little imagination, today's visitors can visualize a New Deal–era work camp, complete with cabins for families that still line the resort's old roads, the Fontana Village community church, and even the old grocery-store conveyor belt that served the residents during construction.

At the dam and the resort, I experienced a haunting feeling of loss. I could see beneath the fresh coats of paint, disc golf courses, and resort restaurants into a bygone era nearly eighty years ago when residents of mountain communities forfeited their homeplaces for electricity to support the war. Part of their sacrifice included the postwar promise of economic improvement by creating a new access point to recreational spaces created by the impoundment. While some tourist dollars followed, many residents believed that they had been shortchanged by the government, changing the narrative of those dispossessed—especially the descendants—from sacrifice to loss.

The loss of mountain communities in the Fontana Basin centered on a fight to build the Road to Nowhere and was a deeply personal and visceral issue for many descendants of the original inhabitants. The fuel for contention was based on collective and distorted memories of those who were removed as children from the area and the narratives both they and their descendants constructed over time. Many of them created an imagined memory of life on the North Shore prior to TVA which was based on nostalgia. Their sadness was real, but their memories were distorted by a romantic view of an idyllic life stolen by a faceless enemy in Washington that seemed fine with ignoring the suffering of those displaced.

Appalachian Atlantis: What Was Lost Under the Water

When Heath Shuler decided to run in the 2006 election for North Carolina's Eleventh District in the US House of Representatives, he was well aware that the largest issue that he would be facing from a constituent standpoint would be to get the Road to Nowhere finally built or to bargain a large enough settlement to ease decades of perceived federal government deception. The Bryson City native and mountain Democrat ran as a "Blue Dog" centrist who believed in fiscal responsibility. He had to balance the economic interests of a dispossessed and economically stagnant region with a desire to move that same region forward, even if it meant promoting ideas that hinted towards progressivism. This fight was made all the more intense given Republican incumbent Charles Taylor's unique position of power on the House Appropriations Committee and desire to get the road finally completed. In effect, Shuler stood in between the two worlds of mountaineer and "modern man"—raised in the coves off Lands Creek with humble beginnings but educated at the University of Tennessee, afterwards playing five years in the NFL, finishing his psychology degree, and starting a successful real estate business in Knoxville. In a very real sense, Shuler was caught between the past and the present, the mountains and the city, and, with the Road to Nowhere issue, resistance and reconciliation.

Linda Hogue, a lifetime local and descendant of a dispossessed family, was on the other hand still very much tied to the land on which she had been raised and moved away from when she was a little girl. Hogue was born exactly at the time of removal from the Fontana Basin in the early 1940s, and her family had deep roots in Swain County. Her father worked on the dams of the Tennessee Valley Authority (TVA) and pastored churches in North Carolina and Tennessee. Her husband's great-grandfather pastored Forney Creek Baptist Church. Despite her travels, however, Hogue always considered Swain County home and communicated that sharply to her interviewers. Overall, she was hopeful that the North Shore Road would be built, saying she was "playing to win."[2] What "winning" meant exactly was up for interpretation, but what was decidedly real was that Hogue, as well as many other former North Shore residents, experienced a real sense of loss at having been removed from the land where generations had lived, died, married, wept, and scratched out a living. What was unclear was who was going to pay the price for this loss and when.

America's attention was recently turned back to Appalachia when J. D. Vance published *Hillbilly Elegy* (2016), a memoir directed at revealing the author's origin story and unlikely rise to affluence and status. As Elizabeth Catte pointed out, however, Vance did little more than perpetuate familiar though cleverly disguised stereotypes that Appalachians have rejected for over a century. As a result of Vance's work, in addition to the 2016 presidential election of Donald Trump on the backs of stalwart Appalachian supporters, the rest of America has once again become interested in trying to figure out just what to do with "Appalachia." Appalachia is an uneven area that seems more problem than poetry, more backward than backbone of American culture. Coupled with this interest, however, is a renewed discovery of loss.[3] Appalachia has long fallen victim to extractive industries seeking to make a quick buck and move on. The logging and coal mining industries created a pattern of dependence that made living in Appalachia akin to trading room, board, and scrip for a southern sharecropper's stake.[4]

New Deal agencies in the 1930s and 1940s had some very paternalistic notions about the backwardness of mountain dwellers, while at the same time romanticizing those same people as some sort of pure American strain of pioneer individualism. In TVA removal profiles, the government authorities were baffled by and condescended to North Shore residents, but they also held them in esteem as some lost American wonder. These files reflected an accurate picture of the people they were interviewing, albeit through a subjective lens. Most mountaineers had no stake in this potential game of romanticism and revelation; they just wanted money, access to education, and a way to improve their station in life. Most interesting, by the last decades of the twentieth century, descendants of these displaced mountaineers had picked up the narrative that they may indeed be as exceptional and unwavering as the projected narratives said they were. Somewhere in this timespan of about seventy years (1940s–2000s), it seems that a group of mountaineers absorbed the paternalistic descriptions and reappropriated these stereotypes to support their narratives of loss.

Historiography of the Road to Nowhere

The Road to Nowhere has been the focus of some intellectual study. Several scholars have argued that this "site of memory and loss" was a case study of how the federal government handled conflict with disillusioned local communities. Existing scholarship offers insights into how locals processed what they lost and gained through the construction of Fontana Dam and resettlement of the residents, but none of these works specifically focused on the theme of loss with the Road to Nowhere. Some historians asserted that the fight to build the Road to Nowhere was Swain County's own "Lost Cause" narrative, which allowed the affected communities to rally around a common purpose.

Stephen Wallace Taylor demonstrated that Swain County was left behind in development compared to other locations ringing the park. More specifically he argued that Bryson City, the county seat of Swain County, lagged far behind Gatlinburg, Pigeon Forge, and Cherokee in terms of economic prosperity tied to tourism in the Great Smoky Mountains National Park (GSMNP). Taylor revealed in his epilogue, however, that Swain County was doing fine by the 1990s with a new scenic railroad, "neatly swept" streets, and tourists "charmed by the town's quietness and quaintness."[5] Taylor challenged the notion that Swain County had lost out on economic development; instead, the county arrived at a point of economic prosperity more slowly than its neighbors but in a sustainable manner that was much less tied to Appalachian stereotypes of development.

Karl Rohr's dissertation, "The Road to Nowhere and the Politics of Wilderness Legislation," fused cultural and political concerns to argue that the Road to Nowhere saga was a story of defining man's role in nature. Further, he believed that the Road to Nowhere was a test case for wilderness designation and management in national parks. He tackled the phenomenon of cemetery visitation and the role of the North Shore Road in defining community, arguing that the road became a sort of glue that held locals together.[6] Rohr's community-driven narrative and wilderness arguments were valid, but the road also served as a geographic and emotional landmark. The Road to Nowhere, or the promise of it, created new memories associated with the 1945 emptying of the North Shore which were then recast, refined, and transferred into activism centered on the narrative of loss.

Laura Kerr's "A 'Road to Nowhere'? The Political Ecology of Environmental Conflict over the North Shore Road in the Great Smoky Mountains National Park," served as a case study for the field of political ecology. This work argued that the pro-construction movement was not an anti-environmental campaign but an effort by local residents of Swain County to restore economic and political power.[7] In effect, Kerr argued that it was not necessarily the houses, railroads, roads, and graves that were lost but the political and economic power of Swain County residents in the latter part of the twentieth century. At the same time, Kerr accused TVA of more or less robbing the majority of the thirteen hundred families along the North Shore by giving them on average $37.76 per acre for their land.[8] Kerr's work is missing what many of the TVA removal profiles intimate, which was that many North Shore and Fontana Basin residents were willing to relocate because of new opportunities wrought by a modernizing economy. Kerr even admitted that the fight to build the road was "overwhelmingly dominated by local residents who have no relatives who were displaced by Fontana Dam."[9]

Lost Cause on the Little Tennessee: Background to the Road to Nowhere

The story of the Road to Nowhere is inextricably tied to the construction of Fontana Dam during World War II. As part of the project, between 1941 and 1945, TVA removed 1,300 families from the flood zone and North Shore area of the Fontana Basin. About 700 of these families were transients, workers who had arrived and settled temporarily for construction purposes as part of the over 7,000 workers at the Fontana construction site.[10] Nevertheless, there were 600 families who either rented or owned land in the area before dam construction commenced. There were 216 families that lived along the North Shore, the area that TVA would eventually transfer to the GSMNP. The Tennessee Valley Authority, created in 1933, had unprecedented powers in the Tennessee Valley region to promote reservoir projects to control flooding and produce inexpensive power. As the war progressed, TVA associated their projects and their electric power with the larger effort to beat Hitler and other authoritarian regimes. One TVA promotional poster read, "We are building this dam / To make the power / To roll the aluminum / To build the bombers / To beat the bastards."[11]

TVA represented a significant economic force in Western North Carolina. When coupled with the financial interests of the nearby Aluminum Company of America (Alcoa), TVA rendered local economies almost completely dependent on the agency. This scenario was nothing more than a change of scenery for North Shore residents, who had been dependent on extractive industries since the first logging and mining booms in the late nineteenth and early twentieth centuries. Not surprisingly, locals were just as willing to work for these new organizations as they had for the mining and logging firms decades earlier.

At the same time that TVA and Alcoa were carving their spheres of influence on the Little Tennessee River, the Great Smoky Mountains National Park took shape. The GSMNP was formed from 1,132 small farms and 18 other large tracts from 1928 to 1940 with the purpose of preserving an Appalachian ecosystem and promoting tourism.[12] Though seemingly at odds, the GSMNP, Alcoa, and TVA all had common interests—the accumulation of land for preservation or resource use for the betterment of the country in general. Also, the three entities engaged in dizzying land swaps, which at that time did not alarm residents or community leaders of the affected localities. Regional newspapers such as the *Bryson City Times* and *Jackson County Journal* celebrated the introduction of tourism dollars from Fontana Lake and the GSMNP, and applauded the jobs created by Alcoa and TVA.[13]

As part of the compensation for the removed residents, on July 30, 1943, representatives of TVA, the Department of the Interior, the state of North Carolina, and Swain County signed a three-part agreement. First, the agreement called for construction of a new road linking Bryson City and Deals Gap (near Fontana Village) to replace North Carolina State Highway 288, which would be buried almost completely under the new Fontana Lake. Second, the agreement approved the transfer of forty-four thousand acres on the North Shore of Fontana Lake from TVA to the Department of the Interior as an addition to the Great Smoky Mountains National Park. Finally, TVA agreed to give $400,000 to Swain County to pay off outstanding bonds dating back to the original construction of the old Highway 288. The construction of the new road, however, came with an enormous caveat. It was only to be built "as soon as funds are made available for that purpose by Congress after the cessation of hostilities in which the United States is now engaged."[14]

At the time of the agreement, many Bryson City residents were ecstatic. Bryson City would become the gateway to the southern part of the GSMNP, and they were more or less completely assured of tourism dollars, a higher tax base, and modern infrastructure. Additionally, residents would be able to see their family homesites and beloved graveyards where their ancestors were buried. In effect, these residents could go home to their former home whenever they desired. Additionally, the promise of the road eased over the realities of what North Shore residents were losing. The real tangible losses could be calculated in acreage, buildings, roads, trees, and gravestones, which were significant but not insurmountable, especially for a population that was used to adjustment based on changing economic conditions. What North Shore residents were afraid to lose, however, was their sense of home and attachment to a very real place that gave them their identities. The road would be a literal pathway for displaced residents to return to their identities; the lack of follow-through in road construction, therefore, constituted another real moment of loss for displaced citizens and their descendants.[15]

The road was never built, at least not all of it. The seven-plus miles that were paved, including a twelve-hundred-foot tunnel at the end, became a site of loss for a later generation of Swain County residents. Many of the disaffected residents and descendants of the removed led a vocal grassroots campaign to get the road finished despite any environmental or financial cost.[16] Swain County residents in the late twentieth century came to believe that the federal government, as represented by TVA and the Department of the Interior, had actually conspired to steal the forty-four thousand acres along the North Shore. This new generation began to "mis-remember" the earlier experiences of the original residents, which fueled an anti-government sentiment and created a narrative of economic and political loss.[17]

TVA's removal profiles, however, indicated that nearly all of the original thirteen hundred or so families living in the Fontana and North Shore area generally supported TVA's dam project and settled elsewhere with relative ease. There were slight differences in the experiences of transients and the original inhabitants, the latter of whom are especially important to consider because they would have been the ones to create the narrative of loss at the time of removal if indeed one existed. It was the memories of the later generations, however, that truly developed the Road to Nowhere "Lost Cause" narrative. This line of thinking emerged from a need to "return to their homeland," which was in most cases not true since the majority of those in the later generations were older transient residents, descendants of those same transients, or had lived along the North Shore as young children. Thus, the loss that many pro-road advocates experienced was not just framed around a loss of economic and political power but also out of a perceived loss of identity and heritage that the North Shore came to symbolize. This intersection of memory and loss was a very powerful catalyst in garnering emotional support for advocates who wanted to finally finish the Road to Nowhere. The irony of the controversy was that in the process of fighting for a return to their homelands the later generation of Swain County residents found what they had seemingly lost—community, a common mission, and a fight for meaningful identity.

Abandoned Appalachia: The Communities along the North Shore

The American West does not have a monopoly on ghost towns. In fact, many townships in the Fontana area were all but vacant by the onset of the Great Depression, though they are not as associated with ghost-town myth as places like Mineral Park, Hackberry, or Caribou in the West. Proctor, at the mouth of Hazel Creek, was one of the towns that was deserted quickly during the 1920s. A booming lumber town in the early twentieth century, Proctor was by all estimates on the upswing, boasting playhouses, a girls' basketball team, a company-built schoolhouse, and a pool hall.[18] Local residents were drawn to these community-based centers.

W. M. Ritter and other lumber lords in the area offered something that many locals had never experienced before: dependable and regular (although low) wages. Residents along the North Shore no longer had to rely on the fluctuations of seasonal husbandry; they could go to work for a wage or "scrip" and enjoy the modern conveniences found only in nearby urban centers such as Asheville and Knoxville. But the darker side of this relationship with the Ritter Lumber Company was that mountain residents had officially put themselves at the "mercy of the market," which was in this locale a monoculture of timber harvesting.[19]

Mountain residents got their first true glimpse of sustained industrial activity through the introduction of logging. The effects of the timber industry on just about every area of life cannot be overstated. Historians have described how easily mountain residents "willfully exchanged" their rural lives for camp life in timber operations.[20] The longest of these transitions centered on how Swain County residents moved from farmers to wage earners. By the early twentieth century, a growing population in the southern mountains contributed to less available farmland, environmentally destructive farming practices such as hillside farming, and an additional strain on local natural resources.[21] For mountain farmers and their extended families, the draw of reliable wages seemed to be a better path to follow than that of the uncertain agrarian life. It did not matter that the majority of these logging companies were based in the Northeast; logging was a reliable job. Lumbermen in North Carolina earned only $0.12 per hour while working a sixty-three-hour workweek, a schedule that showed the extent to which mountain men and women were willing to seek reliable, modern living standards. Logging allowed mountain residents the opportunity to earn extra spending money while entering into the national economy. One such man, Carl Woody, used the lumber camps as a temporary job in order to earn a remaining $200 that he put down on a home he was planning on buying. With the introduction of the timber industry, mountain residents tapped into an international market to provide for themselves and their communities.[22]

In the end, however, logging operations left the area damaged in many ways. Most notable was the environmental catastrophe that soon followed the retreat of timber "robber barons" from the deep coves of the Appalachians. Those who decided to stay after the timber companies left dealt with the skeletal mountain balds, poor soil, and runaway erosion. Wood supplies were all but wiped out, further decreasing the availability of building and heating supplies. Farmers turned to grazing livestock to make the land more economically viable, which in turn further decreased the quality of soil. Lumber companies "brought death to communities,

TVA caseworkers documented many communities which were displaced by the waters of Fontana Dam. Pictured is the Epps Springs school near the Bushnell community. F. E. Ketchen, "Bushnell Community Study—Population Readjustment—Fontana Reservoir," 1944, TVA Pamphlet Collection, MS-0631, box 2, Betsey B. Creekmore Special Collections and University Archives, University of Tennessee, Knoxville.

as deforestation, a decrease in farm size, and an end to woodland pasture accompanied the loss of the forest."[23] Mountain people were tied to their landscape, so a loss in the environment coincided with a loss of a sense of place. Nevertheless, this loss was not the result of the strangling touch of the modern industrial complex; some mountain residents welcomed this change, gladly accepting the opportunities that local industry could afford both intellectually and economically.

Those townships that expanded as a result of timber exploitation included Proctor, Ravensford, Judson, Bushnell, Japan (pronounced "Jay-pan"), and Townsend. When employers such as the Ritter Lumber Company pulled out in 1928 and moved to the nearby Nantahala Gorge west of the North Shore, however, many of the communities became ghost towns. Within a few years, the movie theater and pool hall in Proctor shut down, people began to scatter, the daily train ceased its operation, and those who did stay attempted to farm the cutover land that in a few short years was all but sterile due to poor soil and erosion. This transition back to the farm officially ended the possibility of a subsistence lifestyle for mountain residents since the once sustainable old-growth forest could no longer support the traditional lifestyles of mountain residents such as herb gathering, hunting, and woodland pasturing.[24]

The lifestyle of the stereotypical mountaineer in the early twentieth century was driven by national economics and community life. As historian Ron Eller pointed out, the lumber years did little to ignite a sustainable modern lifestyle for mountain residents. In fact, the time when lumber companies were most active in the area, around 1890 to 1930, was marked by a trinity of negative consequences: an attitude of long-term dependence, inadequate social services, and absentee land ownership.[25] These three negative forces conflicted with the stereotypical picture of the mountaineer as the self-sustaining master of his homestead and land, which was the idyllic picture that many mountaineer descendants would construct in the late twentieth century.

The four major communities that made up the area around Fontana were Proctor, Bushnell, Almond-Judson, and Stecoah, and all had somewhat different cultures and removal experiences. The initial estimate for the number of families living in these areas was woefully underestimated at just 275. By the end of TVA's census, however, the total reached 1,310 families, 216 of which lived on the North Shore. This discrepancy reflected the elusiveness and isolation of mountain residents as well as an influx of transient workers. All told, TVA's initial figures were only 20 percent of the total final number of families in the removal areas; 600 or so of these families lived in the communities before dam construction, and 711 were transient.[26] Proctor had 163 families, Bushnell had 205, Almond-Judson had 143, and 54 families were relocated from Stecoah.[27]

Perhaps the most established area along the North Shore was the Proctor community. The town was bordered west to east between Welch's Ridge and 20-Mile Ridge, from the south by the Little Tennessee River, and the Great Smoky Mountains National Park to the north. This area included perhaps the most widely known watershed in the Smokies—Hazel Creek. The Proctor community also included Fairfax, Ritter, Fontana, Welch Cove, New Fairfax, Bone Valley, and Eagle Creek. By 1943, Proctor had 1,800 people, still a high figure given the desertion of the lumber industry (some of these people were transient workers for dam construction). Interestingly, only 10 percent of the community was flooded by Fontana Lake, but the rest of the inhabitable land was cut off by the loss of Highway 288. The Proctor community had some modern industries, including a copper mine and sawmill, which enabled it to retain a core population ever after timber companies left. Additionally, TVA reports described Proctor as "no wild mountain country"; it had Alcoa, WPA (Works Progress Administration) jobs, and a cigarette factory to help people make a living. Despite these industrial opportunities, there was some ambivalence about the removal of its residents. TVA conceded that locals "may be better off on the little pieces of land so many of them love so much" since by entering more modern economies they would almost be certain to attach themselves to a "guarded dependency."[28]

Even though removal would be a difficult transition, the majority of residents who lived in Proctor were ready for a change. Only 18 residents from the original 163 families went to school past the eighth grade, and only 2 managed to make it to college. These predominantly Baptist families made next to nothing from farming; in fact, farming accounted for only a small fraction of the total income of Proctor residents per year, barely eclipsing $80 per year on average. Proctor's pre-dam inhabitants made only $1,100 per family on average, which was 55 percent of the average income for transient families that fell to just under $2,000 annually. In fact, of the 2,300 families in all of Swain County, 1,894 were eligible for economic relief. Given the discrepancy between income levels, it was understandable that "native" North Shore residents recognized that removal offered them greater economic opportunities. Thus, there was not much to lose economically by packing up and moving on, especially given that farming on the land they mostly rented was not a viable career path. TVA acknowledged this economic disparity. One TVA fieldworker labeled residents "clammish natives." He noted that most of the relocated families seemed "very satisfied" about their new opportunities but were sad to leave.[29]

Residents of the neighboring Almond-Judson community were particularly willing to leave their homesites for better educational opportunities. The community included seven neighborhoods stretching between the towns of Wesser and Bushnell. This area was extremely mountainous and near the convergence of the Nantahala and Little Tennessee rivers. As early as 1880, there were 150 families in Almond-Judson since it was the central hub of the lumber industry in that area. By 1924, however, the community drastically downsized after the Nantahala Power and Light Company bought most of the land in preparation for building a dam in the area.[30]

In 1944, there were 166 families in Almond-Judson, 143 original and 23 transient. TVA fieldworkers described the residents as "native stock . . . practically isolated from the rest of the world," a "thrifty race," and "friendly, congenial, religious, hard-working, and law-abiding." Near the towns, TVA fieldworkers reported that people were progressive and made a fair living. The Southern Railroad ran through the area next to the Little Tennessee River but was dismantled and relocated to the South Shore of Fontana Lake after 1945. Most of the trading was done in Bryson City, but there were eight small grocery and general merchandise stores in the area. Most of the families lived in isolated log cabins. Only five houses had electricity, and less than 5 percent had running water.[31]

TVA fieldworkers noted the importance of education in the Almond-Judson community. Most telling was the comment that many of the inhabitants "have become extremely conscious of the advantages of an education." In fact, 187 of the 189 children attended school in the Almond-Judson community in 1941, and 162 out of 166 heads of the family could read or write, which was higher than the state average.[32] The Almond-Judson community revolved around church and school. Over 400 attended the local high school and elementary schools in 1941. A bus transported 200 of these children to school every day, reflecting the presence of a modern convenience that even these more remote communities enjoyed. There were three Baptist churches, some of which had "old time singing conventions" and competing choirs. Two of these Baptist churches were dissolved as a result of the inundation of the community, and some members found themselves nearly six miles and a mountain away from the nearest Baptist church.[33]

Similar to the residents of Proctor, less than 30 percent of the members of the Almond-Judson community received a major part of their incomes from agriculture. Many worked odd jobs in order to gain as much money as possible for their above-average-sized families. Of the 166 original families living in the area, 33 percent of them had lived there their entire lives. The region was economically destitute, a reality reflected in the fact that 30 of the 177 employed members of original families opted to work for TVA. Another 51 residents worked for the WPA, the CCC (Civilian Conservation Corps), or the NYA (National Youth Administration). By the end of 1943, the number of gainfully employed residents working for TVA increased to 89, which was roughly an 80 percent increase in just a few years. Only 3 workers were employed by a local industry, the Carolina Woodturning Company, in Bryson City. Average income for an original, farming inhabitant was $478 a year while a nonfarmer made $999 a year. When compared to the average transient worker, who earned $1,612 a year, Almond-Judson residents made only 62 percent of what their transient neighbors made (a comparable figure to Proctor).[34]

TVA fieldworker Arnold Hyde noted that "Employment in the community is highly diversified" between industrial and agricultural enterprises. Such a statement indicated that many mountain residents in this community were determined to get whatever income was available.[35] TVA fieldworkers feared that Almond-Judson residents would "lose identity" when removed from their property and that many families had faced "major readjustment problems," including finding new schools, churches, and trading centers. Also, TVA fieldworkers believed that many in the Almond-Judson area would be forced to relocate due to the high rate of ownership of Swain County lands by the federal government. Others were forced up onto the steep ridges and balds surrounding Fontana Lake. Still, TVA was adamant that the inhabitants of Swain County did "not fully appreciate as yet" the economic importance of the GSMNP, the national forests, and the nearby Cherokee Reservation.[36] Although it was uncertain what TVA meant by their "not fully appreciating" statement, the residents of the Almond-Judson community realized that moving would bring better educational and economic opportunities, two major arenas of life that these residents had been trying to improve upon for years. Unfortunately, this progress would come at the expense of their original homesites, which was a very real loss, though bearable in the face of new opportunities.

Stecoah was the last of the major communities affected by the Fontana Dam project. This well-populated area was located in the northeastern part of Graham County on the South Shore of Fontana Lake. The community attitudes and economies on the opposite side of the basin were very similar to those along the North Shore. The community consisted of four small hamlets—Japan, Tuckasegee, Sawyer's Creek, and Stecoah. Only fifty-four of the three hundred families were removed because of Fontana Lake. The area was enclosed by the Cheoah Mountains and the Little Tennessee River and was described as "steep and rugged with the valleys densely populated but the fertile land sparsely occupied." TVA fieldworkers described the community's inhabitants as "hail and hardy people," proud, independent, garrulous, sometimes timid, and "would-be nation builders." Feuds were unheard of in the region, and murder was incredibly rare.[37]

Modern industries and education were linked to progress in communities like Stecoah. One major difference between Stecoah and the Almond-Judson community was the decreased percentage of school attendance. In fact, only 84 percent attended school in 1941–42. The high school and elementary schools in Stecoah were noted as being "modern in every respect." Public school enrollment was three hundred in 1941, and 80 percent were transported by bus. Fieldworkers noted that homes were in extremely poor condition and only two were painted. Further, for many houses there was no running water, pigs ran loose, and the outhouses were located over streams. The TVA profile for Stecoah explained: "Progress has been retarded" in previous years since road access via Highway 10 began only fifteen years prior.[38] Most people traded in Robbinsville and Bryson City, and the Stecoah economy was strictly dependent on agriculture. The average yearly income of a farm family was $408.43, a figure inflated due to 30 percent of those farmers receiving public assistance. The only industries in the area were small, portable sawmills. Perhaps most significant was that, in 1942, TVA employed thirty-seven members of the fifty-four families who were removed from the area. This figure reflected the desire for families to provide economically even if their employers were also their evictors. Only thirty-three of the seventy-nine affected families were farmers, and none of the transients farmed. A farmer made $362.69 a year while a nonfarmer in the same area earned close to $1,200 a year.[39]

Similar to the situation in Proctor and Almond-Judson, farming income in Stecoah was well below that of nonfarming, amounting to only 30 percent of the latter figure, which was even lower than the percentages of other communities in the area. TVA planners viewed the Fontana project as an opportunity for transportation and development for those who were dependent on farming income. TVA fieldworkers described the massive reservoir as containing "new opportunities for dissatisfied families." They also noted that locals "recognized the futility of the struggle with property in their present environment" and would be "freed from restricted circumstances."[40]

After surveying the communities, TVA employees appraised each tract according to its proximity to a trading center, ability to produce crops, or presence of improvements to the land (such as houses or barns). TVA bought 1,064 tracts for an average price of $37.76 per acre, which was close to $12 an acre more than for the initial wave of purchases by the Department of the Interior for the GSMNP a decade before. The majority of families who left the Fontana area moved to bordering counties and states, including Tennessee and Georgia. Of the 600 original families, 269 remained in Swain and Graham Counties and 527 stayed in North Carolina. Of the 711 transient families, only 184 remained in Swain and Graham counties. In effect, many more original families remained around the North Shore than their transient neighbors. TVA maintained that there was an 18 percent increase in farm residence after the land was cleared. There was also a 32 percent increase in homeownership, a figure that may be misleading because many residents along the North Shore rented much of their land in the area and owned land in neighboring communities unaffected by the dam project.[41]

Getting Out of "The Hole": The People Who Left the North Shore

Despite what TVA's community profiles asserted about the communities around Fontana, it was the individual families who had the most to lose by leaving the land they had lived on (either through owning or renting) for generations. These families had an enormous range of responses to removal, but the key commonality among all of them is that, even though they recognized their loss in the face of "improvement" and support for the war effort, these families did not publicize this loss in any widespread or effective manner. We must assume, therefore, that those who were actually removed had more to gain than lose or they recognized the inevitability of their displacement and made the most of a difficult situation. The loss communicated by future generations in Swain County, however, was much more passionate, and they pointed to real moments where their economic and political power was severely downgraded relative to their North Shore forebearers.

A statistic that may reveal the perceived lack of loss among North Shore residents at the time of removal was that only six residents chose to enter condemnation proceedings. These six ended up suing TVA in a case that made it all the way up to the US Supreme Court in 1946. These six plaintiffs were Columbus Welch, John Burns, Fred Lollis, Arnold Bradshaw, Philip Goodenow Rust, and Cole Wyatt. The real leader of these plaintiffs was Philip Rust, a wealthy northern businessman whose dreams of creating a mountain estate from logged-over land became more of an experiment in ecological regeneration than a home. A graduate of MIT and husband to an heir of the Dupont Chemical Company fortune, Rust was an anomaly on the North Shore, although his intention of creating a sustainable mountain retreat seemed to be in earnest. The other litigants against TVA were either his employees or close neighbors—except Welch—and represented a small threat. The land that these six plaintiffs owned was located around Noland Creek, a relatively small strip of the forty-four thousand acres close to Bryson City. It may be possible that others living on the North Shore were interested in joining the suit, but significant financial, legal, or educational barriers would have prevented them from joining or filing additional suits. Unfortunately, sources do not exist to substantiate these potential barriers to legal battles that North Shore residents faced.[42]

Even though the level of resistance was small along the North Shore, the complexities of individual removal narratives were incredibly diverse. Instead of saying that there was a simple "approval/disapproval" choice by residents would be oversimplifying the decision-making process for families who were losing their homes. It is much more appropriate to view their experiences along a spectrum of acceptance and loss. Some families, such as Ed and Sarah Anthony, had family members who were split in their desire to move. Anthony did some farming, but he also worked for the Southern Railroad and WPA. TVA caseworkers noted that Sarah was willing to talk to them and wanted to leave their rented land in the Bushnell community. TVA caseworkers also noted the poor condition of the house and the fact that the family looked malnourished.[43] Similarly, Ollie Ammons, the wife of L. W. Ammons of Almond-Judson, expressed a desire to "get out of that hole," as she called her home in the North Shore area. She was isolated and doing pretty much all of the work on her own since her husband was driving all day and her children were in school. L.W., on the other hand, was content to stay on the land he rented (from the McGaha family), doing the various odd jobs that came along, whether from TVA, WPA, or local industry. In the end, the family moved to Bryson City to a new homesite where TVA actually constructed a new road so that the Ammons family could access their new land. At no point did TVA workers note that the Ammons family requested a road back to Almond-Judson so they could return to where they had just moved from.[44]

Like the majority of North Shore residents, the Jenkins, Chicklelee, Walker, and Styles families voiced absolutely no opposition to resettlement and communicated that they were not only unified in their willingness to move but perhaps even excited to start over in closer proximity to government agencies and local industries. Will Jenkins was a farmer and logger who made close to $1,400 a year and sold his 190-acre plot of land near Forney Creek for close to $5,000 before moving fifteen miles away to raise cattle.[45] Andy Chicklelee preferred to keep the job he had at the Southern Railroad instead of purchasing new land for farming. He had been employed by the railroad for nearly nineteen years and simply wanted to be able to continue working although he battled some health problems, such as rheumatism. He moved to the other side of Almond-Judson and rented land from TVA for $5 per month, which gave him close proximity to his job. Chicklelee was Cherokee, and his situation was exceptional given that he was not living in the Qualla Boundary and was making approximately $1,200 a year in industries that were mostly available only to whites. TVA caseworkers did not have a patronizing attitude to Chicklelee based on his race, saying instead that he was "exceptionally friendly" and widely respected by his peers in the community.[46]

Likewise, Game Walker, Chicklelee's son-in-law, did not resist TVA's removal orders. His fight was focused on securing the most money possible for the improvements he made on the land he rented near Japan. TVA noted that both he and his six children looked malnourished when they arrived to evaluate his property, an observation that can possibly be explained by the fact that he made only $400 per year between raising livestock and driving a truck for TVA. Curiously, his box house and furniture burned down just before he was set to move some six miles away in April 1945. No case for arson was ever presented by TVA as a cause for this fire.[47]

Finally, Mary Styles expressed great thanks to TVA for its assistance in helping her family relocate, noting that life "was a hard fight at very little profit." What is most surprising is that her husband, Jim, was a game warden for Philip Rust, the wealthy New Englander who pushed for the lawsuit against TVA and lost. He made close to $1,000 a year working for Rust but still did not join in the lawsuits against the federal government. This rift in resistance, from one of Rust's employees, shows how the vast majority of North Shore residents supported moving and did not necessarily evaluate the loss of removal as more significant than the gains they would receive by starting over.[48]

The process of moving from renter to owner along the North Shore was a relatively easy process since most residents owned land on which they did not live. W. W. Jenkins, who had lived his life around the Noland Creek area, was the head warden and keeper of the Rust property and made close to $1,800 a year while living rent-free on Rust's land. At his income level, his family "enjoyed every comfort of the city dweller." Jenkins had planted close to forty thousand white pine and walnut trees. TVA said he "freely expresses . . . that he does not desire to relocate." Once again this reluctance may have been due more to his high-income and rent-free living situation than an attachment to the idea of "home." After Rust and the other plaintiffs lost their suit against TVA, the land he occupied was condemned, and he moved to his own land in Bryson City.[49]

TVA reported a 32 percent increase in home ownership as a result of removal for residents along the North Shore. The agency did not describe the process by which the level of homeownership increased. With the example of W. W. Jenkins, it is possible to view how such a transition from renter to owner occurred. Many North Shore residents rented the land they lived on because it was economically beneficial for them at the time; they were able to live closer to their jobs and therefore cut costs associated with commuting. Also, a few large landowners such as Rust, the Coburns, the Cables, and the McGahas' heirs owned much of the land along the North Shore. After receiving money for the improvements on the land they rented, many residents moved to small pockets of land they already owned in nearby communities and built new structures. Further, if the land was in the reservoir area or along the North Shore, they sold it to TVA and moved to other available property in Swain or Graham counties. Thus, a TVA-classified "renter" may have transitioned to an "owner," though no major amounts of money were exchanged because many of these "renters" already had owned land. The transition was based on TVA's classification processes, which may have inflated the home-owning statistics in their final reports.[50]

The details of these landholding changes do not support the accusation that TVA "stole" the land of North Shore inhabitants.[51] In fact, a small collection of families owned a majority of the land in the Fontana Basin. What the families did lose was the ability to rent in close proximity to their jobs. After TVA transferred the land to the GSMNP, however, these jobs were no longer available, so North Shore families did what they had done for decades: move to locations that held other employment opportunities. TVA caseworkers documented the removal stories of dozens of residents, including the Collins, Bradshaw (Fred and Arnold), Fuller, Hyatt, Green, Burns (John, Jim, and Gainey), and Heddon families. The only form of loss that these family members communicated was economic since those who resisted were tied to the Rust enterprise of constructing a mountain preserve. The fact that they did not communicate any loss, however, does not preclude the fact that these families did indeed lose something very tangible: their homes, jobs, access to cemeteries, and natural environment. The evidence demonstrates that the majority of them perhaps did not care enough to fight to stay, although it is also plausible that many saw the federal government as too large of an adversary to actually beat in court.

TVA fieldworkers noted the race of families, but there is no evidence that African American families were displaced because of the Fontana project. African American families had previously lived near Peachtree Creek in Swain County and worked for the nearby Ritter Lumber Company as well as Alcoa's Cheoah Dam project during World War I. But by the 1930s, the African American population on the Upper Tennessee River Valley had largely disappeared. A review of TVA case files for removed families did not yield any evidence of African American families in the surveyed region.[52]

There were African American workers at the Fontana Dam site, but they were not local. Historian Stephen Wallace Taylor noted that many skilled African American workers, between ninety-six and one hundred, were recruited from outside the mountains to work on the Fontana project in order to comply with Executive Order 8802 that called for the use of all manpower in federal projects regardless of race. African American workers were initially excluded from mountain dam projects at Norris, Appalachia, and Hiwassee but were a large part of valley projects at Wheeler, Chickamauga, and Muscle Shoals. During the Fontana project, African American workers had menial jobs and faced discrimination from white workers. The first night that African American workers occupied their dormitory, a local mob attempted to burn the structure. Afterwards, TVA officials assigned guards to protect the African American dormitory.[53]

Discontent and Loss on the North Shore

From 1978 to 2010, the fight to build the North Shore Road became a fight to return home and regain what was lost, and in the process to equip a new generation with a mission to reconstruct a community that had been gone for over thirty years. It did not matter that this new group never saw the road completed; they "won" back what was lost because they were able to construct a narrative of loss that gave meaning to their present. The eventual $52 million settlement was proof that their cause was justified, at least to many locals. The group that was most influential in communicating this idea of loss was the North Shore Cemetery Association, later called the North Shore Historical Association. This group gained the most attention by carrying out a traditional folk holiday at cemeteries in the GSMNP called "Decoration Day."

Discontent along the North Shore started well before Decoration Days began in the late 1970s. In 1962, Democratic Congressmen Roy Taylor, a World War II veteran and graduate of the University of North Carolina at Asheville Law School, wrote to Conrad Wirth, the director of the Park Service, that residents were "getting upset over this road delay."[54] Three years later, the *Asheville Citizen* newspaper rallied to the cause of the locals highlighting the poverty of the area, but also the responsibility of the government to construct roads to "open up" the area.[55] The newspaper pointed out that the nascent wilderness movement was morally misdirected since it took away the chance for those on the ground to regain lost economic opportunities. North Shore residents had an ally in North Carolina's governor, Dan Moore, who in 1966 said outright that the National Park Service had a "legal and moral obligation to build the transmountain road."[56] The tension between the surging wilderness advocacy movement—focused on an almost militant preservation policy—and local economic developers defined much of the fight to build the Road to Nowhere for decades.

Also, in 1966 a series of public hearings allowed advocates from both sides of the debate to speak. The hearing commissioners received nearly seven thousand letters from around the country, most of which were against road construction in any form. During the meeting in Gatlinburg in 1966, three hundred people voiced their opinions on the proposed road that would connect Bryson City to Townsend. Advocates for construction argued that a road would reflect the true purpose of the park, which was to be "for the permanent enjoyment of the people," as written on the 1940 Newfound Gap plaque.[57]

Road proponents interpreted the potential for wilderness designation as inherently exclusive for the majority of visitors, since the vast number of the GSMNP's annual guests viewed the "wilderness" only from their car windows. Supporters of the road believed that wilderness supporters were a marginal group of elitists bent on securing wilderness designation for their own personal enjoyment. Some speakers, such as M. G. Roberts from Cocke County, Tennessee, went so far as to suggest that wilderness designation would "crucify the hopes and rights of four-and-a-half million auto visitors by those who are lost in the wilderness."[58] In effect, wilderness legislation would exclude those people who lost the most in removal from returning to regain a sense of place and identity from their ancestral homesites.

During the 1966 hearings, the scientific community led the charge against road construction. The scientists highlighted the rapid recovery of the flora and fauna in the park while subsequently recommending a road around the park instead of through it.[59] Other conservationists addressed the idea of the park existing for the enjoyment of the people by suggesting that development did not necessarily mean that more people would be able to enjoy the GSMNP's natural treasures. Dozens of hikers and visitors highlighted the beautiful natural scenic qualities of the GSMNP and called for wilderness designation inside the park's boundaries. One such speaker issued a startling metaphor of the situation when he rhetorically asked: "If a church needed more parking spaces, would the parishioners destroy the sanctuary to allow a bigger parking lot?"[60] By framing the landscape of the GSMNP in sacred terms, wilderness advocates equated religious-like significance to the act of preserving the Smokies. Such arguments caught the ear of Secretary of the Interior Stewart Udall. On December 10, 1967, he publicly announced his opposition to the idea of a transmountain road. Udall's decision would set the precedent for the Department of the Interior's opposition toward road construction for decades to come.

Between 1967 and 1975, both wilderness advocates and pro-road factions engaged in an exercise of waiting out the other. Wilderness supporters and the younger generation were hoping for a cash settlement, but Swain County residents still had hope that the road would be finished since even as late as 1970 a portion of the transmountain road was still being paved. Within a few years the wilderness faction won the waiting game. In 1975, leaders of the National Park Service met with Swain County officials at Governor James Holshouser's home and hammered out a settlement. The Park Service offered Swain County more construction projects and a $15 million settlement. Swain County officials countered with a $25 million offer of their own. Each party rejected the other's proposal. Two years later, both sides agreed on a settlement for $9.5 million, including provisions for a new industrial park, school athletic facilities, and the cancellation of a FHA loan. The settlement, which became known as the Andrus Compromise after Secretary of the Interior Cecil Andrus, cleared the US House but was killed in the Senate after Andrus became a lame duck appointee in 1979.[61] The failure of both sides to reach an agreement allowed for the resurgence of the most powerful group of North Shore residents in the twentieth century.

A later generation wove a romanticized sense of loss into the collective imagined fabric of those North Shore residents who had been displaced in the early 1940s by the construction of Fontana Dam. By the 1980s, a new generation of North Shore descendants vocalized this sense of loss in a manner that was not consistent with what the TVA removal profiles documented. By romanticizing their past through selective memory and uniting in the struggle against the federal government and its bureaucracy, former North Shore residents and their descendants reframed their loss in terms similar to those of the neighboring Eastern Band of the Cherokee Nation, going so far as to call it their own "Trail of Tears."

The most glaring loss that Swain County residents experienced was the loss of economic power. In many ways, this fight to return home was really a fight to re-store economic sustainability to a county that was completely left behind in any form of modern economic structure. In the late 1970s, Swain County was over 80 percent federally owned, and of the sixty-six thousand acres in private ownership, 80 percent was either flood prone or too steep to develop. Swain County also lost close to $3.8 million in taxable property after the 1943 agreement (equal to over $55 million today), and wages were 76 percent below the state average.[62] Finally, in an almost cruel twist of irony, the $400,000 promised in the 1943 agreement, which was supposed to be used to pay off old Highway 288 road bonds, was never allocated by the state. Thus, Swain County was still making payments on a road in 1975 that had been under water for over three decades![63]

The formation of the North Shore Cemetery Association by Helen Vance and a handful of other locals reflected growing sentiment in favor of celebrating life and communicating loss along the North Shore. The association's quarterly pub-lication, the *Fontana Newsletter*, was one of the most influential factors in the dissemination of new memories thirty-three years after the last resident surren-dered land to TVA. Vance organized the first Decoration Day at Cable Cemetery in the spring of 1978, which sparked interest in community visitation by former North Shore inhabitants and their descendants. Helen Vance, along with her sister Mildred Johnson, both descendants of long-time North Shore residents, arranged for GSMNP rangers to ferry boats full of visitors across Fontana Lake for a day of cemetery visitation and decoration. While there, visitors noticed the deteriora-tion of the graves and made notes for the National Park Service employees, who were supposed to be maintaining the grave sites. Vance mentioned that this event snowballed into a wide-scale visitation program which in the years that followed included hundreds of visitors.[64] After 1978, Decoration Day festivities took on a life of their own as a nearly spiritual experience—the only true way that those who had been removed could return home.

The act of traveling to a Decoration Day was an exercise in returning to a world that had been buried underwater or untouched because of limited access. There were between twenty-six and thirty-three cemeteries in the North Shore area that housed the graves of over eleven hundred former residents. These sites covered a wide geographic area and an even wider net of community connection.[65] After disembarking from their boats, visitors would clean the graves, lay flowers, and then gather for a "dinner on the ground" complete with gospel music, informal church services, baptisms, a feast of Thanksgiving proportions, and an opportu-nity to share memories.[66] These visits usually took place early in the spring before

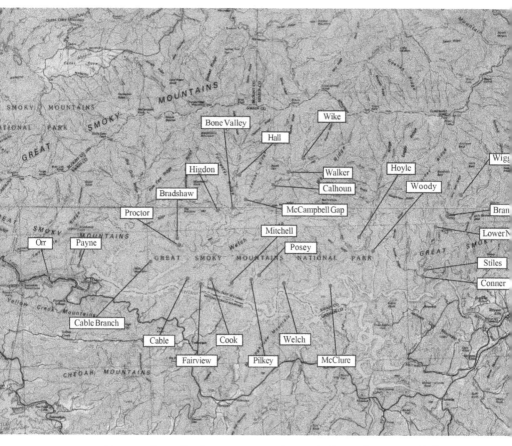

MAP 2. Over two dozen family cemeteries on the North Shore of Fontana Lake have been the sites of recent Decoration Day activities. Map of North Shore Decoration Day cemeteries, in *North Shore Road Environmental Impact Statement* (Great Smoky Mountains National Park: National Park Service, 2006), appendix G, 113.

the cemeteries were overgrown and more difficult to access. The act of visitation was certainly important on a personal level since it gave the descendants of North Shore residents a chance to go back home, but visitation also created a new set of memories and a narrative of loss and redemption that reignited the fight to finish the Road to Nowhere.

The sense of loss brought about by visitation was often an overwhelming experience for cemetery decorators. During these events, visitors expressed a wide array of emotions in response to seeing graves and homesites that many had not laid eyes on for decades. Phoebe Laney Cable made the first visit back to Higdon Cemetery on the North Shore in 1986, visiting the resting place of her newborn son's grave for the first time since she had left that area. She communicated to other visitors the still present pain of thinking about how her son only breathed one time before dying in her arms.[67] Many visitors had actually lived in or around the isolated places almost four decades prior. Thus, they had in their minds a mental image of a community that meant something, not of the wilderness promoted by the National Park Service and only visited by advanced backpackers. One of the Decoration Day visitors in 1989 described a view from the boat crossing the lake as "not much to see. Just tree-covered ridges with occasional clearings, a few aged, unproductive fruit trees . . . a dilapidated house or two, a few junky, rusted automobiles. . . . This is all that's left of a once thriving settlement except for . . . memories."[68]

These memories ultimately bound visitors together. Christine Cole Proctor, a descendent of one of the first white settlers of the North Shore area, reminded readers in the *Fontana Newsletter* that memories "get lost in our mind's cluttered attic . . . are not always pleasant . . . hang around us like a shadow to remind us of our darker side." She personified graves and the graveyards themselves, evoking a scene of the dead calling out to the living in desperation when she said, "When we visit the cemeteries the headstones, even the field rocks, some carved to point upwards, quietly remind us: do not forget us; we are you; you are us."[69] Thus, in an eerie but sincere way, Proctor linked the idea of memory with loss and identity to a graveyard setting. By doing so, her experience showed that graveyards became the epicenters of communing with the past and the only place where descendants could go to see their homes once again.

Due to the heavy amounts of emotion released on Decoration Days, it was not that surprising to see to what extent visitors sacrificed their comfort for a day in an isolated cemetery. The act of visitation was in no way convenient or efficient; it was an experience that was exacerbated by the elderly age of visitors. Still, cemetery goers consistently signed up for the four-hour round trips, which often included afternoon thunderstorms, for a brief respite with their passed loved ones. On one particular day in April 1992, fifty-three visitors decided to walk on the old surface of Highway 288 that emerged out of Fontana Lake due to a drawdown of the water for repairs to the dam. Linda Hogue described the scene in terms reminiscent of the Exodus of the Hebrews, remembering how people aged up to ninety-one walked three and a half miles as "bittersweet memories flooded back as well as an admiration for ancestors." She also made sure to include that one woman walked the entire distance on crutches.[70] Other accounts recalled how groups braved violent thunderstorms, "bundled in ponchos . . . and plastic bags to ward off the stinging rain," as they were transported across the exposed lake.[71]

Many times the *Fontana Newsletter* hinted at a certain "victim" status of these visitors by including articles highlighting the suffering and sacrifice of the pilgrims. By describing visitors' experiences in this manner, a lay reader could then easily jump to identify with a similar "victim" status in relation to the federal government and the failed agreement of 1943. Through visitation and relived memories, past North Shore residents and their descendants came to identify their "homes" as lying permanently within the southern boundary of the Great Smoky Mountains National Park.

Part of the gravitation of North Shore residents to redefine their sense of place was caused by the distress over having lost something valuable and irreplaceable. One observer suggested: "It was their home, their entire history. A strong sense of family and a strong sense of community, that was destroyed forever."[72] This feeling of displacement, especially for many older residents, created a discourse of a "paradise lost" that was real enough to try to replace. When the idea of a monetary settlement was proposed instead of actually building the road, many thought that their homes and heritage were being attacked. Swain County Commissioner David Monteith announced, "My heritage is not for sale. Our folks were promised the road; we have not gotten it."[73]

Monteith had an interesting obsession with tracking down old roadbeds in the Great Smoky Mountains National Park. He claimed that he had found close to six hundred miles of abandoned roads in the area. On one of these roads he found a severed head that he claimed belonged to a man who was unfaithful to his wife. Monteith was actually born in 1946 and not part of the removal, but he still had a strong emotional tie to the North Shore and experienced a sense of loss that may have even been deeper than that of his parents. His father had visited his old homesite, noting how it was not his home anymore. The younger Monteith was often reduced to tears over an event as small as a chimney being pushed over.[74]

For Monteith, the distinction between the road and home was erased as both were equated as one and the same: build the road and a sense of home would be preserved, but fail to build the road and former North Shore residents and their descendants would blow down as easily as a rootless tree.

At the same time, Heath Shuler maintained that Monteith's fight was never about replacing a "lost" heritage but was really about a political fight that pitted Western North Carolina Republicans against mountain Democrats.[75] If Shuler's assertion is accurate, then the fight to build the Road to Nowhere was more than a conflict of loss and selective memory; in effect, the Road to Nowhere would be a red herring for mountain Democrats and Republicans to posture around and manipulate. Other evidence does not support Shuler's claim, but that does not invalidate the argument. Monteith passed away in March 2017, four months before the National Park Service delivered the last check of $37 million to Swain County. This transaction served as the final payout of the cash settlement totaling $52 million. Those who were present at the ceremony mentioned that Monteith would have been proud to see the final check delivered and the settlement completed, which was different from Shuler's assertion that Monteith would never settle. It is completely plausible that Monteith may have had multiple motives and beliefs related to the Road to Nowhere controversy.[76]

Despite the underlying political fight, a new generation of Swain County residents focused on the lost spaces and often performed eclectic rituals to resurrect their past. Dowsing became a prominent technique in later decades for finding lost grave sites. One such dowser was Pete Prince, who made dowsing rods out of coat hangers and found grave sites from the powers of the twitching antennae.[77] Prince learned his technique from Harry Vance, a Christian pastor and husband of Helen Vance, the founder of the North Shore Historical Association. Vance's attachment to dowsing betrayed the relationship between Christianity and mysticism in the mountains, highlighting how mountain residents used a variety of means to find their lost ancestors. Dowsing supposedly responded to "cultural energy," so to Prince and others the practice was not considered occult. This "energy" was then channeled to form memories between visitors of the different graveyards. In other cases, returning mountain residents scraped fungus off of Proctor Bridge to take back home with them. One man pleaded on his deathbed for just one more drink from Hazel Creek since it supposedly had magical powers.[78] All in all, the power of memory and the drive to return was for many mountain residents so strong that they would go to great efforts to preserve some connection to identity along the North Shore. More simply, these believers created physical manifestations of memory and identity.

Many of the pro-road advocates, who adhered to the concept that the North Shore was their "home," supported the narrative that Swain County residents were the "original" inhabitants of the area. Of course, the Smoky Mountains had been inhabited for centuries, most recently by the Cherokee Nation, but for many, the area around the Little Tennessee River was an unsettled wilderness first tamed by white North Shore residents in the nineteenth century. Ray Hooper, a *Fontana Newsletter* contributor who resided in Moultrie, a small town in southern Georgia, wrote in 1989:

> Before the tourists came; before the mountains became the "in" thing for people who "rough it" in Winnebagos. . . . We knew the mountains. We knew the thrill of wandering now forgotten pathways across the mountain tops, where it seemed you could see forever and touch the sky. We knew the valleys, hushed except for the murmur of a stream wandering down to the river. But most of all, we knew the people, as they were before the coming of the New Deal. . . . Gone, but they are there in memory, tough as the hickory of their ax handles, yet gentle as a mountain breeze. They were part of the hills, clinging close to the land and to their God.[79]

Hooper made it clear that the landscape meant much more to collective memory than a place to grow crops or build a house. Indeed, Hooper's descriptions made the landscape and those who had lived there the same thing, tied to the overarching power of a God who sustained both. Just as the ground absorbed the dead when they died, so did the mountains absorb the living as they both worked and played. Hooper also took time to confirm that those who did the "in" thing in their Winnebagos actually had no idea what the Smokies were really about. In effect, Hooper criticized the ignorance of passersby while reaffirming his and his family's rightful place in the mountains.

The sense of loss from North Shore residents was even more acute since many saw their former mountain homestead communities as an isolated American utopia. The decision by the National Park Service not to build the road preserved the space and solidified a memory of a simpler and better time. At the same time, proroad advocates believed that building a North Shore Road represented a tangible way to return to a lost America and to a meaningful life that was irreplaceably lost. The gulf of separation between the "paradise" of the early twentieth century and the modern society of the late twentieth century was a recurrent theme throughout the *Fontana Newsletter*. The Road to Nowhere stood as a viable symbol to try to recreate some sort of link back to a place of identity and abundance. The irony of the situation, however, was that the demands of pro-road construction supporters linked residents with their dead ancestors through graveyard visitation.[80]

Most surprising was the difference in experiences of loss communicated between older generations who were born or had spent their childhood on the North Shore and those who were raised with the reality of the GSMNP as a newly created entity. The younger generation was able to objectively separate the cost of building a road from the emotional effects of "going home." In a 2004 interview, twenty-four-year-old Trevor Lanier noted that he did not feel like the road would do any good after sixty years of empty promises. Lanier had been to Decoration Days and had experienced the stories of loss yet was still hesitant to support building the road. He expected the amelioration of loss would come through storytelling instead of a construction project that may or may not benefit his family and the region.[81]

Perhaps the greatest legacy of Helen Vance and the North Shore Historical Association was that people started visiting graves together instead of on an individual or family basis. Christine Cole Proctor stated that there was no real decrease in visitation in the years immediately following the removals from the North Shore. What was different was that prior to the Decoration Days of the late 1970s people would visit individually because they were "self-conscious" of asserting their claim to the dead. Proctor described the feeling as similar to "getting your hand smacked." Vance was credited for opening the door to North Shore residents and their descendants, allowing families and entire communities "to go home again." Proctor was six when she left the North Shore (Forney Creek) for Whittier and then Bryson City. She remembered that it was sad for her and her neighbors when TVA moved all of them, but also admitted that there was not much of a social life in the area where she grew up. Decoration Day was the apex of that missing social atmosphere, and so Proctor reconnected with her community consciousness and memories. Proctor recalled, "I just could not get over the way you feel . . . people meshed together" when remembering her first Decoration Day. Nevertheless, Proctor's hope for a road to make visits easier and fulfill a promise which ultimately failed with the settlement of 2010.[82]

The end of the saga of the Road to Nowhere was a slow series of events that led to the impossibility of building any sort of road through the GSMNP. Although the North Shore Historical Association was able to garner a wide range of support, there were very few outside voices that pressured the government to live up to its end of the bargain. In a 2002 article in the *Asheville Citizen-Times,* Bob Miller, spokesman for the Great Smoky Mountains National Park, said, "I've got about 2,000 letters (and emails) against the road, and the process has not started yet."[83] Thus, the environmental movement eventually won out over the small but vocal group of road proponents. In 2002, its final year of publication, the *Fontana*

Newsletter included articles acknowledging that the road was probably never going to be built. In the fifteen-year run of the publication, only nine articles focused on why the road should not be built. Six of those articles were published during the publication's final six months. The *Fontana Newsletter* ceased publication in 2002 due to the age of its staff members and the realization that the road would never be built. The somber tone of the final issue in winter 2002 conceded a lost battle, but still called to preserve the heritage of the North Shore, even if the road was never built.[84]

In the early 2000s, leaders in Swain and Graham counties initiated a detailed environmental study of the North Shore. The final environmental impact study, released in 2004, was an exhaustive document providing cultural background around the North Shore area as well as predicted costs associated with further construction. The report effectively crushed the option of building the road by revealing that construction would cost over $550 million, a figure well above what the Federal Highway Administration was willing to pay.[85]

Besides the monetary cost associated with finishing the road, the National Park Service later decided to settle because the environmental risk associated with construction, including acidic run-off from Anakeesta rock, would be much too damaging. One anti-road advocate went so far as to comment that "anybody that's ever hiked those slopes and has any background in soil conservation must instantly recognize this as madness."[86] Also, a modern highway, NC 28, had already been built on the South Shore of Fontana, which linked Bryson City with the Fontana area. Many residents of Asheville, Knoxville, Robbinsville, and Gatlinburg spoke out against the road; they saw it as foolish both fiscally and environmentally.

On December 28, 2007, the National Park Service's Record of Decision decided in favor of a monetary settlement to be paid to Swain County instead of completing the road. In February 2010, the Department of the Interior budgeted $52 million dollars for the settlement. The funding would go to support schools, infrastructure, and jobs in Swain County. The final installment was paid in the summer of 2018, just months before the deadline for the settlement to be completed. This action effectively ended the debate over the Road to Nowhere.[87]

The loss that North Shore descendants experienced should not be diminished just because they did not reach adulthood in the towns that were buried by Fontana Lake. In many ways, their loss was more acute since, relative to their parents, they did not have as much of a say in their relocation. Also, the hope of a brighter future with cash-in-hand that the original inhabitants experienced when they were relocated did not deliver the optimistic future that was promised.

The descendants of the displaced also believed that the federal government had abandoned them.

Today, Bryson City, the address for the most outspoken supporters of the road, is no longer "losing" from an economic or political perspective. Many days, the town is full of tourists wishing to spend a day on the Great Smoky Mountains Railroad and experience a mountain town that has not been overly commercialized like neighboring Gatlinburg and Cherokee. In many ways, Bryson City's slow growth has created a sustainable development that highlights the values of a small Appalachian town, instead of a series of caricatures exploited by forms of tourist capitalism unconcerned with the stereotypes that Appalachians constantly fight.

Additionally, Bryson City native Heath Shuler served as US representative from North Carolina's Eleventh Congressional District from 2007 to 2013. In that post, Shuler worked to finalize a settlement in favor of mountain residents, which revised the decades-old narrative that the federal government was ignoring the plight of a constituency they had willingly fleeced. The loss of the North Shore descendants will always be tainted by the politics of the region. As Shuler pointed out, the narrative of loss may have been created out of a need to restore political and economic power to a group of citizens who saw government bureaucracy created by a Democratic-led New Deal coalition as a farce at best and devilish at worst. This political fight pitted neighbors against each other and diverted their memories in a selective fashion. As Laura Kerr pointed out, the continual loss of political power is a very effective mechanism at driving constituents to action and vaulting rhetoric.[88]

The October 2018 issue of *Our State* magazine included an article about a North Carolinian who was searching for an opportunity to go to the most remote place in the state just to see how far he could truly get "off the beaten path." After researching nearby roads and population centers, he found the location on the flank of a ridge on the North Carolina side of the GSMNP, just northwest of the Road to Nowhere (the exact location is never disclosed).[89] I found this man's trek for remoteness both ironic and humorous in light of the Road to Nowhere story. I can imagine that the original inhabitants of the area would have thought such a quest foolish in the 1930s as they attempted to grapple with how to get a paycheck and food on the table, probably from a government agency. Also, the idea of searching for isolation in their actual backyards probably would have been perceived as a sort of lunacy on the part of the adventurer. Why on Earth would someone want to walk over their own homesites just to *stand* around in the woods where there were not any people?

Those who left the North Shore in the 1940s were leaving to go to an actual *somewhere* with more opportunity. The fact that their abandoned homes and fields would one day be another's site of recreation, a place just to "get away," would have been at odds with the desires of 1940s residents to "get out of that hole." It would have also been at odds with the desires of descendants to return to their roots and experience some healing from their stories of loss. In the end, many residents of Swain and Graham counties traded their homes for recreation that a new generation of Americans would be available to enjoy; their stories of loss and abandonment came at a price that those who tread the trails around abandoned graveyards deep in the Smoky Mountains would be wise to remember. After all, it is in memories that landscapes are most assuredly present.

Any Who See the Valley Would Regret Its Loss Forever

The Keowee-Toxaway Project, Duke Power, and Loss in Northwestern South Carolina

AUSTIN GREGORY

Oconee County, South Carolina, located in the northwest corner of the state, is the only county to share a border with the mountainous regions of both North Carolina and Georgia. Until the middle of the twentieth century, the rivers of Oconee County drew people, industry, and tourism to this remote area of the Appalachian Mountains. Today, "Visit Oconee SC," the local tourism and marketing organization, have branded the area as the "Mountain Lakes" region of South Carolina for the county's three major lakes, Keowee, Jocassee, and Hartwell, and its location in the foothills of the Blue Ridge Mountains. Historians Michael Hembree and Dot Jackson explained that, through human influence, the eastern rivers of Oconee County were transformed from "whitewater to deep waters" when in 1965 Duke Power announced its plan to dam the Keowee River. In doing so, they created two lakes that would be used for recreation as well as reservoirs for hydroelectric power generation for much of the western Carolinas.[1]

On January 2, 1965, Duke Power Company president W. B. McGuire met with more than four hundred civic and political leaders from Oconee and Pickens counties at the Clemson House in Clemson, South Carolina. There he announced Duke Power's plans for a $700 million energy complex along the waterways between Pickens and Oconee counties. The project would consist of two dams on the lower portion, one between Pickens and Oconee counties and the other just above the town of Newry, to form the reservoir that later would be called Lake Keowee. A third dam, much higher than the others, would create Lake Jocassee in the northern portion of Oconee County. McGuire projected that, once completed, Lake Keowee would have a surface area of approximately 17,700 acres with

Duke Power Company's Keowee-Toxaway Project included three dams and two
resulting lakes. Lake Keowee and Lake Jocassee provide water for a hydroelectric
station, a pumped storage facility, and a nuclear station. Artist conception of Duke
Power Company's Keowee-Toxaway Project near Seneca, S.C., ca. 1960s, Asheville
Postcard Company, South Carolina Postcards Collection, University of South
Carolina, South Caroliniana Library.

388 miles of shoreline, and the smaller Lake Jocassee would have a surface area of nearly 8,000 acres with 92 miles of shoreline.[2] A headline from the *Seneca Journal and Tribune* proclaimed that "Lake Jocassee will be deepest in the state!" and second deepest in the Carolinas behind the reservoir created by Fontana Dam in Western North Carolina.[3] The lakes provide energy for the Keowee Hydro Station and the Jocassee Pumped Storage Facility, and water to cool the three reactors of the Oconee Nuclear Station.

The Duke Power Company had its eye on the Keowee River for nearly fifty years before the company announced that it would flood the valley. As early as 1916, Duke Power (then called Southern Power Company) drafted preliminary project designs and made land purchases at the future dam sites. In 1963, eighteen months before the official announcement, Duke Power formed the South Carolina Land and Timber Corporation. This subsidiary company, "very unobtrusively, acquired property throughout the project area, still without public knowledge of what was coming." Following the public announcement of the project, the South Carolina Land and Timber Company changed its name to Crescent Land and Timber Corporation and its leaders declared their connection to Duke Power.[4]

The lakes displaced residents, businesses, and churches in the Jocassee Valley and even more along the Keowee River. Actual footage of the exhumation of graves at Mount Carmel Baptist Church in the Jocassee Valley was featured in the 1972 film adaptation of the James Dickey novel *Deliverance*.[5] The promise of tax dollars and tourism opportunities convinced many local residents and leaders that this project would bring economic prosperity to the county and the region. Duke Power's project and influence have redefined the county and the South Carolina Upcountry. This dominant narrative ignores the culture that existed before the project. Thus, the displaced residents and their children are unable to connect with the places they once called home as well as their own past.

Lakes Keowee and Jocassee attract thousands of visitors each year and have drawn many people from outside the county to make the area their home. Almost as soon as the lakes were at full pond, private retirement communities sprang up around Lake Keowee, along with hundreds of expensive private residences which stood in contrast to the modest homes that served the sharecroppers and mill-working families of Oconee County for many decades. Piper Peters Aheron expressed her discontent, as well as acknowledgment of the economic contributions the lakes have made to Oconee County. She explained, "these independent communities presently restrict county resident access as a whole, but doubtlessly,

Duke Energy has added much to the overall economy of the upcountry."[6] The area surrounding Lake Jocassee has been protected from development by state parks and habitat preservation sites created through land donated to the state by Duke Power after the project was completed, while Lake Keowee continues to see an overwhelming amount of private property development.

Duke Power completed the dams, nuclear station, and reservoirs (Lakes Keowee and Jocassee) approximately fifty years ago. This gap of time has made it difficult to locate the displaced residents who dealt directly with Duke Power in the 1960s. There are, however, descendants of the displaced who remember the loss of their family homeplace while children or teenagers. Other descendants of the displaced have absorbed the first-hand stories and made them into their own memories of life before the Duke Power project.

This examination of loss of community and culture in the remote northwestern corner of South Carolina relies on five oral history interviews with those who were directly affected by the displacement of families for the Keowee-Toxaway Project. Two of the interviewees, Debbie Fletcher and Claudia Whitmire Hembree, have published books on the Jocassee Valley which include pictures and detailed descriptions of their families, who lived in the area for many generations. Harry McCall's family had a summer home in Jocassee, and he and his brothers continue to own property and operate businesses in the area. Although Duke Power made an unsuccessful attempt to purchase property from Mike Wilson's family, they watched as their neighbors sold theirs and moved away. Lastly, Wilma Crocker Thompson's family sold their fifty-acre farm early in Duke's purchasing efforts, something she regrets to this day. The recollections of these five individuals fifty years after displacement help create a clearer picture of community loss, regional gain, and the power of memory.

Unlike the preceding stories of displacement by the federal government, the Keowee-Toxaway Project demonstrated how a private company worked with local and state government officials to use power and influence at a time when the federal government, especially the US Army Corps of Engineers, faced public opposition for similar water-control projects. It was an epic struggle of a nearly unstoppable private company with full support from government officials pitted against dozens of mountain farming families who had few resources available to oppose their removal. Those displaced by the Keowee-Toxaway Project experienced both the loss of their property and communities to make way for regional progress.

Early Twentieth-Century Oconee County

Harnessing the power of the rivers of the South Carolina Upcountry came long before Duke Power changed the face of Oconee County. Northern textile manufacturers began moving into the area as early as 1814 to set up mills along the area's many waterways, while also taking advantage of lenient labor laws and wages half that of their New England counterparts.[7] The state of South Carolina issued the first charter to construct a cotton mill in Oconee County to William Ashmead Courtenay, a Civil War veteran from Charleston, South Carolina, in 1893. The Little River, which fed into the Keowee, lured Courtenay to Oconee County to build his factory because of the water source needed to power the equipment and for the local labor supply. He named the town Newry after the town in Northern Ireland from which his family emigrated in the 1790s. All activities in Newry centered on the work schedule of the mill, and the bell, imported from Ireland, told the residents when to wake up, when to eat, and most importantly, when to begin work. The mill, named the Courtenay Manufacturing Company after its founder, was already on the decline when Duke Power announced the Keowee-Toxaway Project in 1965. The Little River dam ultimately protected Newry from inundation by the waters of Lake Keowee, but the town lost many adjoining acres, including the town's textile-league baseball field. The town was spared from inundation and even survived the closing of the mill in 1975. Michael Hembree explained that "the Duke project left Newry practically in the shadow of the massive Oconee Nuclear Station."[8] Today, the town still stands, and some of the mill's abandoned brick structures are visible from the highway that crosses the dam which saved the town from inundation.

A handful of books document the early history of the region. Debbie Fletcher's *Whippoorwill Farewell* (2003) and *Lake Jocassee* (2014) both tell the stories of those who once lived in Jocassee, provide details of the Camp Jocassee for Girls, and discuss the history of the lodge owned by her maternal grandparents. Fletcher grew up in Columbia, South Carolina, but spent her summers at the family's home in Jocassee.[9] In *Jocassee Valley* (2003), Claudia Whitmire Hembree provided an extensive look at the Jocassee Valley before Duke Power covered the landscape with water. She described the Cherokee who once lived in the valley and recounted the legend of Jocassee, the daughter of Attakullakulla, who drowned herself in the Keowee River after the death of her lover. Hembree noted that this story is similar to other regional tales such as Lover's Leap in neighboring Pickens County and Issaqueena, a tale of a Cherokee maid leaping from a waterfall, in Oconee County, a few miles north of Walhalla. She included information on Philadelphia botanist

William Bartram, who explored the valleys in 1775, and French botanist André Michaux, who followed him a decade later. Hembree's book also provided an extensive review of the families who lived in the valley, including her own.[10]

According to Hembree, beginning in the late 1800s, timber companies began to purchase land from private owners and to solicit proposals for dams along the Keowee River. She claimed that the announcement of the Keowee-Toxaway Project fulfilled a prediction made by her father, Homer Whitmire, in the 1920s: "One day they're going to build a dam down at Arthur and Rosa Johnson's house and Jocassee will be gone forever!"[11] When the US Geological Survey installed gauging stations to monitor water levels and flow near Camp Jocassee on the north end and near Chapman Bridge on the south end of Jocassee shortly before Duke announced the project, it signaled an alarm to residents that something was about to happen to their rivers.[12]

There are few works focused on the area now covered by Lake Keowee. In *The Forgotten Society of the Keowee River Valley: A Biography of a Sharecropper* (2008), Jerry Vickery documented the life of Johnny V. Hester and his family, white sharecroppers who lived in the Keowee Valley during in the mid-twentieth century. In the introduction, Vickery wrote that Hester's story is "of a sharecropper's existence in what was at one time an extremely backward, rural corner of Oconee County, South Carolina," where "land that was tilled by mule with the lowest rung on the society ladder behind the plow stock, the sharecropper."[13] Vickery stated that the Hester family "never owned a foot of ground, but toiled endlessly hundreds of acres from the first part of the century until their final exit in the early 1960s prior to the rivers' demise."[14] His purpose was "to tell a story of an essential downtrodden society that was part of the Keowee Valley life segment, which up until now has totally been overlooked and forgotten."[15]

Because they did not own the land they were living on and working, sharecroppers such as the Hester family were left out of any negotiations as Duke Power and their subsidiaries purchased land in the Keowee River Valley. Even if consulted, they would not have received the financial benefits as the landowners did. Although the Hester family moved to Easley, in neighboring Pickens County, a safe distance from the impending inundation in 1959, this work highlights the narrative of the sharecroppers at the lower end of the South Carolina Upcountry socioeconomic ladder.

In *Keowee: The Story of the Keowee River Valley in Upstate South Carolina* (1995), Michael Hembree and Dot Jackson included information on the Lower Towns of the Cherokee, eighteenth-century European explorers, and the early German settlers who came into the northwest corner of South Carolina after the American Revolution. Hembree and Jackson argued that the South Carolina Land and Timber Company was formed in 1963 for the explicit purpose of acquiring land for the Keowee-Toxaway Project and not for timber rights as the company's name would suggest.[16] The most poignant portion of their telling of the story comes from a quotation by former resident Dennis Chastain, a teenager at the time of the project, who recalls his family's final trip into the Jocassee Valley before it was flooded in 1973. Chastain says, "It was kind of sad. I remember very well the experience of riding up there and knowing that within a matter of days or weeks all that would be under water. You get out on Jocassee now on a boat, and people really don't have a sense of what's under there. There's a whole world under that lake."[17] Chastain compared Jocassee to Cades Cove in the Great Smoky Mountains National Park: "it was just about as pretty a place as you can imagine."[18] Chastain also claimed that, had the valleys not been flooded, the area "would be one of the most unique natural resources in the eastern United States" because "you'd have 15 to 20 miles of whitewater on four major rivers. It could have been one of the premier national parks in the country."[19]

Other books on local history of the area were published shortly after the announcement of Duke Power's project. Among them are Nora Nimmons Field's *The High Falls Story* (1966), which describes one of Oconee's first villages and community gathering places, much of which (including the waterfall for which the area is named) is now under Lake Keowee.[20] Another work on local history, Pearl McFall's *The Keowee River and Cherokee Background* (1966), tells the history of the Cherokee Lower Towns that existed in Oconee County from the sixteenth century through the American Revolution.[21] Based on the year of their publication, these two works seem to have been published in response to the Keowee-Toxaway Project and the impending loss of culture and history.

Most recently, Christopher J. Manganiello included the Keowee-Toxaway Project in his discussion on the inextricable connection between water and power in the South in his *Southern Water, Southern Power: How the Politics of Cheap Energy and Water Scarcity Shaped a Region* (2015). Manganiello explained the creation of water reservoirs across the South as the work of "New South capitalists, New Deal regional planners, and Sun Belt boosters" who desired to "spur industrial development, consolidate or challenge corporate power, and deliver a multitude of economic and social benefits to urban customers, rural citizens, leisure seekers, and shareholders." He also argued that, by doing so, "corporate and state operatives attempted to conquer environmental conditions such as flooding, drought, and a lack of quality indigenous fossil and mineral fuel sources." The Duke Power Company capitalized on the more than 100,000 acres of land along the Keowee River that their agents had purchased between the 1920s and 1960s. The company garnered enough public and local government support to challenge the public power-generating model in favor of a corporate model that supposedly would provide endless streams of tax revenue to the local economy.[22] The public model, exemplified by TVA, features government control and operates with government subsidies and taxpayer funds; the corporate model, rooted in free enterprise, relies on private control of property and a profit model.

Pre-Removal Snapshot

During the first half of the twentieth century, the majority of Oconee County residents made their living as farmers or by working in one of the county's textile mills located in Newry, Seneca, Walhalla, and Westminster. In the 1920s, nearly one-sixth of white South Carolinians worked in the mills; Black workers were largely barred from work on the factory floor until the 1960s, except as custodians. Conditions in the mills were not much better than the fields as management dramatically increased machinery speeds in the 1930s. Workers at the Lonsdale Mill in Seneca joined thousands across the region when they went on strike in 1934. When Duke Power built the dams and nuclear station of the Keowee-Toxaway Project, the textile industry in South Carolina had declined because of competition from overseas mills in Latin American and Southeast Asia which could produce textiles at a much lower cost. By 1970 only 4,700 of Oconee's 41,000 residents were employed in one of the county's nine mills.[23]

The *Farm Plat Book and Business Guide: Oconee County, S.C.* (1953) provides a wealth of data on Oconee County farms in the early 1950s. In 1953, there were 3,288 farms in the county with the average farm size being about 75.5 acres. A total of 248,309 acres of the county's 428,800 acres, approximately 58 percent, were considered farmland. The primary crops were cotton, small grain, corn, aromatic tobacco, pimiento peppers, peaches, and apples. The county then was the largest apple producer in South Carolina. The population of Oconee County in 1953 was 39,050.[24]

Farming in Oconee County was a difficult way to make a living, especially for sharecroppers and renters. Johnny V. Hester provided detailed insight into the life of his sharecropping family in the Keowee River Valley. When Hester was born in 1939 the family was living in a tenant house along the banks of the Keowee River.

He calls their three-room home "an average house for tenants with rough painted clap weather boarding on the outside nailed to rickety studs" and no "finished interior walls nor an overhead ceiling, just sheets of tin tacked to exposed rafters."[25] The family gathered water from a spring located approximately forty yards from the house and that flowed from the earth into a bowl likely chiseled from the rock by Native Americans.[26] The Hester family kept to themselves and did their best to "dig out a meager subsistence from the soil," while remaining "oblivious to events happening outside this remote rural area of Oconee County, South Carolina."[27]

Debbie Fletcher credited Jerry Vickery's book for giving her insight into the side of the valley with which she was unfamiliar. Fletcher explained that the Keowee Valley had been "farmed to death" and consisted of "ugly red hills, scars." Her grandparents, lifelong residents of the Jocassee Valley, were "probably much better off than a lot of people there" while "most of the people that lived there were little farmers [who] struggled" and "lived hand-to-mouth."[28]

Claudia Whitmire Hembree maintained that her family, the Whitmires, were "the first there and the last to leave" the Jocassee Valley. According to her, they were also the first white residents to farm the Jocassee Valley in 1812 and, on November 16, 1967, Claudia Whitmire Hembree's brother Dan and his wife Sybil were the last to leave the valley before it was inundated.[29] Her book *Jocassee Valley* detailed the lives of dozens of families who called the valley their home.[30]

The remainder of the homes in the Jocassee Valley, including the home maintained by the McCalls from Charleston, South Carolina, became summer residences for families living outside the South Carolina Upcountry. Harry McCall recalled the hardships endured by the full-time residents that the summer residents never fully experienced, such as terrible storms and brutally cold winters. McCall explained that the area was a "summer home place," and "in the wintertime it was cold, dead, and the way it was when the sun went down, it was like those mining towns in West Virginia."[31]

For all the harshness and restricted accessibility involved with living in such a remote area, Claudia Whitmire Hembree recalled her family being remarkably well connected to the rest of the world. The influx of summer residents into the Jocassee Valley influenced the full-time residents greatly. She remembers that her grandfather A. L. Whitmire subscribed to four newspapers, including the *Atlanta Journal* and the *Greenville News,* and was an extremely well-read man with a home full of books.[32]

There are many slightly conflicting perceptions of the area from the midtwentieth century. Some saw the area as remote, backward, and lifeless as residents endured the harshness of everyday life. Others saw the beauty and the wildness of it and enjoyed summers at the Camp Jocassee and viewed the area as a welcome escape from city life in Charleston or Columbia.

Duke Power's Removal Process

There are varying narratives on Duke Power's methods for purchasing the land necessary for the dams and the land that would be flooded by the Keowee-Toxaway Project. The Oconee History Museum calls the company's methods "unobtrusive," which implies that the removals were necessary and that the process occurred without incident or opposition.[33]

Interviews with those removed emphasized, however, that the Oconee County residents who sold their property early in the process later realized they had been deceived by the Duke Power Company. The residents who faced displacement either favored the project or had no pathway to oppose it. Thus, with little or no opposition, Duke Power was able to move quickly in the removal process.

Duke Power's most effective land-purchasing tactic was the use of well-known locals as buying agents. Debbie Fletcher explained that, "during the negotiations, one man was snookered into selling his land because they didn't represent themselves as Duke. They represented themselves as somebody who wanted to buy the land to have a sheep farm because there was a particular kind of sheep that would do well really well in that environment."[34] Mike Wilson recalls these local agents as "'money people' that everybody knew" whom Duke Power contracted "to go around and be their front-man because, of course, people are going to be more receptive to a local than they are somebody from outside."[35]

Claudia Whitmire Hembree remembered the local agent, Luke Winchester from Pickens, South Carolina, who made her family an offer on their twenty-two acres of land in the Jocassee Valley. Her family were compelled to sell its land because, as she said, "I think in life you have to pick your fights. We were dealing with a huge company and that's why we just said, well, as my brother said, 'it's a done deal.'"[36] By the time Duke Power came to make an offer, the Whitmires' property was in the names of the Whitmire children, who then had to meet with Winchester to discuss the buyout. Hembree, along with her five siblings, believed they had no other option but to take the offer given to them. The Whitmire family appeared to have little faith in negotiating with the power company.

Mike Wilson remembered that most of the people living in the Keowee area were older and maintained small gardens and pastures only where there were once fields of corn and other crops. This general decline in farming along the Keowee River would have provided further motivation for residents to sell their land. Wilson had a great aunt and uncle who owned land along the Keowee River. The local agents came to these older folks living in Keowee and told them that the land was being bought by groups who intended to farm the land again.[37] The residents then sold their property with the nostalgic expectation that their land would be restored, only to see it flooded and lost to the rising water of Lake Keowee.

By first concealing its intentions and identity in the land-purchasing process, Duke Power's agents gained an upper hand in negotiations with residents and thus, after the company announced the project, set terms favorable to the company after the announcement. Debbie Fletcher remembered the first time her family was approached about selling their property:

> The lodge had this huge front porch and I remember I was on the porch, just piddling around on the porch and this car drove up and a man with a white shirt got out and I remember he had his sleeves rolled up to here. . . . That's when he told us he was from Duke Power . . . and that they had plans to build a dam and the valley was going to get flooded and they needed to make arrangements to buy our property. It's my understanding from my brother and from others that they approached us first because we were the largest land owner of property that was going to be totally inundated and I'm sure they thought that if they got us taken care of first then the others would fall in line.[38]

Another tactic Duke Power used involved targeting land owned by people who had summer homes in the area before making offers to those living along the Keowee River or in the Jocassee Valley full-time. Mike Wilson said, "by the time they had that much land, they could condemn your place and give you what they thought it was worth. So, it's best to deal with them or get condemned. And they had already geared up to start that."[39] The fear of condemnation proceedings, through the power of eminent domain, appears to have persuaded many people living in the Keowee River Valley to sell their property to Duke Power and South Carolina Land and Timber Company quickly and without much bargaining.

Debbie Fletcher recounted that her family's real mistake was taking Duke Power's offer too quickly. Her uncle Buck thought that if they sold quickly, they would get a better deal. Some families, however, did get a better deal when they negotiated with the power company. After family members inquired about swapping their land in the valley for lakefront property on either Lake Jocassee or Lake Keowee, Duke representatives told them that Jocassee was "too remote" and would be used for the pumped storage facility and that swapping for property on Lake Keowee was out of the question. Then, after the publication of her book *Whippoorwill Farewell* (2003), Fletcher met a doctor living in Easley, South Carolina, who claimed that Duke Power swapped the 135 acres he owned in Jocassee for a parcel of the same size on Lake Keowee with approximately two miles of shoreline. This news was devastating to Fletcher.[40]

Seneca Journal and Tribune staff writer Rooche Field published an article on January 13, 1965, shortly after Duke Power Company president W. B. McGuire publicly announced the project, titled, "When Reservoir Is Built: Will Lovely Jocassee Valley and 'Oconee Bell' Be Only a Memory?" Field called Jocassee the "little Switzerland of the South" for its secluded beauty. The article featured a picture of Camp Jocassee and included an interview with the camp's owner, Mrs. Morris Brown of Walhalla. In addition to the four-acre girls' camp, Brown also owned 166 acres in the Jocassee Valley. She explained, "I haven't sold my land yet. An agent for Duke Power offered me one hundred dollars an acre without seeing the land, but the value of the land far exceeds that amount. This land is valuable." Field continued the article, saying, "Nestled among the deep blue of the surrounding mountains and refreshed by the swift flow of the Whitewater River, Jocassee is a place of loveliness regardless of the season and is set apart from the noisy world of man. Any who see the valley would regret its loss forever."[41]

Harry McCall's family, owners of a summer home in Jocassee, also benefited from swapping its land in Jocassee for land on Lake Keowee. By doing so, the family avoided paying taxes on the price Duke offered them for their land and modest summer home. However, the family's experience with Duke Power was not all positive as they also spent many years involved in legal battles with the company and with property owners living in the subdivision that was later developed around them. Duke Power even claimed that the McCalls were trespassing on property the company had signed over to them years before. Harry McCall said that, with the amount of money and resources at Duke Power's disposal, "they would bankrupt you.... Duke Power has enough money that if they want to sue you because they don't like your name, by the time you go to court and you pay four or five hundred dollars for lawyer's fees, you'd be thinking about changing your name." The only thing that saved the McCall family was that the first judge sided with them and this precedent helped the family in later trials.[42]

Duke Power made an offer on the Wilson family's property only after purchasing the adjoining five-hundred-acre farm owned by the Finley family, an offer that Mike Wilson says his father quickly refused. Duke Power was not simply purchasing the land that would be inundated; it was buying thousands of acres that would remain above the waterline. Wilson said "a lot of that was where the lake didn't back all the way over and cover it. They told [residents] they had to have that, too, and they couldn't keep it." He also recalled that families who could afford lawyers were able to keep some of their land that was not inundated. Wilson said he believes residents were taken advantage of, but "land around here was dirt cheap back then and so they got more than they would have got if another local person had bought it from them."[43] Wilma Thompson also remembered friends and neighbors to whom Duke Power made offers, even though their land was not scheduled to be inundated. She told me that Duke Power wanted their land only because it was going to be lake-front property on Lake Keowee when the project was completed.[44]

From Farmland to Lakefront Property

Later interviews with descendants of the removed families confirmed that Duke Power paid residents approximately $250 per acre of farmland and, in some cases, a little more for their homes or for usable timber. Thompson said that her father always believed that he was "getting the short end of the thing." She believed that they were probably getting a better deal than most of her neighbors as her parents received $20,000 for their fifty-two-acre farm, including their farmhouse and other structures adjacent to Cane Creek. Her parents gave her older brother and sister one-acre plots each of the original fifty-two acres that her parents purchased several years prior. Each of them had already built homes there and, when Bruce Rochester came to purchase their property, he offered her siblings each $7,500 for their land and homes. Assuming that Duke paid her parents the same amount for the acre of land where their home was located, they would have been paid approximately $255 per acre for the remaining forty-nine acres of pasture, garden, and farmland.

Land that Duke Power purchased for around $250 per acre soon became prime lakeside real estate and, by the middle of the 1970s, gated communities such as Keowee Key were selling that same property for $25,000 per acre.[45] The price for a lakefront lot with no structures in Oconee County today is easily ten times that amount.[46] Harry McCall said his neighbor on Lake Keowee at present has his lakefront home and property on the real estate market for nearly $500,000. Mike Wilson said the mood shifted "when Duke went into the realty business and started selling off all the land that taxpayers had helped buy and loading it down with people."[47] Wilson meant that residents were not happy that Duke Power developed the land bought from Oconee County residents, especially because the company was involved in building subdivisions and gated communities marketed to retirees from outside the region. Harry McCall also saw how these new arrivals, primarily from northern states and Florida, affected property prices. He said "the northern people have come in and it's almost like a little New York. A lot of people from Florida moved back up to western South Carolina and North Carolina because the prices in Florida have gone up and the heat and humidity down there. So, everything is going up."[48]

Wilma Thompson also believed strongly about the power shift that happened as a result of the lakes created by Duke Power and the wealthy newcomers who began purchasing land that, prior to the sale to Duke, had been in some Oconee County families for several generations. She said, "I know that a lot of northerners came in and bought land at Lake Keowee. My personal feeling is, I know they've got money, but it seems to me like they pretty much think that they've got more say-so than anybody else because they live on the lake and their property is a lot more valuable than a lot of other people's property."[49]

As Lakes Keowee and Jocassee became a major attraction for retirees from other parts of the country, Oconee County began to see changes not only in its physical landscape, but in demographics, politics, and financial well-being of the county's residents. This was in contrast to the people who lived on the river prior to Duke Power's project. In fact, very few locals could afford to live on Lake Keowee. Even one of these early newcomers attracted by the cheap lakefront property saw the effect the Keowee-Toxaway Project had on the area. Alice Badenoch, author of *Keowee Key: The Origins of a Community* (1989), wrote that residents "must have felt that some sort of flood gates had been opened as they watched their landmarks disappear and witnessed the rapid influx of population."[50]

Dividing Communities

The lakes separated long-standing communities on both sides of the Keowee River. Mike Wilson recalled, "We had a lot of people who went to our church that lived on the river. Most of them lived on the other side. Even though that's Pickens County, everybody considered them being from Salem. Once the lake backed up, seems like almost all of them ended up moving to Pickens or Easley or Six Mile. So, we didn't see them anymore. They used to come to church, homecoming and stuff like that. That's about the only time you saw them anymore."[51]

He also said of his changing sense of community: "When I was growing up, I knew everybody around Salem. If I saw a dog on the side of the road, not only did I probably know whose dog it was, I probably knew its name. And then it got to where I didn't know hardly anybody up there anymore. So, you know, things change."[52] Intentional or not, as lakes replaced the river, communities were dismantled as residents made their way to higher ground, many moving to other communities in Oconee, Pickens, and Anderson counties.

Striking images of the displacement of Oconee County residents as a result of the Keowee-Toxaway Project appeared in local papers. For example, a *Seneca Journal and Tribune* article titled "It'll Be Under Water Pretty Soon" pointed out that the poor farmers from the mountains were not the only ones affected: "You look up suddenly, if you're driving along a road in the Seneca-Clemson vicinity, and you might see a house moving down the road toward you. Houses are being moved from the Keowee lake area. . . . You have to feel sorry for the fellow who bought one of those brick houses in the Lake Keowee area."[53] This article suggested that homes and land continued to be sold in the Keowee area to unsuspecting buyers well into the 1960s. The sellers likely would not have had any more information on the area's future than did the buyers. The homeowners with the financial means had to hire a moving company to pick up their brick homes and move them to a safe location.

Reactions and experiences were mixed among residents living in the Keowee River Valley. Thompson remembers that some of her neighbors did not like what Duke offered for their property and, like her, were not happy about the prospect of their homes and memories being covered by a hundred feet of water. But in her words, "It was going to happen regardless. There wasn't going to be a way out of it. That was it." After her father told her that they were moving out of their house along Cane Creek, she decided that she would take one last look at the house and the property. Thompson said she remembers crying as she walked from the house down to the barn and then to Cane Creek as she thought to herself, "this is the last time I'm going to see this. And it was."[54]

Who Dares Oppose Such a Project?

With passionate vocal support from local government, Duke Power moved forward with land acquisition. There were no documented public forums or other outlets for Oconee residents to voice their concerns or to ask government or company representatives questions about the impending project. Residents had few legal options to halt the project. There were, however, two documented cases in which residents and the federal government questioned Duke Power's actions.

Within a few months of Duke Power announcing its intentions in the Keowee River Valley, President Lyndon B. Johnson's secretary of the interior, Stewart Udall, along with the Tri-State Power Committee, argued that the Keowee-Toxaway Project should be put on hold until its environmental effects could be studied. Duke Power leaders, local government officials, and the many Oconee residents who supported the project, however, were eager to get it underway. Articles in local newspapers immediately attacked Secretary Udall and called any opposition to the project a "Blow to [the] State."[55] An article in the *Greenville News* titled "Get On With Keowee-Toxaway!" said: "Almost without exception, the citizens of South Carolina have welcomed the idea of the Keowee-Toxaway Project since it was first announced in 1965. There were a few dissenters, of course, people who seem to have a psychopathic fear of all private utilities; but sweet reason and forceful public opinion appear to have prevailed."[56] The article cast the supporters as heroes and those who questioned the project as villains.

Local newspaper articles seemed to mock Secretary Udall when he suggested that the area be studied for the possible impact on fish populations. In an article titled, "And There Are Tadpoles Too," the Walhalla-based newspaper, the *Keowee Courier*, agreed that fish populations should be studied; however, it reasoned that "more water would mean more fish and would make the area a virtual fisherman's paradise."[57] What the newspaper failed to address was that some species of fish, such as the trout that lived in the many streams and rivers of Oconee County, would not thrive in the deep, murky, and current-less lakes, as they do in clear, fast-moving rivers. The South Carolina Department of Natural Resources website explained: "Since trout only live in pure, cold water, they are highly sensitive to excessive silt loads, increased water temperatures, and lowered oxygen levels. When improperly conducted, practices such as logging, agriculture, residential development, and dam and highway construction can effectively destroy many trout-producing habitats."[58] Each of these practices increased across the eastern portion of Oconee County as a result of the Keowee-Toxaway Project.

The South Carolina state senator from Oconee County, Republican Marshall Parker, was one of the more vocal proponents of the project. He said that the "shocking action" taken by Secretary Udall and the Tri-State Power Committee could destroy the project, resulting in a $6 million annual loss to Oconee and Pickens counties, $14 million to the state, and $24 million to the federal government, along with a major source of employment.[59] Senator Parker demanded, "Who dares oppose such a project?" State Representative Snead Schumacher, a Democrat, echoed his colleague's stance and argued that any opposition was "a direct disservice to the people of South Carolina" and added "I am irrevocably committed to support the development of South Carolina through private capital in lieu of public funds at any time it can be done."[60] An article from the *Seneca Journal and Tribune* claimed that "protests, vocal and otherwise, are being raised right and left in Oconee this week following the protest made last week by the Secretary of the Interior." However, the article went on to describe protests to Secretary Udall's stance not from groups of organized common folks, but from local elites such as the Board of Directors of the Seneca Chamber of Commerce and from Senator Parker.[61]

Duke Power applied pressure on both local and federal governments in September of 1966 when company leaders asked for an expedited approval process for its initial license to begin the project. The company said that, if it did not receive a decision by the Federal Power Commission (FPC, now called the Federal Energy Regulatory Commission) by October 1, 1966, it would withdraw plans in South Carolina and "move the project elsewhere at great expense."[62] The FPC issued the initial fifty-year license for the Keowee-Toxaway Project on September 26, 1966, a mere twelve days after Duke Power threatened to abandon the project.[63]

Some families did, however, fight Duke Power's apparent self-designated right to do as it pleased in the valley. Debbie Fletcher recalled that her grandfather C. O. Williams received $250 per acre for his land in the Jocassee Valley and a little more for some of the timber. The Williams family also had an agreement with Duke Power that allowed it to keep the property in its name until it became necessary for the completion of the project, most likely as a way to keep possession of the property in case the Jocassee Valley was not inundated as planned. The Jocassee Dam was the last to be completed, and therefore most of the valley remained above water for several years after the start of the project. When it came time to talk with Duke Power about selling their property, she said, "We didn't negotiate well, let me put it that way. My family hardly got anything."[64]

Fletcher's family, one of the few to make any attempt to stand up to Duke Power, did so because the family's two-story log cabin, built by her great-grandfather, was torn down and buried by Duke Power before the sale was finalized. She explained that her family did not have time to retrieve any belongings from the home and that Duke Power "obviously made a mistake because they had not purchased that part of the land yet." Fletcher then said: "it was still our property and Duke knocked it [the cabin] down and buried it. So, we did go to court and got a restraining order against Duke and they were not allowed to come on our land. . . . They had done something pretty egregious." She also said that she heard from former employees of Duke Power that the company did not abide by the restraining order because shortly thereafter "they cut a road up right behind the lodge, across our property."[65]

The actions by Duke Power led to the family taking the case to the South Carolina Supreme Court. Debbie's older brother Jim Richardson was part of the Williams family's legal team that defended Duke Power's lawsuit to acquire a twenty-two-acre tract of land in the Jocassee Valley.[66] This parcel of land was reserved and optioned in December 1965 for purchase within five years of that date only "when the land is required to begin actual construction of the Jocassee Dam." Construction on the Jocassee Dam began in April 1968 and the diversion tunnel, coffer dam, and river diversion completed in October 1969. Five years later, the South Carolina Supreme Court ruled in favor of Duke Power and the Crescent Land and Timber Company, inferring that the land was "[r]equired 'at a point in time simultaneous with the actual commencement of construction of the Jocassee Dam.' Certainly, the acquisition of the land over which to back water is necessary to begin construction of a project of the nature."[67] Jim Richardson explained that, to the best of his knowledge, their case was the only litigation that resulted from Duke Power's land-acquisition strategy and he was also not aware of any condemnations.[68]

Some residents were initially determined to prevent Duke Power from forcibly removing them from their homes. Harry McCall, whose family owned a summer home in the Jocassee Valley, commented that his former neighbor Jack Hinkle was adamant about staying in the valley. McCall said they used to tease Hinkle, saying, "I guess you'll be down inside a pipe and the pipe will stick up three hundred feet and we'll lower food down there to you. He [Hinkle] said 'I'm not leaving,' but when everything was said and done and they realized the new house that they're going to get with the modern conveniences, telephone, television, it was hard to say 'I'm going to stay up here.'"[69] Residents such as McCall, initially opposed to selling their land to Duke Power, in the end saw they had no other option and took what they were offered.

Duke Power's Keowee-Toxaway Project was an enormous undertaking that even fifty years later continues to define Oconee County. There is no official number of displaced residents in any published sources, but overlaying a current map of Oconee County with the lakes and a map with the details from the 1953 *Farm Plat and Business Guide: Oconee County* (which showed the approximate locations of the county's farms), there were approximately ninety farms affected by waters of either Lake Keowee or Lake Jocassee.[70] This number does not include nonfarm residences or renters, which easily puts the number of displaced families well over one hundred.

Construction of the Jocassee Dam which included a hydroelectric powerhouse began in 1968 and was completed in 1971. Jocassee Power House, Keowee-Toxaway State Park, Sunset, South Carolina, ca. late 1960s, from color slides of South Carolina Park, South Carolina Department of Parks, Recreation, and Tourism.

Although completion of the project took years from announcement to complete inundation, residents believed that any efforts to stall the project would be futile. McCall explained, "There wasn't any pro bono attorney going to take it. You're going up against Duke Power that's already got a stack of lawyers and if you're doing this pro bono, which I don't even know if any lawyers did pro bono back then, it would just be a lost cause."[71] Many residents learned about the project and its progress only through reading newspapers or talking to their neighbors.

Debbie Fletcher summed up how these families would have reacted when they heard their family farms would be inundated by reservoirs and how a similar project might be received today: "Those little farmers in the valley, how are they going to take on Duke Power? This whole project was approved in secret. If it was done now there'd be hearings and protests and it will be all over the nation. People would be talking about building this nuclear station. We knew nothing about it, nothing about it until that man showed up and told us about it. We had no opportunity to say anything or protest or write letters or anything."[72]

Wilma Crocker Thompson noted that Oconee County residents were in no position to fight Duke Power. She said: "I think most people were like us. We were poor and we didn't know really much about lawyers and we wouldn't have had money to get a lawyer anyway back then. I imagine most of them were in the same boat we were in and no, they wouldn't have fought it because they figured Duke Power had more say-so and more money behind it and more fighting behind it than they did, and they'd have to just give in to it. It was going to come and that was it."[73]

For most federal and state removal projects, a public hearing stage precedes the acquisition of land from those affected. Often public hearings are dominated by project backers, business leaders, politicians, and those who seek to benefit, but in other cases the voices of concerned residents make a difference in whether the project continues. No documentation exists that any interested party held a public forum to allow residents to voice their concerns or ask questions about how they would be affected by the Keowee-Toxaway Project. The Oconee County Clerk's office does not have records relating to the project and none of the interviews with the displaced families mentioned that any public forums occurred.[74]

One of the few accounts of opposition to the project appeared as an anonymous letter to the editor of the *Seneca Journal and Tribune* published on January 13, 1965:

Dear Sir:

I am one who is not happy to hear of the proposed inundation of the Keowee Valley. Aside from the fact that this beautiful stream will be eliminated, this valley is the cradle of Oconee's beginnings. The first traders lived here: the Indian towns of the

Keowee and Toxaway were here; Fort Prince George was here. All of these sites will be covered by the lake.

Now, I realize that historical considerations will in no wise deter the building of the dams, but I have not yet seen in print any indications that Duke Power Company intends to preserve in any manner this historical heritage of Oconee County.[75]

Duke Power had the money and influence to do as they pleased in this remote area of South Carolina. Residents saw that any attempt to stand up to the company would have been doomed from the start and only cost them time and money that they did not have. No matter how much time these former residents spent there, their connections to this place have encouraged them to write books about the area, collect photographs, and think often of their homes now underwater.

America's Last Period of Gullibility

Some residents, including those not directly affected by the removals, were concerned about losing pieces of the region's history and culture to inundation. The areas scheduled for flooding included a number of Native American sites, landmarks from the British colonization period, and wonderful natural features such as waterfalls. The areas surrounding the Keowee River were all privately owned, some only becoming protected lands after the conclusion of the Keowee-Toxaway Project. This land would join Sumter National Forest on the county's far western border with the Chattooga River, which came under federal control in the 1930s.

Philip Lee Williams worked with his father as a volunteer from the University of South Carolina archeological team that was excavating Fort Prince George before it would be covered by the waters of Lake Keowee. He was extremely upset to see residents of Oconee and Pickens counties losing their homes and their history. Williams described the scene in his book *In the Morning: Reflections from First Light* (2006): "For weeks, crews have been cutting down all the trees in the glorious Keowee Valley because the Duke Power Company, damn their eyes, is about to impound a lake that will flood the area with water a hundred feet deep. . . . The valley, one of the most beautiful in the Southern United States, has been destroyed. I feel literally sick every time I see it. . . . I have come to think of the 1960s as America's Last Period of Gullibility, when it could be over-awed by utility companies to such an extent they would allow their heritage to be raped."[76]

Even those who spent a very limited time in Jocassee remember it for its striking beauty. In a story produced by South Carolina Public Radio from March 8, 2016, naturalist Rudy Mancke remembered his only visit to the valley, in 1965. He said he was "blown away by the biodiversity" of the valley. He talked of seeing the rare *Shortia galacifolia,* or Oconee Bells, on his visit and that Lake Jocassee now covers most of what was once this plant's habitat. He added, "I sure do miss it."[77]

The same local newspapers that praised Duke Power and the state for the new lakes, hydroelectric and nuclear power stations, also suggested what would be lost as a result of the project. A special section of the *Seneca Journal and Tribune* from October 13, 1965, exclaimed, "The Story of Oconee County Is a Story of Progressive People!" This publication highlighted all the things that Oconee residents had to be proud of in their county, including recreational opportunities afforded by Lake Hartwell (another recent addition to the Oconee County landscape by the Army Corps of Engineers only a few years before) and the many rivers that flow through the county, along with the benefits to be provided by the impending Keowee-Toxaway Project. The piece even mentioned some facets of life that Oconee County would lose. Clemson University, along with the city of Clemson, would be annexed by neighboring Pickens County in 1968 when the college worked with Pickens County to move the county line to the center of Lake Hartwell. Camp Jocassee was also highlighted as a place "where hundreds of young girls have spent wonderful summertime hours roaming those same lovely woodland paths that Jocassee herself once trod."[78] The camp was lost to the waters of Lake Jocassee just a few years later.

On July 13, 1966, the *Seneca Journal and Tribune* printed a picture of High Falls, located along the Little River, with the caption: "Probably no spot in Oconee County is more popular these sweltering Summer days than the 'Ole Swimmin' Hole' at High Falls. . . . This beautiful setting lends itself to various forms of summer recreation . . . such as swimming, picnic outings, or just relaxing on the sand beach. Last Friday afternoon, when above photo was made, more than a hundred people visited the falls."[79] Although the article's aim was to highlight the scorching temperatures of summer, there was no mention that in just a few short years this community gathering place would be one of many natural spaces inundated by Lake Keowee.

My mother and her family have called this area near High Falls home for several generations and have owned property since the early 1950s. I have lived for much of my life here as well and have heard my mother recount many times her memories of climbing the falls with her father when she was very young. She never forgets to tell me how slippery the rocks were and how she cannot believe that she never fell in.

Even though Duke Power flooded the area almost two decades before I was born, it is through family stories like this that I feel connected to the pre-lakes version of my childhood home.

Many components of an Appalachian community were lost to the waters of Lakes Keowee and Jocassee. This included not only historic sites such as Fort Prince George or much of the natural habitat for a rare flowering plant, the Oconee Bell, but all the hard work put into clearing land and tilling fields, days spent fishing or swimming in the river, and times spent with friends and family. The Keowee-Toxaway Project and the promises for a new, modern way of life in Oconee County began a new chapter in the lives of South Carolina Upcountry residents. Wilma Crocker Thompson explained, "I enjoyed growing up on the farm. It wasn't an easy life, but I think it helped me to be the kind of person I am today. It was harder back then, but I think it shaped me as a better person."[80]

A Great Future in Store for Oconee

By most local media accounts, Duke Power's Keowee-Toxaway Project had the potential to transform the region into one of national recognition and unparalleled economic growth while keeping much of the natural beauty of the area intact. Although the area's rivers had drawn tourists, campers, and other outdoor adventure seekers for decades, the new lakes were designed to attract a new generation who saw the lakes for boating, waterskiing, and fishing as well as their property development potential. As for displaced residents of Oconee County, some saw the buyout as a means to move away from scratching a living out of worn-out soil or to move their aging parents closer to one of the nearby cities such as Walhalla or Seneca and closer to amenities such as grocery stores, doctors, and other modern conveniences.

Wilma Crocker Thompson remembered that, when she first heard about Duke Power's plans for the Keowee area, she did not like it because she assumed that her family's farmhouse would always be there and be passed on from generation to generation. Yet, as time passed between her father selling their property and their farm's inundation, she realized how much the move would improve the lives of her parents. Thompson said, "I thought Momma might have things easier . . . and then I was okay with it. But I still regret it happened." She also remembered seeing an early map of how the area was going to look and how the project would beautify the area with new parks and the lakes.[81]

Concern for her aging mother was also on Claudia Whitmire Hembree's mind when her family received an offer from Duke Power to buy their land. She explained that the Jocassee Valley was once a "little resort valley," but after World War II, people had the means to travel to other places. She said, "My mother was a widow and, as it turns out, we were sort of glad that she could get out and move to Anderson (South Carolina) and be in a nice community and have access to things and go to church there and [have] a more active lifestyle. I think that was a lot of my concern at the time."[82]

The shores of Lake Keowee quickly became crowded with boat docks and hundreds of private residences, but there were early planning and conservation efforts to protect Lake Jocassee. Duke Power leased 6,800 acres around Lake Jocassee to the South Carolina Wildlife Resources Department, who stocked the area with whitetail deer, turkey, and black bear. The same newspaper article that described Duke Power's recreational plans for the area also noted that Duke planned to lease property to other services such as food, bait and tackle, marine, and boat repair, and provide free public parking and boat-launching access.[83] Opened in 1991, Devil's Fork State Park is currently the only public access point for Lake Jocassee. The state-managed park charges five dollars per adult to enter the grounds.[84]

In 1970, Duke Power donated 1,000 acres of land on Lake Keowee for the creation of Keowee-Toxaway State Park. The park charges no entrance fee and includes one cabin, twenty-four campsites with water and electricity, and two hiking trails that total about five and a half miles in length.[85] The park also includes the Jocassee Gorges Visitor Center, which includes exhibits on the area's biodiversity and history.[86] The 1,000 acres Duke Power donated for Keowee-Toxaway State Park is part of the 33,000 total acres the company has transferred to South Carolina around Lake Jocassee. In 2000, the Richard King Mellon Foundation purchased almost 8,000 acres, which it immediately donated to the state. The winter–spring 2000 issue of the *Jocassee Journal*, published by the South Carolina Department of Natural Resources, said that the purchase, with assistance from the Conservation Fund, is integral to the Jocassee Gorges "becoming a prominent part of the nature-based tourism economy of the Southern Appalachians." South Carolina Department of Natural Resources director Dr. Paul Sandifer called the purchase "the most significant conservation land acquisition in the Southern Appalachians in the latter half of the twentieth century."[87]

Living Up to Expectations

The economic benefits of the Keowee-Toxaway Project, with its two lakes and nuclear station, were mentioned frequently in the local and regional newspapers throughout the project's construction. *Seneca Journal and Tribune* staff writer Martha Navy wrote that the project was going to be a "tax bonanza" for the county and the state. She estimated that the timber harvested from the valleys would be a "billion dollar business ... alone" and that over the next ten years, 450 jobs would be created as a result. *Greenville News* bureau chief for Oconee and Pickens counties also predicted the project would be an economic "bonanza" for the two counties as well as the Upstate.[88]

Another article from the *Greenville News* written by executive news editor Carl D. Weimer and associate editor J. H. McKinney Jr. told readers that Duke's project would provide access to "the hidden valleys and brooding crests of the Blue Ridge Mountains in extreme northwest South Carolina" which "have been in a large measure cut off from mankind's enjoyment" and likened the area to the mythical paradise of Shangri-La.[89] Other articles told the public that the lakes, parks, and wildlife areas would be a major tourist attraction for the region and create a "water sports mecca."[90]

It is difficult to determine estimates on annual tourist visits and dollars. For many visitors, it is often a challenge to find a parking space on a summer afternoon at Devil's Fork State Park (the only public access point on Lake Jocassee), and there seems to be an unending stream of watercraft on Lake Keowee. This anecdotal evidence of my own observations suggests that the lakes have attracted plenty of tourists and locals alike.

Many locals took part in the activities provided by the new lakes soon after the project was completed. Mike Wilson explained that, "back when they first built it, it was nice for us locals to go out there." He remembered riding with his friends from one end of Lake Keowee to the other in the summertime, and they "might not see another boat and there wasn't a house anywhere. And then it finally got to where we sold our jet skis. It got so miserable on the lake because it'd beat you to death, there were so many boats and jet skis everywhere." The common areas where locals had free rein to camp, fish, and swim later became restricted as state and county parks designated areas for specific recreational activities. Wilson, along with friends or family, camped near Fall Creek landing in the summer, and he noticed that eventually one could not park by the water anymore and gates were put up to keep out campers.[91]

As for the economic bonanza promised to the residents of Oconee, in 2004 the Appalachian Regional Commission (ARC) placed Oconee County at a "transitional" economic status. This designation means that the county is transitioning between strong and weak economies and ranks somewhere between the worst 25 percent and the best 25 percent of the nation's counties.[92] The ARC also reported that Oconee County had a poverty rate at or higher than the national average between the years 2012 and 2016.[93] By ARC standards, Oconee County is in much better economic shape than many other areas of Appalachia, but still in the middle of the list.[94]

It is unlikely that, for all the land under its control, Duke Energy contributed as much to the local economy and to local tax revenue as originally promised or at the same rate as other landowners in Oconee County. During his legal battles with Duke Power, Harry McCall wanted to find out how much the company was paying in taxes. He related:

> I talked to them at FERC to try and find out what taxes Duke is paying on this bed. They own the bed of the river. They own it. They bought it, they flooded it. But try to find out what tax Duke Power is paying. . . . It is listed. You've got to call Columbia and it is highly confidential. Duke power has got a lot of pull. . . . The lake encompasses probably thousands of acres and they've got it almost pennies on the dollar is what they're getting it at. And then, like I said, I wanted to find out when we were in that lawsuit with Duke, what they were paying and stuff and it's just almost impossible.[95]

McCall added: "Duke, as long as they held the land, it was listed as farm land. They hardly paid any taxes on it. The minute it is sold, Oconee County now wants any of the back taxes Duke owed for . . . residential. So, whoever buys the land has to pay five years back or something and it's just unreal. You have no garbage collection. You have few things that I take for granted in Greenville like sewer and different things. But it's a changing world here. The old part is moving off with the old timers and the old people. Oconee has had a lot of growing pains real fast."[96]

Former residents also questioned the preservation efforts around Lake Jocassee. Even though she is happy that much of the shoreline of the lake has been maintained, Claudia Whitmire Hembree is still protective of how people talk about the place where she grew up. She explained that during a tour of the Bad Creek pumped storage facility near Jocassee the guide kept referring to the natural resources that had been preserved by Duke Power around Lake Jocassee. She said, "He was talking about resources. I thought, 'what happened to your human resources in all of this?' Because that was a displacement. We were displaced. . . . Whoever was working for Duke did not present very well that there was a lot at stake for the individuals who live there."[97]

⚠⚠

The research materials I collected from oral history interviews, newspaper articles, and other documents point to a general exclusion of displaced residents from the dominant narrative of the Keowee-Toxaway Project. Like many of the residents displaced by the Tennessee Valley Authority and the National Park Service in other parts of the southern mountains, residents of the Keowee and Jocassee valleys later expressed their belief that their families and their culture were devalued and stood in the way of progress. Analysis of the oral history interviews revealed that, even though some former residents continue to see the benefits of the project, they still believe that Duke Power cheated them out of their homes, land, history, and culture. Communities were created while others were dismantled by the project. The memories these former residents have of the area before and during Duke Power's work in the area are now filtered through their life experiences of the last fifty years and how they positively or negatively see those changes.

One of the goals of my study was to determine how Duke Power and local government presented the project to the public and to residents who were to be displaced. The $700 million price tag made the headlines, and local newspapers included this figure in nearly every article as Duke Power gradually announced the extent of the project. Even with the maps of the proposed lakes that were printed in local newspapers following its announcement, many residents found out the power company had scheduled their property to be inundated only when local agents came to their doorstep and made them a seemingly nonnegotiable offer. Duke Power took the upper hand in these negotiations by purchasing much of the needed land through subsidiaries years before the company made its intentions known to the public. Early in the purchasing process, local agents misled residents about their intentions, playing on the residents' attachment to place as they told them the land would be rejuvenated and would become prosperous once again.

Neither Duke Power nor local government provided any type of public forum for residents to ask questions and have input on Duke Power's decision to inundate their land. This ubiquitous disregard for the concerns of residents was shaped by issues of power and socioeconomic standing. Giving residents any kind of agency in the project might have delayed or even canceled the project altogether. Instead, residents believed that they were little farmers who had no chance against a giant corporation and therefore posed little resistance. The only major sources of opposition came from Secretary of Interior Stewart Udall, who encouraged more studies on the environmental effects of the project, and from the Williams family, who tried to keep its property in the Jocassee Valley for as long as possible.

Local media supported the project and mentioned the loss of historic places and structures only as a necessary part of bringing Oconee County into modernity. Tax revenue and the promises of jobs and a steady stream of tourists blinded many to the diverse and historically and culturally significant places they were losing. Although Duke Power has played a major role in providing jobs and upgrading the county's infrastructure to accommodate the nuclear station and lakes, judging by the Appalachian Regional Commission's "transitional" rating for Oconee County, the predicted "bonanza" never placed average Oconee residents at economic parity with the rest of the nation.

Duke Power and county government were overwhelmingly the largest beneficiaries of the Keowee-Toxaway Project. These two groups combined their resources and power to expedite the project and control the narrative that they were the region's saviors. Duke has been selling electricity to the region from these facilities for over forty years and has made tremendous profits. In Oconee County, far from South Carolina's capital and from tourist attractions in the state's coastal regions, Duke Power made $64 million in profits from electricity sales in 2016 alone, which ranks near the top of their list of profitable counties in the state.[98]

Oconee County residents have also experienced some improvements, such as new roads and schools, but according to the most recent data available from the Appalachian Regional Commission, the poverty rate has climbed from 14 percent in 1980 to 18.5 percent in 2016. The poverty rate is higher than the state's 17.2 percent, the Appalachian region's 16.7 percent, and the national 15.1 percent. The ARC also reports that per capita income in the county has remained roughly equal to the rest of Appalachia since 2008 at approximately 80 percent of the national average.[99]

The dominant storyline presents Lakes Keowee and Jocassee as two of the area's greatest assets and Duke Power as its greatest contributor. Oral histories present a much more complex series of narratives that involve displacement, loss of the commons, separation of communities, perceived oppression by wealthy newcomers, and in many cases, a strong sense of regret. The stories told by the displaced residents of Oconee County show another perspective that involves questionable treatment of locals in the buyout process as well as the loss of culturally and histor-ically significant sites. Many of the displaced residents of Keowee and Jocassee have strong connections to the land now covered by the lakes. One of the most mov-ing moments of the interviews came when former Keowee Valley resident Wilma Crocker Thompson told me, "I guess a lot of people think that Duke Power is probably one of the best things that ever happened to this area, but I think it's one of the worst. . . . My memories are there and I hate it's covered up in water."[100]

Conclusion
Can You Go Home Again?

The Meanings of Appalachian Identity,
Displacement, and Memory

STEPHEN WALLACE TAYLOR

I don't wanna to live like a big shot rich man
I don't wanna to live like a branded slave
I just want to give some land to my children
So they won't have to buy my grave.
—Jason Boland and the Stragglers, "Big Shot Rich Man," 2002

Appalachia is a land of stories. Perhaps more than most parts of the United States, the region has been "othered" for more than a century as scholars, missionaries, and politicians sought to explain its supposedly unique and isolated culture, its persistent poverty, and its deviation from alleged American norms.[1] Inhabitants have been virtually cast in amber as static relics of a bygone era, doomed by progress. In that context, "progress" demands their "removal." The very use of the term "removal" suggests an impersonal process and renders the individuals less as people than as an obstacle to be overcome by the protagonist—government, private enterprise, or the very force of progress itself.

Yet the "removal" process is itself quite personal. The loss of a home can be traumatic. It may separate the individual from tangible benefits such as shelter and in many cases income. It also deprives one of a sense of connection to one's neighbors and to one's past. The stories of displacement vary widely, but they have in common the notion that something was irretrievably lost. Exactly what that something was is not nearly as obvious as we might assume.

Some of these stories describe the loss in economic terms. The transition from a setting in which one could, if necessary, support oneself without depending on others to a setting in which a weekly or monthly paycheck is essential to survival is both financially and psychologically difficult. In many cases the land that was taken was the best farmland in the area because of regular deposits of topsoil washed into the riverbottom by rainfall. Often, part of the story is that the price their families received for the land was much lower than what they thought it was worth—or what their neighbors received.

For others, the loss is less tangible. They believe they are cut off from their sense of identity, their family heritage, their community of origin. They may be materially better off than they were before relocation, but the sense of loss is still a defining characteristic for them. They tell stories of land that was in their families for generations, and that was taken from them in the name of the greater good. Some are embittered, but others are merely wistful for an idyllic, perhaps idealized, way of life they remember from their childhood, one they imagine fixed in time. But the image of an unchanging, preindustrial Appalachia is misleading. It was misleading even in the 1930s when the Tennessee Valley Authority launched its Norris Dam project, the first of its type. Michael J. McDonald and John Muldowny described the Norris Basin as being in a "transitional" state between premodern and modern socioeconomic structures in 1933, but they missed the important point that life in Appalachia was more precarious, and more subject to boom and bust cycles, than elsewhere.[2]

In a previous study that covered the period from the 1880s to the 1890s, I wrote:

Many residents . . . far from stuck in time and space, moved about so frequently that their connections to a particular family dwelling or ancestral homeplace lasted no more than a generation. Furthermore, entire communities came and went as industry and employment did.

What most people in this region did was to "get by," whatever that might require at the moment. Getting by might require taking employment in local industries, such as mining and timbering, or working for the Southern Railway. It might also require growing vegetables or cutting pulpwood. It might even require leaving one's family behind and working elsewhere temporarily.[3]

The authors of their respective chapters in this book gathered some of these stories through direct interviews, while others come from earlier scholars as part of the effort to preserve the experiences of those removed. Government workers assembled still other stories, while trying to assess the success or failure of "readjustment" attempts or by journalists trying to reconstruct the lives of long-dead communities. They represent a cross-section, if not necessarily a complete profile, of the effect of forced relocation in Appalachia, but they also illustrate many of the problems historians face when attempting to tell the whole story of the displacement of families from Appalachian lands.

As historians, we aim to tell "the truth." We know that memory is a process of selecting what to remember and what meaning to attach to it. We also know that memories change under influence from subsequent events and evolving external contexts. How, then, do we properly understand the past as it is conveyed through oral accounts, interviews, memoirs, and contemporary media? Of all forms of historical evidence, oral testimony is perhaps the most subjective. But does that make these accounts less useful? The history of the displacement of families is local history, and while the prospect of drawing broad conclusions from detailed case studies is certainly tempting, overgeneralization is unwise. As historian Kate Tiller noted, "The fields of enquiry which are the bread and butter of local history—family, politics, religion, power, prosperity, influence—include some of the most sensitive and contentious areas of recent experience."[4]

Tiller went on to advise caution against oversentimentalizing the past, especially when historians have or develop a personal connection to the individuals or events involved. When local history derives from family history, these relationships may dominate the narrative to the exclusion of broader themes. Similarly, when the practice of history melds with public commemoration, audiences often filter what they see through a romantic lens, intentionally or otherwise. Since Appalachian history is inseparable from the present story of Appalachians continuing to try to build lives for themselves, historians must look not only at the past itself, but at how the present retells and reinterprets the past.[5]

Alessandro Portelli, in his attempt to understand the competing narratives of the death of Luigi Trastulli, found that, as expected, oral accounts differed considerably. But more to the point, he found that they differed in *predictable* ways—according to a rather complex set of patterns. Portelli discovered that "chronological displacement" (placing events in a different order or in a different context than that in which they occurred) was surprisingly common among oral accounts. He also found that "rank-and-file narrators [were] less matter-of-fact, more epic, and more imaginative" than those whose memories reflected their participation in some sort of official or leadership capacity.[6]

Portelli's analysis concluded that "memory manipulates factual details and chronological sequence in order to serve three major functions: symbolic, psychological, and formal." Rather than weakening the value of oral accounts, and the reports derived from them, Portelli asserts that these patterns of manipulation actually tell historians more about the *meaning* of the events than about the events themselves. They are thus a gateway into the minds of participants. This, then, calls for a more sophisticated and nuanced approach to the gathering of oral accounts as well as their interpretation.[7] Portelli explained: "[W]hat is really important is that memory is not a passive depository of facts, but an active process of creation of meanings. Thus, the specific utility of oral sources for the historian lies, not so much in their ability to preserve the past, as in the very changes wrought by memory. These changes reveal the narrators' effort to make sense of the past and to give a form to their lives, and set the interview and the narrative in their historical context."[8]

The present volume relies on a mixture of oral testimony and other sources to tell the stories of people who were forcibly removed from their homes either by government action or (in the case of Keowee-Toxaway) private enterprise acting with the support of government. While the experiences of these people varied in a number of ways, they are fundamentally narratives of loss. But what, exactly, is the nature of the loss? Was it material and easily quantifiable? Was it primarily emotional? Are there patterns that determine how those who lived through it, and their descendants, will remember and commemorate it?

The first people to lose Appalachian land to the federal government were the Cherokee of North Georgia, Western North Carolina, and East Tennessee. Ironically, many of the white settlers who moved into the open tracts beginning in the 1830s were displaced from the same land by the federal government in the century that followed. The story of the Cherokee Removal, which became known as the "Trail of Tears," is an essential and canonical element in the great American national narrative. Southerners, in particular, were strongly attached to the romanticized version of the Cherokee Removal, as it mirrored and complemented their own "Lost Cause" mythology. Southerners venerated Seminole leader Osceola because of his supposed similarities to Robert E. Lee, and their monuments to the "lost" Catawba and Pascagoula tribes reflected their preoccupation with doomed romantic causes. Indeed, it was southerners who popularized the term "Trail of Tears," conflated the experiences of all of the removed southeastern tribes under the Cherokee umbrella, and recast the narrative accordingly.[9] As Theda Perdue explained: "Collapsing all of removal history into one sentimental narrative featuring the Cherokee simplified the past for non-Indians while, in effect, denying the suffering of many other native peoples. But it was not the Indians whom white southerners were really interested in—it was themselves. By mourning the tragedy of removal, southerners absolved themselves of guilt for the actions of their ancestors and responsibility for the plight of Indians who remained."[10]

The removal narrative popularized by southerners quite explicitly blames the federal government for the tragedy, which conveniently dovetails with the "states' rights" interpretation of the Civil War that became virtually canonical in southern civil religion in the postbellum era. By casting southerners and Native Americans alike as victims of a power-hungry federal government run amok, this mythology effectively cements an allegiance of identity between the two groups. Memory and commemoration thus meld into fiction seamlessly.[11]

The tendency to romanticize history is even more prevalent when either money or political influence is at stake. The Cherokee outdoor historical drama *Unto These Hills* is a staple of the tourist experience for those visiting the town of Cherokee, North Carolina. Created just after World War II, it presents a highly romanticized version of the events surrounding the Trail of Tears. Noble Cherokee, misled by unscrupulous federal agents, are driven out of their homeland, except for a handful who hid in the wilderness and fought back in a doomed effort to preserve traditional ways of life. Many members of the Eastern Band of the Cherokee found *Unto These Hills* reductionist and frankly insulting. In the 1990s, the Eastern Band hired a native author to update the script to more accurately reflect the group's post-removal life and culture, not merely persisting and surviving but adapting and in some cases even thriving in these new circumstances. But tourists were disappointed. They wanted to see the "noble savage" mythology, inaccuracies and all. Attendance figures dropped precipitously, and eventually the script was rewritten again to meet the expectations of the visitors whose dollars translated directly into economic benefits for the local population.[12]

While the story of the Eastern Band of the Cherokee is in many ways unique, later groups displaced by federal action often identified with the Trail of Tears and co-opted it for their own purposes. The setting is an idealized, almost Edenic mountain community, the people are generally like-minded and congenial, and daily life is challenging but rewarding. The federal government is cast—always—as the villain in these stories. The brave struggle of the individual seeking to remain free is a narrative of a doomed hero. While such a story, possessing clear lines between good and evil, is undoubtedly appealing, it is of course heavily sentimentalized and frequently at odds with the actual lived experience of those whom federal actions displaced.

Countering this hero narrative is the progress narrative, in which government, informed by the expertise of scientists, engineers, and economists, mobilizes itself for the common good, and those who oppose it are cast as stubborn, backward-thinking, or willfully uninformed. This narrative, whose proponents included the Tennessee Valley Authority, the US Forest Service, and the National Park Service, became the dominant one promulgated through regional and local newspapers, with the endorsement of local elites.

These local elites played a crucial role in "selling" federal projects to their communities, and in relaying local concerns back to the responsible agencies. The extent to which these individuals were committed to their role, and their competence in performing it, would help determine whether the project would be completed with the cooperation of locals or over their objections. Their attitudes, perhaps even more than the policies of the agencies they worked for, would linger as a source of either good or ill will.

From the beginning, government agencies charged with responsibility for what TVA called "population readjustment" or "removal" frequently hired local people as intermediaries, relying on the personal attributes of these individuals and their relationships with the rest of the community to ease the transition and perhaps streamline negotiations. Charged with responsibility for comprehensive regional development, TVA's mission encompassed scientific agriculture, navigation, flood control, and even recreation in addition to the centerpiece, inexpensive electric power through the construction of hydroelectric plants. In part because of its expansive mission, TVA attracted reformers of many different types and served as a mechanism through which, it hoped, the nation's "number one economic problem" would be "fixed." TVA's showpiece, its proof-of-concept project, was the Norris Dam, located on the Clinch River some twenty miles north of the city of Knoxville. Norris Dam was to be the first dam built by the agency, and while other construction projects would be larger or more controversial, none would displace as many families. The basin flooded by the creation of the dam was composed of land of variable quality, mostly unsuitable for large farms, but it did support a good number of small family farms that faced increasing population pressure as relatives from urban areas moved "back home" to avoid starvation.

Since Norris Dam was TVA's first project, it bore the weight of expectations heavily. As the agency was itself experiencing internal conflict over its mission, while simultaneously engaging in centralized planning for which there was no federal precedent, the agency inevitably sent out mixed messages about what residents could expect. Honest miscommunication was frequent, and it was compounded by attitudes of condescension on the part of TVA planners, including Arthur E. Morgan, who chaired the agency's board of directors.[13]

At Norris, which included a massive hydroelectric dam and a small planned community for white residents to occupy in the following decades, the process of planning for resettling displaced families was fraught with difficulties. Morgan's vision of resettlement was driven by his idealization of family farms and his desire to use TVA to showcase "model community development" for the future.

Unfortunately, such a vision proved difficult to implement because of the rapid pace of land acquisition and construction—and the poverty of many of the area's residents. Other agencies with which Morgan hoped to partner seldom subordinated their own agendas to that of TVA, and more pragmatic administrators found him difficult to work with. Tenant farmers proved particularly difficult to relocate, as they had little or no capital available, and the agency moved slowly in creating a separate office to assist them.[14]

In some of the less remote parts of the Tennessee Valley, the farm population included significant numbers of African American farmers, most of whom—unlike their counterparts in the Deep South—owned their own land. While East Tennessee's Black farmers were significantly better off than their counterparts in the rest of the state, they were nonetheless poorer than most white farmers in the area. TVA's early projects at Fort Loudoun and Watts Bar affected notably large African American communities. TVA's relocation-assistance policy during this period involved referring displaced families to local agencies rather than providing direct assistance. Thus, absent any strong federal leadership on behalf of African Americans, the agency effectively capitulated to the social attitudes of local officials rather than attempting to narrow the economic gap between Black and white households.[15]

TVA's muddled approach to providing relocation assistance frustrated even its own officials. In particular, several relocation workers complained that the agency failed to account for informal land-use agreements not formally recorded. This proved to be particularly worrisome for small farmers whose way of life included hunting, fishing, and gathering forest resources. Historian Nancy L. Grant reported that the agency employed only one African American relocation agent for the large swath of northern Alabama affected by Wilson and Wheeler dams, despite 25 percent of the area's population being Black. Unlike their East Tennessee counterparts, these families lived in separate communities from whites, and some 80 percent were sharecroppers. Their already precarious economic situation was made worse by a more rigid set of segregation practices as well. TVA therefore found itself moving entire Black communities, already cut off from white society, into even more remote places in an effort to avoid taking responsibility for any offense nearby whites might feel. Here, too, as in the case of relocating individual families, these efforts appear half-hearted when compared with the assistance provided to white communities.[16]

Later TVA projects at Fort Loudon and Watts Bar, west of Knoxville, employed professional relocation workers, generally white southerners educated in either sociology or agriculture. These officials seldom if ever questioned the prevailing segregationist attitudes and practices, and (whether consciously or otherwise) helped to perpetuate both racial stereotypes and economic disparity. Historian Melissa Walker noted that some forms of assistance were simply unavailable to Black families, regardless of whether they owned or rented their land. She concluded that "TVA's policies and its workers served to dispossess many African American farmowners from locations where they had . . . an unusually good chance of success at achieving the agency's own agricultural vision."[17]

By the time TVA began building Fontana Dam, not quite nine years later, the agency's approach had evolved further. Public statements from the directors, which no longer included Arthur Morgan, were rare. As with Fort Loudoun and Watts Barr, communication with area residents was handled by readjustment workers, hired for the Population Readjustment Division and chosen because of their ties to the region and their education level. These individuals became the face of TVA, for good or ill. Arnold Hyde, a former teacher in Graham County, North Carolina, had one foot in the Little Tennessee River Valley and the other firmly planted among the forces of modernization, thanks to his education at Western Carolina Teachers' College (now Western Carolina University). Of the mountain community of Stecoah, eight miles from his Robbinsville home, Hyde wrote:

> A majority of the homes are in extremely poor condition, which not only reflects something of the economic condition of the family but reflects in many instances the lack of pride as well as initiative in making necessary improvements on the farm. . . . Often the chickens roost in the shade trees in the yard and the pigs run loose around the house. The toilets are placed over open streams, and flies breed unmolested around the house and barnyard. All of these insanitary [sic] practices point to the reluctance of the mountaineer to make modern improvements and develop a cooperative community spirit.[18]

Note that Hyde was not describing an individual household. He used instead a composite portrait—a stereotype—to emphasize the distance between his own expectations and those of the Stecoah residents. Hyde also betrayed his own religious biases when he described an abandoned Methodist church building at Judson that "serve[d] as a stark reminder of the more progressive days when Methodists lived and worshipped among the native Baptists."[19]

If Hyde was impatient with his neighbors, fellow TVA representative Rome C. Sharp, a former teacher from Tennessee, was downright dismissive. Sharp's report on Proctor, the largest community displaced by the Fontana Dam project, asserted that "on the edge of the preserved forest primeval—among the pioneers—for all but a sixth of the people, literacy meant only the ability to sign a relief receipt." Sharp failed to acknowledge that the community he described was built by an Ohio lumber company and had, at its peak, perhaps twelve hundred residents; both Proctor's poverty and its supposed lack of community organization were quite recent developments.[20]

TVA's high-handed management of land acquisition and population resettlement at Fontana and other projects left a bitter taste in the mouths of locals. The reputation of the Park Service suffered because of similar attitudes. As Alyssa D. Warrick recounted, Robert Holland's management of land acquisition for Mammoth Cave National Park created massive ill will through tactics such as tearing down homes that were still occupied. A tense relationship erupted into gunfire and widespread arson, and the long human history of the region was largely erased by the Park Service.

Missteps like those at Fontana and Mammoth Cave were not inevitable. Sarah Mittlefehldt, in her study of the acquisition of land for the Appalachian Trail, found that the "people's path" reflected unusual alliances and led to the establishment of a new model—the public-private partnership. The trail originated from an association of local conservation groups rather than government initiative, but it did benefit from relationships with the National Park Service and US Forest Service, both of which offered expertise and legal assistance. Because the trail was neither dominated by engineering concerns (as the sites for dams or roads might be) nor by grassroots boosters (as park sites might be), the usual conflicts did not materialize; rather, the shifting dynamics of the acquisition process reflected the role of local mediators, especially those with a long history of volunteer involvement.[21]

After more than forty years of development, parts of the Appalachian Trail had become uncomfortably close to public roads, businesses, and other facilities, undermining the quiet atmosphere many hikers desired. The need for route changes, which had previously been addressed in an informal and piecemeal fashion, became more acute, and Congress responded by expanding the authority of federal agencies in the area. This threatened to upset the delicate balance of interests that had maintained the trail since 1925. The passage of the National Trails Act in 1968 placed the trail more firmly within the sphere of Park Service influence, though no single federal agency owned it. Beginning in 1977, the Park Service began to assert more aggressive prerogatives regarding inholdings, including review of any proposed route changes. Landowners fought the Park Service's increased clout through the establishment of the National Park Inholders Association, led by Charles Cushman.[22]

Few people lost their homes to the Appalachian Trail at any point in its history. But the taking of even small parcels changed the way the rest of the land would be used and thus altered the lives of residents in ways large and small. Moreover, the greater role of the federal government after 1968 fueled anxieties about heavy-handed bureaucracy. The Park Service combatted these fears through the use of minimal easements tailored to the needs of individual landowners along the trail, negotiated through the assistance of volunteers whose long relationship with the trail helped allay fears. As Mittlefehldt noted, "long-term volunteers often knew the local terrain and political dynamics more intimately than their federal partners did, and the park service hoped that basing decisions largely on the knowledge and experience of citizen volunteers might help overcome the negative images of federal acquisition programs that had spread throughout the national media." Eminent domain, the sledgehammer in the Park Service's toolbox, was the tool of last resort because of the desire to minimize public outcry—and legal expenses.[23]

Mittlefehldt found that the long-term attitude of area landowners toward the trail was often shaped by the effectiveness (or lack thereof) of these local coordinators. When coordinators became impatient or did not do the difficult work of building relationships, or unintentionally gave the impression that they were directly speaking for the federal government, conflicts often ensued. One notorious example, in the Cumberland Valley of Pennsylvania, became a *cause célèbre* that gained national media attention. The ultimate resolution, she wrote, "became the physical embodiment of both the conflict and the cooperation between local landowners, citizen volunteers, NPS officials, and a wide range of other interests—both local and nonlocal, public and private." The net result of the negotiations, within a few years, was a new model in which the Park Service would concentrate its resources on legal and administrative matters while delegating maintenance, preservation, and future land acquisition to the nonprofit, privately controlled Appalachian Trail Conference.[24]

If the National Park Service's shifting mission sometimes led to overuse of its power, the US Forest Service seems to have had less difficulty. While the NPS's mission targets areas of national significance and sometimes encompasses efforts to remove evidence of human habitation, the Forest Service, housed in the Department of Agriculture, makes no such claims. Rather, its emphasis on conservation, not preservation, makes it a natural ally of landowners so long as their concerns are given adequate voice in the planning process.

Much of the land the National Forest Resources Council initially acquired for Jefferson National Forest was cutover or abandoned mountain land that was of little or no value to the absentee logging and mining companies who held title to it. Thus, there were few small landowners with whom to negotiate, and little farmland to be taken out of cultivation. Government officials presented condemnation as a "friendly" legal process to clarify improperly recorded titles or address inadequately surveyed lands. Once these large holdings had been placed under federal ownership, small holdings generally proceeded with minimal conflict. Residents often received "special use permits" that allowed them lifetime occupancy while relieving them of the burden of property taxes, in contrast to the wholesale depopulation in other areas. Will Sarvis explicitly contrasted the Forest Service's approach to the "massive, concentrated, and aggressive acquisition of a consolidated area" associated with the National Park Service and the Tennessee Valley Authority in their acquisition of lands for Shenandoah and Great Smoky Mountains national parks and the Norris Basin.[25]

Training encouraged Forest Service rangers to integrate themselves as fully as possible into the local community. Their efforts frequently included hiring local residents for fire control—a seasonal but ongoing employment opportunity in contrast to the temporary "boom town" relationship that emerged where TVA built dams. By focusing on sustainability and ongoing mixed use rather than quick exploitation, the Forest Service gained local allies relatively easily, and by leading with a gentle hand rather than governing with technocratic insistence, it encountered much less resistance from locals. Selective timbering, hunting, and fishing allowed local residents both a connection to their existing ways of life and sustainable, managed access to a cash economy. Forest rangers also frequently looked the other way when they encountered evidence of illegal activity such as moonshining. In doing so, they gained the trust of the locals and avoided the perception that the federal government was an enemy of Appalachian families.[26]

As with the Jefferson National Forest, the Blue Ridge Parkway's success or failure would rest largely on the relationships between government officials and local community leaders. Before the construction of the Blue Ridge Parkway, the Peaks of Otter community in Virginia was somewhat typical of mountain communities. A range of economic activities took place, from subsistence farming to small-scale commercial farming, logging, and tourist activities. The Mons Hotel coexisted with local farms, purchasing commodities from them and often employing family members on a casual basis. Local residents of whatever economic stripe pursued gains and improved their property as opportunity presented itself. The land itself

changed hands many times, and the areas deemed most attractive for tourism, purchased by outside interests in the 1870s, came back into the hands of local business
interests before being deeded to the Park Service in 1937. The Peaks of Otter Lodge
operates as the only hotel on the Blue Ridge Parkway in Virginia.[27]

The construction of the Blue Ridge Parkway, more than thirty years in the making, altered residents' options for economic gains. It also gave the Park Service the
lead in presenting the area's history. The Park Service worked diligently to present
an attractive landscape, but its efforts included demolition of relatively modern
structures and the creation of intentionally rustic ones to replace them. The history
to which visitors were exposed was thus highly selective, overly romanticized, and
ultimately alienating. Like their Cherokee counterparts whose history was reduced
to melodrama in *Unto These Hills,* the locals whose stories were essentially erased
from the Peaks of Otter story told by the Park Service expressed their displeasure
and attempted, with limited success, to take control of their own narrative.[28]

Unlike Peaks of Otter, much of Grandfather Mountain in North Carolina
remained in the hands of an absentee landowner when construction of the Blue
Ridge Parkway began. Far from the sturdy yeoman mountaineers that even scholars of Appalachia regarded as the archetype of the region, the owners envisioned
exploiting the mountains from afar, for their timber and mining resources. Wealthy
industrialist Hugh MacRae, of the coastal city of Wilmington, led the Linville
Improvement Company, which began developing the area around Grandfather
Mountain in 1875. His son Nelson MacRae had managed the growth of the up-
scale Linville resort community while timbering paid the bills, and locals, including a small number of African Americans, worked for low but steady wages. The
MacRaes had attempted to get Grandfather Mountain designated as the center
of a national park in the Appalachian South, but they lost out to the promoters
of the Great Smoky Mountains National Park. After that and several subsequent
attempts to sell the land to the federal government failed, logging efforts accelerated in an effort to prop up the company's finances as the nation struggled with the
Great Depression.[29]

After the deaths of Hugh and Nelson MacRae, Nelson's nephew Hugh Morton
came into possession of the property at a time when its scenic value and its economic value were very much in question. Under the advice of his brother-in-law
Norman Cocke, Morton came to distrust the Park Service. Morton's tenure coincided with the post–World War II tourism boom, and he sought to redevelop
the Grandfather Mountain area through private efforts alone. Through legal ma-
neuvers and an astute public relations campaign, Morton successfully portrayed

The National Park Service shaped the rural Peaks of Otter community as a tourist destination for motorists traveling the Blue Ridge Parkway. The privately operated Peaks of Otter lodge is the only hotel on the Blue Ridge Parkway. Peaks of Otter, Abbott Lake, by David Haas, ca. 1990s, Historic American Buildings Survey/Historic American Record/Historic American Landscapes Survey, Library of Congress Prints and Photographs Division, Washington, DC.

himself as both an environmentalist and a champion of private property rights while casting the Park Service as the "big government" villain. He also profited handsomely from an image of the area as relatively untouched by human hands, even though it had less than two decades earlier been so heavily logged that it was nicknamed "Stump Town" and Morton had spearheaded the environmentally destructive expansion of the privately owned toll road to the mountain's summit. Morton's mythic "mountain that didn't deserve to be conquered" boasted a visitor center with a gift shop, a snack bar, and a two-hundred-seat assembly hall. As historian Anne Whisnant put it, "Twinned with the ubiquitous swinging bridge icon was the mountain's new mascot, a black bear named Mildred . . . at once evoking the (now safely captured) wildness of the 'unconquered' mountain and the warm fuzziness of sentimentalized, marketable nature."[30]

While Morton's behavior was perhaps duplicitous, it could be legitimately seen as a response to Park Service accommodation policies which Whisnant claims "seemed determined to shut out local entrepreneurs." One of the most important selling points for national parks, at least to local residents, was economic benefit, and many, including Morton, regarded the Park Service as both dishonest and obstructionist in its awarding of exclusive concessions.

From these examples we might conclude that it is possible to maintain a positive and mutually beneficial relationship between the agency responsible for taking land and those who were affected directly by it. Conversely, the misuse of authority or any displays of detachment or arrogance by government officials certainly fed distrust and allowed it to fester. But it is also possible that people remember their losses differently for other reasons.

About six hundred people once called the town of Butler, Tennessee, home. More than a half-century after the town was inundated for the creation of Watauga Lake, some of them—and some of their descendants who were not yet born when the dam was built—still do. An annual "Butler Days" homecoming celebration commemorates the town's demise. As media historian Christie Kleinmann demonstrated, the stories of the town's life and death as reported in local newspapers have undergone significant changes. As Kleinmann explained, "the variance of a shared memory suggests that memory is a dynamic discourse that retells the past based on an individual's perception of the *present*."[31]

While TVA began to plan and build support for the construction of Watauga Dam in the late 1930s and early 1940s, local newspapers described the project in glowing terms, lauding both flood control and the potential for job growth through cheap electricity. More distant newspapers emphasized instead the project's contribution to the coming war effort. Neither local nor regional news-papers made any substantial mention of what Kleinmann calls "the Butler resident perspective." A massive flood in 1940 helped spur local support for the project, and accounts of the damage became more sensationalized after TVA placed the dam on hold due to wartime shortages.[32]

The resumption of the project after the war yielded another round of booster-ism, but this time journalists acknowledged the price of progress. Regional and na-tional newspapers applauded the town's "sacrifice" in the face of inevitable change, while local outlets continued to assert that "Butler residents were giving up little and gaining much" from the project. Residents appear here as sturdy but ultimately doomed pioneers from a bygone era. By the time the dam was finished and the town inundated, the dominant storyline credited TVA with bringing hope to a town that was dying anyway due to the loss of rail access.[33]

Repair work on the dam in 1983 led to the draining of the lake and the un-covering of the original townsite. This time, the story was different. Local press interviewed residents displaced by the project, and their accounts emphasized what they saw as their own helplessness and TVA's unfairness. They sometimes described Butler in exaggerated terms, as a "prosperous" or "bustling" town with "ten stores," minimizing the hardships they had experienced there. By 1998, press coverage associated with the fiftieth anniversary of the dam and coinciding with another maintenance round showed at least one resident asserting that govern-ment employees would be killed by angry residents if they had done what they did "this day and time."[34]

Like their counterparts at Butler, those displaced by Fontana Dam have held frequent reunions to commemorate their loss. Their grief was exacerbated by sev-eral factors. First, much of the land TVA took for Fontana was not inundated, but merely cut off from road access. TVA deeded that land (the North Shore land) to the Park Service, also promising the construction of a replacement road to al-low access to the former townsites, which included numerous cemeteries. Between 1943, when the agreement was finalized, and 2018, when the controversy was finally settled, area residents nursed a sense of grievance against the federal government over the matter. For many of these residents, the North Shore Road symbolized a federal government that was out of touch with its constituents, and that alienation merged local concerns over the road with broader currents in American political life, as when Ronald Reagan asserted that "government is not the solution to the problem—government is the problem."[35]

In 1948, the town of Butler, Tennessee, in Johnson County was relocated to higher ground to make way for Watauga Dam and reservoir. During drought or lake drawdown, descendants of the displaced organize homecoming events to visit the original site of the town. Watauga Lake/Town of Butler, Tennessee before flooding from Watauga Dam, June 1, 1947, TVA's Historic Photograph Collection, Records of the Tennessee Valley Authority, Record Group 142, National Archives, Atlanta.

Bitterness over the outcome of the Fontana Dam project took multiple forms. Two of these are particularly interesting. The controversy over the designation of certain parts of the Great Smoky Mountains National Park as permanent wilderness—especially the North Shore of Fontana Lake, which TVA had confiscated and then deeded to the GSMNP in 1944—inspired the creation of a group called Citizens Against Wilderness in the 1980s. The group used the then-unfulfilled North Shore Road agreement as an excuse to demand that forty-four thousand acres be removed from the park and opened for private industrial development. In their view, environmentalists had conspired with the state of Tennessee to keep North Carolina's portion of the park underdeveloped.[36]

While Citizens Against Wilderness focused their attention on lost potential for economic development, the North Shore Cemetery Association, later renamed the North Shore Historical Association, emphasized access to the affected land for descendants of those buried in cemeteries there. By emphasizing what they believed they had lost, and by placing a sympathetic face on the cause in the person of the North Shore Historical Association's president, Helen Vance, the group gained much public sympathy. Vance, a personable and sympathetic character, became the face of the Fontana removals, collaborating with journalists to create an image of the lost communities of the North Shore that was romantic, idyllic, and tragic. Vance and others also sued TVA, the Department of the Interior, Swain County, and the State of North Carolina, asserting that these government entities had violated their First Amendment right to free exercise of their religious beliefs, by making it inconvenient or impossible for them to visit the graves of family members.[37]

While the district court dismissed the suit, its very premise—that visiting graves is an inherently religious practice—is intriguing. For some displaced residents, their lost land represents lost economic opportunity, lost potential, or a lost (if perhaps exaggerated) past prosperity. For others, the loss is as much spiritual or psychological as it is economic. Perhaps, as in other "narratives of the fall," part of what they have lost is the innocence of youth itself, and their nostalgia for that carefree life melds seamlessly with their grief over lost loved ones and lost economic opportunities.[38] As Matthew Chisholm explained, the recent final government payment to Swain County did not fully bring closure to the controversy. As Helen Vance put it, "It's not too much to ask, to go back home, is it?"[39]

Vance's question reverberates throughout all of Appalachia. The stories found here are compelling and sometimes tragic. They may also tell us, as Portelli suggests, more about the storyteller than about the events as they took place. Appalachians, like other Americans, saw the possible advantages that could be delivered by a pro-active, reform-minded federal government in the early decades of the twentieth century. They saw the nation's priorities shift toward military superiority on land and sea, in air and in space. They saw Americans land on the moon. They saw disillusionment with a government that seemed increasingly alienated from those it served as the Great Society of the 1960s gave way to Vietnam, Watergate, and economic malaise. They heard Ronald Reagan declare that less government is a better government.

They did not just see these developments. They lived them. And then they told their stories. Along the way, they made their antecedents into heroes who built their lives out of timber and soil, and into victims who were swindled out of their birthright by an impersonal, even evil, Leviathan. They identified with Native Americans while minimizing or forgetting entirely the experience of African Americans in Appalachia. They erased from their stories elements they could not explain, or did not want to explain, thus memorializing an Appalachia that was simpler, more prosperous, ethnically homogeneous, and at times so idealized as to bear little resemblance to the circumstances under which their parents, grandparents, and great-grandparents actually lived. They decided that they could not go back to the home that few of them had ever known, but through memory they and their descendants could return to an imagined past that never was.

Contributors

MARGARET LYNN BROWN is associate professor of history at Brevard College in Brevard, North Carolina. The author of *The Wild East: A Biography of the Great Smoky Mountains National Park*, Brown teaches environmental history, the history of wilderness, and engages her students in oral history projects. She writes a monthly blog on nature and history.

MATTHEW CHISHOLM is a high-school humanities teacher at Montford Hall in Asheville, a therapeutic boarding school for boys in recovery. Previously he taught history and started the Adventure Racing Program at Christ School, an Episcopal school for boys near Asheville. Chisholm received an MA in environmental history from the University of North Carolina, Charlotte, in 2012 with a focus on memory in the Southern Appalachians. He received the McClung Award in 2016 for his article "The Arrival of the Road to Nowhere: Memory and Myth in the Great Smoky Mountains' North Shore Road Controversy" in *The Journal of East Tennessee History*. He lives in Weaverville, North Carolina, with his wife, daughter, and twin boys.

AUSTIN GREGORY is a native of Oconee County, South Carolina, and is a recent graduate of East Tennessee State's Appalachian studies master's degree program.

SAVANNAH PAIGE MURRAY is a visiting assistant professor of rhetoric and writing studies in the Department of English at Appalachian State University, where she teaches expository writing, writing across the curriculum, business writing, and technical writing. In 2020, she earned a PhD in rhetoric and writing at Virginia Tech. Murray's research focuses on commons environmentalism, Appalachian rhetoric, and environmental discourses. Her work has appeared in journals such as *Appalachian Journal*, the *Journal of Appalachian Studies*, and *The Journal of East Tennessee History*.

RUSSELL OLWELL is associate professor of education and associate dean at the School of Education and Social Policy, Merrimack College, North Andover,

Massachusetts. He is the author of *At Work in the Atomic City: A Labor and Social History of Oak Ridge, Tennessee* (2014), as well as books about nuclear nonproliferation and youth mentoring. His latest work focuses on early college and dual enrollment as strategies for educational change.

KATRINA M. POWELL is professor of English at Virginia Tech. She is the author of *The Anguish of Displacement: The Politics of Literacy in the Letters of Mountain Families in Shenandoah National Park* (2007) and *Identity and Power in Narratives of Displacement* (2015). Her current work focuses on the dissemination of displacement and refugee narratives and the ethical dimensions of collecting those narratives in alternative spaces. With support from the nonprofit Voice of Witness, she is conducting an oral history and edited book project called "Resettled: Beginning (Again) in Appalachia."

AARON D. PURCELL is professor and director of Special Collections and University Archives at Virginia Tech. He has published several books in the fields of history and archives, including, as editor, *The Digital Archives Handbook: A Guide to Creation, Management, and Preservation* (2019); *Donors and Archives: Building Successful Donor Programs in Archives* (2015); *Arthur Morgan: A Progressive Vision for American Reform* (2014); as editor, *The New Deal and the Great Depression* (2014); and *White Collar Radicals: TVA's Knoxville Fifteen, the New Deal, and the McCarthy Era* (2009). He has served as the editor of *The Journal of East Tennessee History* since 2009. Purcell is completing a book of edited Civil War letters from an Ohio surgeon and working on a book about the environmental and economic development of Cumberland Falls in Southeastern Kentucky.

STEPHEN WALLACE TAYLOR is professor of history at Middle Georgia State University. He holds a PhD from the University of Tennessee, and his current research focuses on authenticity and commemoration in public memory. He is the author of *The New South's New Frontier: A Social History of Economic Development in Southwestern North Carolina* (2001).

ALYSSA D. WARRICK was born and reared in the Missouri Ozarks before earning her undergraduate degree in history from Truman State University. She completed her PhD in history at Mississippi State University and is currently teaching at Montgomery College in Maryland.

Notes

Introduction

1. This quote appears on the dedication plaque of the Rockefeller Memorial; see https://www.pigeonforge.com/great-smoky-mountains-national-park/rockefeller -monument/.

2. Franklin D. Roosevelt, *The Public Papers and Addresses of Franklin D. Roosevelt* (New York: Macmillan Co., 1941), vol. 9: 370 (first quote), 370–71 (second quote).

3. Existing TVA removal records available in TVA Record Group 142, National Archives and Records Administration, near Atlanta, include several Whaley families (with different spellings), but none are listed for the Norris project.

4. Daniel S. Pierce, *Great Smokies: From Natural Habitat to National Park* (Knoxville: University of Tennessee Press, 2000), 172; Daniel S. Pierce, "The Barbarism of the Huns: Family and Community Removal in the Establishment of the Great Smoky Mountains National Park," *Tennessee Historical Quarterly* 57 (Spring–Summer 1998): 76.

5. Daniel S. Pierce's interview with Glenn Cardwell on March 21, 1995, is the main source for the Whaley family's removal story. Pierce referred to this interview in both his book and his article on the creation of the Great Smoky Mountains National Park in the above note.

6. Alessandro Portelli, *The Death of Luigi Trastulli and Other Stories* (Albany: State University of New York Press, 1991).

7. Durwood Dunn, *Cades Cove: The Life and Death of a Southern Appalachian Community, 1818–1937* (Knoxville: University of Tennessee Press, 1988); Ronald J. Foresta, *The Land Between the Lakes: A Geography of a Forgotten Future* (Knoxville: University of Tennessee Press, 2013).

8. Kathryn Newfont, *Blue Ridge Commons: Environmental Activism and Forest History in Western North Carolina* (Athens: University of Georgia Press, 2012); Sara M. Gregg, *Managing the Mountains: Land Use Planning, the New Deal, and the Creation of a Federal Landscape in Appalachia* (New Haven, CT: Yale University Press, 2010).

9. Michael J. McDonald and John Muldowny, *TVA and the Dispossessed: The Resettlement of Population in the Norris Dam Area* (Knoxville: University of Tennessee Press, 1982), 67–68.

10. For studies of the Cherokee Removal and the effects of cultural dislocation on the Cherokee Nation, see Brian Hicks, *Toward the Setting Sun: John Ross, the Cherokees, and the Trail of Tears* (New York: Atlantic Monthly Press, 2011); William L. Anderson, ed., *Cherokee Removal: Before and After* (Athens: University of Georgia Press, 1991); Wilson Lumpkin, *The Removal of the Cherokee Indians From Georgia* (New York: Arno Press,1969); John Ehle, *Trail of Tears: The Rise and Fall of the Cherokee Nation* (New York: Doubleday, 1988); John R. Finger, *The Eastern Band of the Cherokees, 1819–1900* (Knoxville: University of Tennessee Press, 1984); Theda Perdue and Michael D. Green, *The Cherokee Nation and the Trail of Tears* (New York: Penguin Books, 2007).

11. Overview sources of the historical development and application of eminent domain include David Schultz, *Evicted! Property Rights and Eminent Domain in America* (Santa Barbara: ABC-CLIO, 2010); Richard A. Epstein, *Takings: Private Property and the Power of Eminent Domain* (Cambridge, MA: Harvard University Press, 1985); James W. Ely, *The Guardians of Every Other Rights: A Constitutional History of Property Rights* (New York: Oxford University Press, 2007); "History of the Federal Use of Eminent Domain," https://www.justice.gov/enrd/history-federal-use-eminent-domain; William B. Stoebuck, "A General Theory of Eminent Domain," *Washington Law Review* 47 (1972): 553–79; Errol E. Meidinger, "The Public Uses of Eminent Domain: History and Policy," *Environmental Law* 11 (Fall 1980): 1–66.

12. See Kyle Scott, *The Price of Politics: Lessons from Kelo v. City of New London* (Lanham, MD: Rowman and Littlefield, 2009); Dana Berliner, *Public Power, Private Gain: A Five-Year, State-by-State Report Examining the Abuse of Eminent Domain* (Washington, DC: Institute for Justice, 2003); Douglas A. Boyd, *Crawfish Bottom: Recovering a Lost Kentucky Community* (Lexington: University Press of Kentucky, 2013).

13. *United States Code Annotated,* Title 16. Conservation, Chapter 12A-Tennessee Valley Authority, § 831C. Corporate Powers Generally; eminent domain; construction of dams, transmission lines, etc., section, H, I (quote).

14. "Theodore Roosevelt and Conservation," National Park Service, https://www.nps.gov/thro/learn/historyculture/theodore-roosevelt-and-conservation.htm; "American Antiquities Act of 1906, 16 USC 431–433," National Park Services, https://www.nps.gov/history/local-law/anti1906.htm; Douglas Brinkley, *The Wilderness Warrior: Theodore Roosevelt and the Crusade for America* (New York: HarperCollins, 2009).

15. Dyan Zaslowsky and T. H. Watkins, *These American Lands: Parks, Wilderness, and the Public Lands* (Washington, DC: Wilderness Society).

16. Douglas Brinkley, *Rightful Heritage: Franklin D. Roosevelt and the Land of America* (New York: Harper Perennial, 2016), 590–608.

17. See Christopher J. Manganiello, *Southern Water, Southern Power: How the Politics of Cheap Energy and Water Scarcity Shaped a Region* (Chapel Hill: University of North Carolina Press, 2015).

18. General planning. This photograph is included in the series as a vivid document on the impingement of the Twentieth Century technology upon the neglected and backward rural scene. The meter on the wall of the rural shack indicates that is now receives its share of electricity from the power carried overland by the huge TVA (Tennessee Valley Authority) transmission line. TVA program must resolve the conflict between modern and ancient ways of life so that individuals, similar to those which are show in the picture, will be benefited. US Farm Security Administration/Office of War Information Black and White Photographs, 1933-1945, Library of Congress Prints and Photographs Division.

19. "Appalachian Counties Served by ARC," Appalachian Regional Commission, https://www.arc.gov/appalachian-counties-served-by-arc/.

20. Ben Pounds, "New K-25 Center Opens!" *Oakridger,* March 2, 2020, https://www .oakridger.com/news/20200302/new-k-25-center-opens; K-15 Virtual Museum, http://www.k-25virtualmuseum.org/.

1   Loss, Betrayal, and the Power of Stories

1. Dunn, *Cades Cove,* 179.

2. G. Walter Gregory to John D. Rockefeller, June 18, 1928, box 9, folder 9, Great Smoky Mountains Conservation Association Records, Great Smoky Mountains National Park Archives, Townsend, TN (GSMNP Archives).

3. Margaret Lynn Brown, *The Wild East: A Biography of the Great Smoky Mountains* (Gainesville: University of Florida Press, 2000), 96–97.

4. The eighty dollars per acre Gregory received for his land was among the highest rate paid. Brown, *The Wild East,* 96–97.

5. The capitalization of "Sacrifice" is in the original document. John Oliver to Harold Edwards, July 10, 1936, box 3, file 3, Condemnation of Lands: *Tenn. v. John Oliver et al.,* GSMNP Archives; Dunn, *Cades Cove,* 254.

6. Jim Gaines, "Sevier County's Fall Tourism on Track for Record Receipts," *Knox News,* August 30, 2018, https://www.knoxnews.com/story/money/business /2018/08/30/sevier-county-tourism-outlook-strong-fall-2018/1085784002/; "Great Smoky Mountains National Park sees record visitation"; *AP News,* February 22, 2019, https://www.apnews.com/845955bb7a08453384b1oeeabda45072.

7. Bruce J. Weaver, "What to Do with the Mountain People?": The Darker Side of the Successful Campaign to Establish the Great Smoky Mountains National Park," in *The Symbolic Earth: Discourse and Our Creation of the Environment*, ed. James G. Cantrell and Christine L. Oravec (Lexington: University Press of Kentucky, 1996), 173.

8. Richard Starnes, *Destination Dixie: Tourism and Southern History* (Gainesville: University Press of Florida, 2012), 280.

9. R. L. Noland to Ed Lloyd, April 10, 1930, enclosure, Floyd Store Ledger GRSM10299, GSMNP Archives.

10. Teresa Maples interview with Mrs. Ray Bohanon and Ruth Maples Hunter, November 23, 1981, box 1, folder 8, Great Smoky Mountains National Park Collection, Betsey B. Creekmore Special Collections and University Archives, University of Tennessee, Knoxville (Creekmore UTK).

11. Mark Coleman interview with Calvin Shields, July 21, 1997, box 1, folder 61, Great Smoky Mountains National Park Collection, Creekmore UTK.

12. Philip E. Coyle interview with Linton Palmer, July 27, 2004, Western Carolina University Oral History Collection, GSMNP Archives.

13. William Myers to Arno Cammerer, April 15, 1933; William Myers to David Chapman, April 19, 1933, all in box 3, file 25, Land Acquisition, GSMNP Archives.

14. John Foster Hays, "A History of Incendiary Fire in the Great Smoky Mountains National Park, 1931–1988," master's thesis, University of Southern Alabama, 1993, vii, 21–22.

15. Ibid.

16. Ibid., 28, 30, 37.

17. Philip E. Coyle interview with Mildred Thompson, Gladys Wright, and Lucille Cooke, February 18, 2004, Western Carolina University Oral History Collection, GSMNP Archives.

18. Jill Breit interview with Lucille Beck, June 28, 2005, Ravensford Project, Oral History Project, GSMNP Archives.

19. Matthew Tant interview with William Eugene Lequire, October 24, 1997, box 1, folder 48, Great Smoky Mountains National Park Collection, Creekmore UTK.

20. Ibid.

21. Brown, *The Wild East,* 71, 181; Philip E. Coyle interview with Gudger Palmer, August 10, 2004, Western Carolina University Oral History Collection, GSMNP Archives.

22. Coada was born in 1924, so he would have had a young child when he left Cades Cove. Mark Cole interview with Lee Roy Coada, July 22, 1997, box 1, folder 24, University of Tennessee Oral History Project, GSMNP Archives.

23. Lucinda Ogle, handwritten speech, 1994, box 2, folder 16, Lucinda Ogle Collection, Creekmore UTK.

24. Alan Jabbour interview with Shirley Crisp, August 3, 2004, box 62, folder 6, Western Carolina University Oral History Collection, GSMNP Archives.

25. Alan Jabbour and Karen Singer, *Decoration Day in the Mountains: Traditions of Cemetery Decoration in the Southern Appalachians* (Chapel Hill: University of North Carolina Press, 2010), 181, 182, 186.

26. Email from Michael Aday to Margaret Lynn Brown, May 21, 2019, in author's possession.

27. Philip E. Coyle interview with Larry Vickery, August 2, 2004, box 62, folder 5, Western Carolina University Oral History Collection, GSMNP Archives.

28. *Tennessee Valley Authority v. Welch et al.,* Legal Information Institute, Cornell Law School, https://www.law.cornell.edu/supremecourt/text/327/546.

29. Brown, *The Wild East,* 162–65.

30. Myrtle L. Laney, "Just Thinking of the Past," *Fontana Newsletter,* July 1986.

31. Philip E. Coyle interview with Helen Vance, September 5, 2002, box 1, folder 7, Western Carolina University Oral History Project, GSMNP Archives.

32. Ibid.

33. *Fontana Newsletter,* September 1986.

34. Ibid., Summer 1990.

35. Ibid., October 1987.

36. Email from Michael Aday to Margaret Lynn Brown, June 10, 2019, in author's possession.

37. *Smoky Mountain Times,* July 3, 2018.

38. "North Shore Heritage Memories," https://web.archive.org/web/20180324035637 /http://northshoreheritagememories.com/.

39. This story is told in detail in Finger, *The Eastern Band of Cherokees.* For an important work about how removal is remembered and memorialized by the National Park Service, see Andrew Denson, *Monuments to Absence: Cherokee Removal and the Contest over Southern Memory* (Chapel Hill: University of North Carolina Press, 2017).

40. Kevin Murphy interview with Bob Blankenship, August 11, 2004, Ravensford Tract Oral History Project, GSMNP Archives.

41. *Waynesville Mountaineer,* August 25, 1995.

42. Coyle interview with Vickery, August 2, 2004, Western Carolina University Oral History Collection, GSMNP Archives.

43. "Memories of Fish Trap Branch," *Fontana Newsletter,* Summer 1990.

44. Ibid.

2 At the Bottom of the Loyston Sea

Epigraph: Quoted in James Overholt, ed., *These Are Our Voices: The Story of Oak Ridge, 1942–1970* (Oak Ridge, TN: Children's Museum, 1987), 21–22.

1. TVA, *The Norris Project: A Comprehensive Report on the Planning, Design, Construction, and Initial Operations of the Tennessee Valley Authority's First Water Control Project* (Washington, DC: Government Printing Office, 1940); "Norris," TVA, https://www.tva.gov/Energy/Our-Power-System/Hydroelectric/Norris -Reservoir.

2. "Our History, Philosophy and Mission," Museum of Appalachia, at http://www .museumofappalachia.org/about-us/; Kathleen George Graves and Winnie Palmer McDonald, *Our Union County Heritage Vol II: A Pictorial–Genealogical Album*

of *Union County* ([Maynardville, TN]: K. G. Graves, 1981), 275; "John Rice Irwin,
Curator and Cultural Preservationist, Class of 1989," August 1, 1989, MacArthur
Foundation, at https://www.macfound.org/fellows/366/.

3. Glenn Irwin removal file, September 7, 1934, box 33; John Irwin removal file,
September 7, 1934, box 33; both in Tennessee Valley Authority, Family Removal
and Population Readjustment Case Files, 1937–48, Records of the Tennessee Valley
Authority, Record Group 142, National Archives, Atlanta (RG 142, NARA).

4. Glenn Irwin removal file, September 7, 1934, box 33; John Irwin removal file,
September 7, 1934, (quote), box 33; John Irwin removal file, October 15, 1935, box
45, all in Removal and Readjustment Files, RG 142, NARA; US Census, 1940,
Tennessee, Anderson County, Civil District 8, 6A; John Rice Irwin interview
with Keith McDaniel, June 17, 2011, Center for Oak Ridge Oral History, http://
cdm16107.contentdm.oclc.org/cdm/singleitem/collection/p15388coll1/id/66/rec/5.

5. "Hiking," Big Ridge State Park, https://tnstateparks.com/parks/activity-detail
/big-ridge-hiking.

6. "Lenoir Museum Cultural Complex," Norris Tennessee, Norris Dam State Park,
http://www.cityofnorris.com/id61.html; "Interpretative Programs and Events,"
Norris Dam State Park, Tennessee State Parks, https://tnstateparks.com/parks
/activity-detail/norris-dam-interpretive-programs.

7. C. Herman Pritchett, *The Tennessee Valley Authority: A Study in Public
Administration* (Chapel Hill: University of North Carolina Press, 1943), 313–24.

8. David E. Lilienthal, *TVA: Democracy on the March* (New York: Harper and Brothers,
1944), 139–40; Howard Segal, "Down in the Valley: David Lilienthal's *TVA:
Democracy on the March*," *American Scholar* 64 (June 1995): 424–25.

9. Philip Selznick, *TVA and the Grass Roots: A Study in the Sociology of Formal
Organization* (Berkeley: University of California Press, 1949), 262–66.

10. Donald Davidson, *The Tennessee, Volume II, The New River: Civil War to TVA* (New
York: Rinehart and Co., 1948), 257 (quote), 237–38, 254–57.

11. M. Harry Satterfield, "The Removal of Families from Tennessee Valley Authority
Reservoir Areas, *Social Forces* 16 (December 1937): 258–61.

12. Charles J. McCarthy, "Land Acquisition Policies and Proceedings in TVA—A Study
of the Role of Land Acquisition in a Regional Agency," *Ohio State Law Journal* 10
(Winter 1949): 49 (first quote), 47 (second quote), 47–49, 63; William Prather,
"'The Color of This Life Is Water': History, Stones, and the River in *Suttree*," *Cormac
McCarthy Journal* 4 (2003): 42–43; Charles McCarthy, "TVA and the Tennessee
Valley," *Town Planning Review* 21 (July 1950): 129 (third quote).

13. See Erwin C. Hargrove, *Prisoners of Myth: The Leadership of the Tennessee Valley
Authority, 1933–1990* (Knoxville: University of Tennessee Press, 2001); Aaron D.
Purcell, *Arthur Morgan: A Progressive Vision for American Reform* (Knoxville:
University of Tennessee Press, 2014); William Bruce Wheeler and Michael J.

McDonald, *TVA and the Tellico Dam, 1936–1979: A Bureaucratic Crisis in Post-Industrial America* (Knoxville: University of Tennessee Press, 1986).

14. See Michael J. McDonald, "V. Tennessee Valley Authority Records," *Journal of Agricultural History* 58 (April 1984): 127–37.

15. Tennessee Valley Authority, "Population Readjustment Handbook," March 1940, 2, box 75, in RG 142, NARA. In recent years, the National Archives and Records Administration partnered with Ancestry.com to create online access to over 19,500 removal files from TVA's official records. The digital content, which is freely available to anyone with an Internet connection, amounts to over 81,000 searchable pages worth of material. The files cover removal projects in Alabama, Georgia, Mississippi, North Carolina, Tennessee, and Virginia. Ancestry.com also offers access to cemetery relocation records, 1933–90, which amounts to a staggering 172,537 scanned pages of material. This official material alongside other searchable government sources such as the US Census, also searchable through Ancestry.com, makes it possible for researchers to recreate and analyze families and entire communities. "Records of the Tennessee Valley Authority (Record Group 142)," National Archives and Records Administration, https://www.archives.gov/research/guide-fed-records/groups /142.html; "U.S., Tennessee Valley, Family Removal and Population Readjustment Case Files, 1934–1953," Ancestry.com, https://www.ancestry.com/search/collections /4903/; "Tennessee Valley Authority Cemetery Relocation Files, 1933–1990," Ancestry.com, https://www.ancestry.com/search/collections/60427/.

16. McDonald and Muldowny, *TVA and the Dispossessed*, 67–68, 264–66.

17. Portelli, *The Death of Luigi Trastulli*, 2 (first quote), xiii (second quote), vii–ix, 1–3; McDonald and Muldowny, *TVA and the Dispossessed*, 29–68.

18. Michael Rogers, "TVA Population Removal: Attitudes and Expectations of the Dispossessed at the Norris and Cherokee Dam Sites," *The Journal of East Tennessee History* 67 (1995): 89–92, 99–105.

19. See TVA, *The Norris Project*.

20. Marshall A. Wilson, "Families of the Norris Reservoir Area," May 1949, 8–9, Calvin M. McClung Historical Collection, Knox County Public Library, Knoxville, Tennessee (McClung Historical Collection), http://cmdc.knoxlib.org/cdm /compoundobject/collection/p15136coll4/id/3692/rec/4; Kathleen George Graves and Winnie Palmer McDonald, *Our Union County Heritage* (n.p.: n.p., 1975), 2–5.

21. Wilson, "Families of the Norris Reservoir Area," May 1949, 12, 147–48, McClung Historical Collection; Graves and McDonald, *Our Union County Heritage* (1975), 17, 24; Kathleen George Graves and Winnie Palmer McDonald, *Our Union County Heritage: A Historical and Biographical Album of Union County—People, Places, and Events* ([Maynardville, TN].: Kathleen George Graves, 1978), 26; Eastin Morris, *The Tennessee Gazetteer or Topographical Dictionary* (Nashville: W. Hasell Hunt and Co., 1834), 92; *Goodspeed's History of Tennessee Containing Historical and Biographical*

Sketches of Thirty East Tennessee Counties (1887; rpt., Nashville: Charles and Randy Elder Booksellers, 1972), 850, 1151; William G. Tharpe and Norman L. Collins, eds., *From Hearth to Hoe: Union County, Tennessee, 1910–1940* (Maynardville, TN: Union County Historical Society, 1985), 4; *Official Register of the United States, Containing a List of the Officers and Employees in the Civil, Military, and Naval Services on the First of July, 1895* (Washington, DC: Government Printing Office, 1896), vol. 2: 346; William G. Tharpe, *To Loy's Cross Roads: Union County—Tennessee* ([Maynardville, TN: Union County Historical Society], 1989), 79; William H. Thomas, "Helve Hammer Story Revives Memories of Historic Bold Valley, *Knoxville Journal*, August 30, 1964, 13.

22. Tharpe and Collins, eds., *From Hearth to Hoe*, 5–6; Michael J. McDonald and John Muldowny, "Loyston in the 1930s," *Tennessee Valley Perspective* 2 (Spring 1972): 23–24; Tharpe, *To Loy's Cross Roads*, 74; Graves and McDonald, *Our Union County Heritage, Historical and Biographical Album*, 118.

23. U.S. Census, Union County, Tennessee, District 4, Civil District 0007 (Northwest Part), 1A–10A.

24. Ibid., 3B, 4B, 7A.

25. Tennessee Valley Authority, "Social and Economic Characteristics of Six Tennessee Valley Reservoir Areas," April 5, 1940, 28–29, TVA Pamphlet Collection, MS-0631, box 1 (Creekmore UTK); McDonald and Muldowny, *TVA and the Dispossessed*, 127–36.

26. TVA, "Social and Economic Characteristics of Six Tennessee Valley Reservoir Areas," 28–32, Creekmore UTK. Robert E. Lowry, "A Review of Social and Economic Conditions in the Five-County Norris Area, Summary and Recommendations," December 28, 1939, 3–4, 8, box 949, Office of the General Manager Administrative Files; L. L. Durisch and Laverne Burchfield, "Families of the Norris Reservoir Area, A Presentation of Basic Data," July 17, 1935, 9 (quote), 3–5, box 47, Regional Studies Correspondence; George F. Gant, "Consumption in Selected Population Groups in the Norris Area," May 21, 1935, 1–4, box 48, Regional Studies Correspondence; Robert Lowry and Paul Cadra, "Local Social and Economic Effects of the Norris Dam Project," August 8, 1938, iii–vi, viii, box 45, Regional Studies Correspondence, all in RG 142, NARA.

27. T. J. Wooten, "Some Social and Economic Characteristics of Selected Counties Within the Norris Dam Area," December 1933, 1–2 (quotes), box 48, Regional Studies Correspondence, RG 142, NARA.

28. Lowry and Cadra, "Local Social and Economic Effects of the Norris Dam Project," v, box 45, RG 142, NARA.

29. McDonald and Muldowny, *TVA and the Dispossessed*, 142; Tharpe, *To Loy's Cross Roads*, 93.

30. McDonald and Muldowny, *TVA and the Dispossessed,* 89.

31. Enos F. Miller removal file, September 13, 1934, box 34; L. E. Norton removal file, September 5, 1934, box 34; James P. Miller removal file, October 7, 1934, box 47, all in Removal and Readjustment Files, RG 142, NARA.

32. J. A. Greenlee removal file, September 11, 1934, box 32, Removal and Readjustment Files, in RG 142, NARA; TVA, "Social and Economic Characteristics of Six Tennessee Valley Reservoir Areas," 7, 11–12, 30, Creekmore, UTK; Lowry, "Review of Social and Economic Conditions in the Five-County Norris Area," December 28, 1939, 3–5, box 949, Office of the General Manager Administrative Files, in RG 142, NARA.

33. US Census, Union County, Tennessee, District 4, Civil District 0007 (Northwest Part), 1A-10A; TVA, "Social and Economic Characteristics of Six Reservoir Areas," 6–7, 30, Creekmore, UTK; T. Levron Howard, "Some Social and Economic Characteristics of Selected Counties Within the Norris Dam Area," December 1933, 14–15, box 48, Regional Studies Correspondence, RG 142, NARA.

34. Melissa Walker, "African Americans and TVA Reservoir Property Removal: Race in a New Deal Program, *Agricultural History* 72 (Spring 1998): 420–21; Nancy L. Grant, *TVA and Black Americans: Planning for the Status Quo* (Philadelphia: Temple University Press, 1990), 77–83, 87–88.

35. William Hutchenson removal file, September 8, 1934, box 33; Freeman Sharp removal file, August 15, 1934, box 35; Hershel Nelson removal file, September 11, 1934, box 34; George Witt removal file, September 6, 1934, box 36, all in Removal and Readjustment Files, RG 142, NARA.

36. James Mitchell removal file, September 5, 1934, box 34, Removal and Readjustment Files, RG 142, NARA.

37. C. M. Claiborne removal file, August 16, 1934, box 31; Aubrey Graves removal file, September 20, 1934, box 31; Arthur Sinard removal file, December 31, 1935, box 50; James P. Miller relocation file, October 2, 1935, box 47; Andy Heatherly removal file, October 15, 1935, box 44, all in Removal and Readjustment Files, RG 142, NARA; Tharpe, *To Loy's Cross Roads,* 95–96.

38. Charley Cooper removal file, September 14, 1934, box 31; Charles Cooper removal file, October 30, 1935, box 42, both in Removal and Readjustment Files, RG 142, NARA.

39. Hubert Grissom removal file, September 8, 1934, box 32; Robert Kidwell removal file, August 15, 1934, box 33, both in Removal and Readjustment Files, RG 142, NARA.

40. Kelly George removal file, September 14, 1934, box 31, Removal and Readjustment Files, RG 142, NARA.

41. L. G. Hill removal file, August 17, 1934, box 32; Isaac Anderson removal file, September 11, 1934, box 29, both in Removal and Readjustment Files, RG 142, NARA.

42. McDonald and Muldowny, "Loyston in the 1930s," 24 (quote), 25; Tharpe, *To Loy's Cross Roads*, 74.
43. McDonald and Muldowny, "Loyston in the 1930s," 23 (quote), 25–27.
44. Ibid., 23 (quote).
45. Tennessee Agricultural Extension Service, *Proud Past, Promising Future: A Narrative History of the Tennessee Agricultural Extension Service, 1914–1989* (Knoxville: Tennessee Agricultural Extension Service, 1994), 13, 115, https://utia.tennessee.edu/ext/wp-content/uploads/sites/5/2020/02/ProudPastPromisingFuture_OCRed.pdf. Phoebe Sharp removal file, August 17, 1934, box 35; M. Harry Satterfield and William Davlin, "A Description and Appraisal of the Relocation of Families from the Norris Reservoir Area," September 23, 1937, 8–9, box 48, Regional Studies Correspondence; TVA, "Population Readjustment Handbook," March 1940, 4–5, box 75, all in RG 142, NARA.
46. Tennessee Valley Authority, "Classification of Families in the Norris Flowage According to Assistance Necessary for Relocation," January 23, 1935, 1–2, 10–11, box 48, Regional Studies Correspondence, RG 142, NARA.
47. McDonald and Muldowny, *TVA and the Dispossessed*, 175. TVA, "Activities of Reservoir Family Removal Section, Coordination Division, Norris Reservoir Area," January 1937, Family Relocation Administrative Files, box 9; Satterfield and Davlin, "Description and Appraisal of the Relocation," September 23, 1937, 10–11, box 48, Regional Studies Correspondence; TVA, "Population Readjustment Handbook," March 1940, box 75, all in RG 142, NARA.
48. Joe Thomas removal file, December 2, 1935, box 51, Removal and Readjustment Files, RG 142, NARA.
49. Oscar Oaks removal file, October 15, 1935, box 48, Removal and Readjustment Files, RG 142, NARA.
50. Claude Graves removal file, September 30, 1935, box 32, Removal and Readjustment Files, RG 142, NARA.
51. Wayne Hutchinson removal file, October 15, 1935, box 45, Removal and Readjustment Files, RG 142, NARA.
52. Mrs. E. Q. Hill removal file, August 14, 1934, box 32; Walter Craig removal file, August 17, 1934, box 31; Plummer Irwin removal file, September 13, 1934, box 33, Removal and Readjustment Files, all in RG 142, NARA.
53. Rhoda McCoy removal file, August 17, 1934, box 34, Removal and Readjustment Files; Durisch and Burchfield, "Families of the Norris Reservoir Area," July 17, 1935, 12; T. Levron Howard, "Tenant Families of the Norris Flowage, 1935, 12, 76, all in box 47, Regional Studies Correspondence, RG 142, NARA.
54. Mrs. Julia Carrol removal file, September 10, 1934, box 30; Arlie Branum removal file, September 10, 1934, box 30; Sillus Raley removal file, November 21, 1935, box 49, all in Removal and Readjustment Files, RG 142, NARA.

55. W. T. Hunt, "Report of Relocation and Removal of Families from Reservoirs in the Tennessee Valley," 1953, box 75; Satterfield and Davlin, "Description and Appraisal of the Relocation," September 23, 1937, 1–2, box 48, Regional Studies Correspondence; Lowry, "Review of Social and Economic Conditions in the Five-County Norris Area," December 28, 1939, 1–11, box 949, Office of the General Manager Administrative Files, all in RG 142, NARA.

56. Ralph Leighton Nielson, "Socio-Economic Readjustment of Farm Families Displaced by the TVA Land Purchase in the Norris Area," master's thesis, University of Tennessee, 1940, 86, 136. Satterfield and Davlin, "Description and Appraisal of the Relocation," September 23, 1937, 14–16, box 48, Charles M. Stephenson, "Relocation of 1,834 Families from the Norris Purchase Area," August 19, 1935, 3–5, box 45, Regional Studies Correspondence, both in RG 142, NARA.

57. Charles E. Elkins removal file, September 24, 1935, box 42; Will A. Elkins removal file, October 24, 1935, box 42; John Q. Sweat removal file, January 2, 1936, box 50, all in Removal and Readjustment Files, RG 142, NARA.

58. "Fire Has Burned 70 Years In Rural Home," *Knoxville News-Sentinel,* October 12, 1931, 3; E. R. Lindamood removal file, September 17, 1934, box 33, Removal and Readjustment Files, RG 142, NARA.

59. Lee Davis, "Lindamood Home Fire Will Keep Burning," *Knoxville News-Sentinel,* October 28, 1934, C-7.

60. "Lindamood Doesn't Have to Move Yet," *Knoxville News-Sentinel,* November 13, 1934, 12; Wilson, "Families of the Norris Reservoir Area," May 1949, 132 (first quote), 131 (second quote), McClung Historical Collection; E. R. Lindamood removal file, October 29, 1935, (third quote), box 46, Removal and Readjustment Files, RG 142, NARA; "City Sights Give Ras Lindamood Thrill But He Fails to Find New Song Book," *Knoxville News-Sentinel,* March 13, 1937, 6; "Ras Lindamood of 'Eternal Fire' Is Dead," *Knoxville News-Sentinel,* December 6, 1942, 21; Bert Vincent, "Strolling," *Knoxville News-Sentinel,* December 9, 1963, 19; Bert Vincent, "Strolling," *Knoxville News-Sentinel,* October 31, 1952 ,9; Bert Vincent, "Strolling—Old Home Torn Down," *Knoxville News-Sentinel,* March 12, 1946, 17; Vic Weals, "Home Folks: Water and Wilderness," *Knoxville Journal,* July 29, 1958, 16.

61. Tharpe, *To Loy's Cross Roads,* 97; Thomas, "Helve Hammer Story," 13; TVA, *The Norris Project,* 531–32.

62. "Loyston Folk to Meet," *Knoxville News-Sentinel,* May 26, 1937; "New Loyston Homecoming Celebrated," *Knoxville Journal,* May 26, 1937, 9 (quote); "Loyston Pilgrimage," May 18, 1952, *Knoxville Journal,* 1-D, 3-D; Tharpe, *To Loy's Cross Roads,* 98; Graves and McDonald, *Our Union County Heritage* (1975), 120–22.

63. Bob Fowler, "Museum to Preserve Loyston Playhouse," *Knoxville News-Sentinel,* August 11, 2008. Jimmie Hubbard removal file, August 16, 1934, box 33; Jim Hubbard removal file, October 4, 1935, box 44, both in Removal and Readjustment Files, RG 142, NARA.

64. Davidson, *The Tennessee, Volume II,* 229 (quotes), 228–30; Carroll Van West, *Tennessee's New Deal Landscape: A Guidebook* (Knoxville: University of Tennessee Press, 2011), 153–55, 219–22.

65. "Norris Lake to Eject Residents After 70 Years," *Johnson City Press-Chronicle,* June 30, 1935, 10-D; Carson Brewer, "Worst Drought Making Lakes Barren Holes," *Knoxville News-Sentinel,* January 15, 1956, 1 (quote).

3 The Gift of Good Land

1. Katrina M. Powell, ed., *Answer at Once: Letters of Mountain Families in Shenandoah National Park, 1934–1938* (Charlottesville: University of Virginia Press, 2009), 69 (quotes).

2. Ibid., xvi (first quote), xv–xvi (second quote).

3. Scott Hess, "Imagining an Everyday Nature," *Interdisciplinary Studies in Literature and the Environment* 17 (Winter 2010): 85–112.

4. See Darwin Lambert, *The Undying Past of Shenandoah National Park* (Boulder, CO: Roberts Rinehart Publishers, 1989); George Pollock, *Skyland: The Heart of Shenandoah National Park* (n.p.: Virginia Book Co., 1960); Sue Eisenfeld, *Shenandoah: A Story of Conservation and Betrayal* (Lincoln: University of Nebraska Press, 2015); Audrey Horning, *In the Shadow of Ragged Mountain: Historical Archaeology of Nicholson, Corbin, and Weakley Hollows* (Luray, VA: Shenandoah National Park Association, 1994); Powell, ed., *Answer at Once.*

5. For a history of Native American removal from wilderness lands in the West see, Isaac Kantor, "Ethnic Cleansing and American's Creation of National Parks," *Public Land & Resources Law Review* 41 (2007): 42–62.

6. Ethan Carr, *Wilderness by Design: Landscape Architecture and the National Park Service* (Lincoln: University of Nebraska Press, 1999), 303.

7. Sevren R. Gourley, "Towards Ethical Stewardship: Balancing Natural and Historic Cultural Resources in National Parks," *Virginia Environmental Law Journal* 35 (2017): 553.

8. Ibid., 554.

9. See Richard West Sellers, *Preserving Nature in the Parks: A History* (New Haven: Yale University Press, 1997).

10. Henry D. Shapiro, *Appalachia on Our Mind: The Southern Mountains and Mountaineers in the American Consciousness, 1870–1920* (Chapel Hill: University of North Carolina Press, 1986).

11. Katherine Ledford, "A Landscape and a People Set Apart," 47–66, in *Confronting Appalachian Stereotypes: Back Talk From An American Region,* ed. Dwight B. Billings, Gurney Norman, and Katherine Ledford (Lexington: University Press of Kentucky, 1999).

12. Mandel Sherman and Thomas R. Henry, *Hollow Folk* (New York: Thomas Y. Crowell Co., 1933), vii (quotes), v.

13. This lack of working with residents is countered by more recent efforts to work with indigenous communities in forming contemporary parks. See Dawn Chatty and Marcus Colchester, *Conservation and Mobile Indigenous Peoples: Displacement, Forced Settlement, and Sustainable Development* (New York: Berghan Books, 2002).

14. See Audrey J. Horning, "When Past Is Present: Archaeology of the Displaced in Shenandoah National Park," February 26, 2015, https://www.nps.gov/shen/learn/historyculture/displaced.htm.

15. Derek G. Ross, "Common Topics and Commonplaces of Environmental Rhetoric," *Written Communication* 30 (2013): 125 (quotes).

16. Wendell Berry, *The Art of the Commonplace: The Agrarian Essays of Wendell Berry* (Berkeley, CA: Counterpoint Press, 2003), 299 (quotes).

17. Ibid., 303.

18. Ross, "Common Topics," 115 (quotes).

19. Carr, *Wilderness by Design*, 6.

20. Hess, "Imagining an Everyday Nature," 86 (quotes).

21. Ibid., 96 (first quote), 97 (second quote), 102 (third quote).

22. Powell, ed., *Answer at Once*, 78.

23. Terry Gifford, *Reconnecting with John Muir: Essays in Post-Pastoral Practice* (Athens: University of Georgia Press, 2006), 13–14.

24. Ibid.

25. Thomas J. Schoenbaum, *The New River Controversy* (West Jefferson, NC: MacFarlane Press, 2007), 57.

26. National Committee for the New River, "The Struggle for the New River," box 19, folder 3, National Committee for the New River Records, 1912–2004, W. L. Eury Appalachian Collection, Appalachian State University, Boone, North Carolina (NCNR, Appalachian State).

27. Stephen William Foster, *The Past Is Another Country: Representation, Historical Consciousness, and Resistance in the Blue Ridge* (Oakland: University of California Press, 1988), 135.

28. Ibid., 109.

29. "A Day of Prayer for the New River," box 17, folder 6, NCNR, Appalachian State.

30. Sidney Gambill, "Statement of Sidney Gambill," 6, box 19, folder 1, NCNR, Appalachian State; *Designation of New River Segment as a Component of the Wild and Scenic Rivers System: Hearing Before the Subcommittee on National Parks and Recreation of the Committee on Interior and Insular Affairs*, House of Representatives, 94th Congress, 2nd Sess., H.R. 12958 and H.R. 13372 (Washington, DC: Government Printing Office, 1976), 187–88.

31. Schoenbaum, *The New River Controversy*, 3, 170.

32. Memo, National Committee for the New River, "To: Membership, From: Edmund I. Adams [NCNR President]," box 17, folder 4, NCNR, Appalachian State.

33. See Savannah Paige Murray, "'United We Stand, Divided We May Be Dammed': Grassroots Environmentalism and the TVA in Western North Carolina." *The Journal of East Tennessee History* 87 (2015): 47–63.

34. Powell, ed., *Answer at Once*, 125 (first quote), 127 (second and third quotes).

35. Ibid., 74 (first and second quotes), 136 (third quote).

36. Rob Nixon, *Slow Violence and the Environmentalism of the Poor* (Cambridge, MA: Harvard University Press, 2013), 17.

37. Ibid.

38. Ibid., 17–18 (quotes).

39. Gourley, "Towards Ethical Stewardship," 522 (quote).

40. For example, Shenandoah National Park has made great strides in representing the cultural history of the park. In the early 2000s it created an exhibit at Byrd Visitor Center, and in 2017 it created an educational website focused on the cultural history of the park. "History & Culture," Shenandoah National Park, Virginia, https://www.nps.gov/shen/learn/historyculture/index.htm.

41. See Ann Mitchell Whisnant, *Super-Scenic Motorway: A Blue Ridge Parkway History* (Chapel Hill: University of North Carolina Press, 2010).

42. Eisenfeld, *Shenandoah*.

43. Ned Ellerbe interview with Katrina M. Powell, 2003, in author's possession.

44. Shenandoah National Park, "Exploring Shenandoah National Park History—One Tract at a Time," National Park Service, https://nps.maps.arcgis.com/apps/webappviewer/index.html?id=81acffc694a24f4692e704051526f61c.

45. See Samantha Senda-Cook, "Materializing Tensions: How Maps and Trails Mediate Nature," *Environmental Communication* 7 (September 2013): 355–71.

46. Hess, "Imagining an Everyday Nature," 107 (quotes).

47. Kerry-Ann Hamilton's September 2020 article in the *Washington Post* discussed the percentage breakdown of whites and people of color in the national parks. She explained: "According to recent National Park Service data, 77 percent of visitors to the 419 national parks are White. People of color make up 42 percent of the U.S. population, but according to the most recent survey, 23 percent of visitors to the parks were people of color." Hamilton urged the National Park Service "to diversify, or they risk becoming irrelevant and indefensibly exclusionary." As part of this transition, the National Park Service has made recent efforts to create a more inclusive organization and tell more diverse stories at the parks. Further, leaders have recognized current challenges in communities of color, especially related to the environment, health care, and social justice. Kerry-Ann Hamilton, "National Parks Are Travel's Next Frontier in the Movement for Racial Equality," *Washington Post*, September 17, 2020. See also Alex Harmon, "Shenandoah National Park and the

Racialization of Progress," in *Contested Commemoration in U.S. History: Diverging Public Interpretations*, ed. Melissa M. Bender and Klara Stephanie Szlezák (New York: Routledge, 2019), 14–33.

4 Contested Sacrifice

1. "Mammoth Cave Presented to U.S. as National Park," *Louisville Courier-Journal*, September 19, 1946, 1.
2. See Mark David Spence, *Dispossessing the Wilderness: Indian Removal and the Making of the National Parks* (New York: Oxford University Press, 2000); Karl Jacoby, *Crimes Against Nature: Squatters, Poachers, and Thieves and the Hidden History of American Conservation* (Berkeley: University of California Press, 2001); Don Lago, *Grand Canyon: A History of a Natural Wonder and National Park* (Reno: University of Nevada Press, 2015); Hal K. Rothman, *America's National Monuments: The Politics of Preservation* (University Press of Kansas, 1994); Robert H. Keller and Michael F. Turek, *American Indians and National Parks* (Tucson: University of Arizona Press, 1999); Pierce, *Great Smokies*; Brown, *The Wild East*.
3. James C. Klotter and Freda C. Klotter, *A Concise History of Kentucky* (Lexington: University Press of Kentucky, 2008), 9; Samuel W. Thomas, Eugene H. Conner, and Herold Meloy, "A History of Mammoth Cave, Emphasizing Tourist Development and Medical Experimentation under Dr. John Croghan," *Register of the Kentucky Historical Society* 68 (October 1970): 323; Duane DePaepe, *Gunpowder from Mammoth Cave: The Saga of Saltpetre Mining before and during the War of 1812* (Hays, KS: Cave Pearl Press, 1985), 10.
4. Robert Davidson, *An Excursion to the Mammoth Cave and the Barrens of Kentucky* (Philadelphia: C. Sherman & Co., 1840), 62–63; Joy Medley Lyons, *Making Their Mark: The Signature of Slavery at Mammoth Cave* (Washington, PA: Eastern National, 2006); William Schumann, "Place and Place-Making in Appalachia," in *Appalachia Revisited: New Perspectives on Place, Tradition, and Progress*, ed. William Schumann and Rebecca Adkins Fletcher (Lexington: University Press of Kentucky, 2016), 4.
5. See David Randolph Kem, *The Kentucky Cave Wars: The Century that Shaped Mammoth Cave National Park* (Cave City, KY: David Randolph Kem, 2014); Robert K. Murray and Roger Brucker, *Trapped! The Story of Floyd Collins* (Lexington: University Press of Kentucky, 1982).
6. Gregg, *Managing the Mountains*, 108; Bob Thompson, "Willis T. Lee's 1925 Visit to the Mammoth Cave Region of Kentucky," *Journal of Spelean History* 38 (July–December 2004): 51.
7. Maurice H. Thatcher to George E. Zubrod, May 15, 1926, box 1, folder 6, Mammoth Cave National Park Association Collection, MS 296, Manuscripts and Folklife

Archives, Western Kentucky University, Bowling Green, Kentucky (MCNPA Collection, WKU).

8. *Final Report of the Southern Appalachian National Park Commission to the Secretary of the Interior, June 30, 1931* (Washington, DC: Government Printing Office, 1931), 18.

9. Ibid., 19.

10. Report of Stanley G. Thompson on the Status of the Mammoth Cave National Park Bill, box 1, folder 6, MCNPA Collection, WKU.

11. Maurice H. Thatcher to George E. Zubrod, May 15, 1926, box 1, folder 6, MCNPA Collection, WKU.

12. Robert Sterling Yard to John C. Merriam, March 22, 1930, box 187, John C. Merriam Papers, Library of Congress, Washington, DC (Merriam Papers, LC).

13. Robert Sterling Yard, Memo to National Parks Association members, n.d., box 86, Merriam Papers, LC.

14. Ibid.

15. "Now for Mammoth Cave National Park," *Louisville Courier-Journal,* May 26, 1926, 6.

16. "An Act to Provide for the Establishment of the Mammoth Cave National Park in the State of Kentucky, and for other purposes," May 25, 1926, Public Law 283, *Statutes at Large,* 69th Cong., Sess. 1 (1926), chap. 382: 635–36; Cecil E. Goode, *World Wonder Saved: How Mammoth Cave Became a National Park* (Mammoth Cave, KY: Mammoth Cave National Park Association, 1986), 25.

17. Local Mammoth Cave historian Norman Warnell estimated that 500 families were displaced. Collins Eke, a geographer, placed the number of removed families closer to 850 based on census data. See Norman Warnell, *Mammoth Cave: Forgotten Stories of Its People* (Fort Washington, PA: Eastern National, 2006), 1; Collins Eke, "Where Did They Go? Analysis of Out-Migration from Mammoth Cave National Park, 1920–1940," master's thesis, Western Kentucky University, 2019, 44.

18. Matthew Brunt, "Analysis of Mammoth Cave Pre-Park Communities," master's thesis, Western Kentucky University, 2009, 4.

19. Eke, "Where Did They Go?" 46.

20. Ibid., 32.

21. "Last Heir to Mammoth Cave Estate Dead, Tract Sale Under Will Seen," *Nashville Tennessean,* August 29, 1926, 1.

22. Max B. Nahm to George E. Zubrod, November 30, 1926, box 1, folder 8, MCNPA Collection, WKU.

23. "Sampson Makes Cave Appeal," *Louisville Courier-Journal,* February 28, 1928, 2.

24. Ibid.

25. Goode, *World Wonder Saved,* 32.

26. George E. Zubrod Speech for Mayor's Meeting, January 7, 1928, box 3, folder 1, MCNPA Collection, WKU.

27. Ibid.

28. Sidney Smith to George E. Zubrod, June 18, 1926, box 1, folder 6, MCNPA Collection, WKU.

29. Max B. Nahm to George E. Zubrod, June 16, 1926, box 1, folder 6, MCNPA Collection, WKU.

30. Sidney Smith to Edward S. Jouett, January 5, 1928, box 3, folder 1, MCNPA Collection, WKU.

31. "Senate OKs Bill for Cave Park Board," *Louisville Courier-Journal,* February 21, 1928, 1–2.

32. George E. Zubrod to John B. Rodes, April 16, 1928, box 3, folder 2, MCNPA Collection, WKU.

33. "Mammoth Cave Worth $496,000," *Louisville Courier-Journal,* August 8, 1928, 1.

34. "Suit Ordered to Condemn Land at Cave," *Louisville Courier-Journal,* May 8, 1928, 1.

35. Eugene Stuart to Huston Quin, George E. Zubrod, and Blakey Helm, May 5, 1928, box 3, folder 3, MCNPA Collection, WKU.

36. See Katie Algeo, "The Puzzling Mr. Janin and Mammoth Cave Management, 1900–1910," in *Proceedings of the Max Kaemper Centennial Symposium and Ninth Science Symposium, Mammoth Cave, Kentucky, October 9–10, 2008,* ed. Shannon Trimboli (Bowling Green: Western Kentucky University, 2008), 11–21.

37. George Newman to Kentucky National Park Commission members, June 21, 1928, box 3, folder 3, MCNPA Collection, WKU.

38. "Mammoth Cave Worth $496,000," 1.

39. "Park Board Objects to Cave Valuation," *Edmonson County News,* August 23, 1928, 1; "Exceptions Filed in Cave Suit," *Edmonson County News,* August 30, 1928, 1; "Cave Appraisal Exception Suit Filed," *Louisville Courier-Journal,* September 4, 1928, 1.

40. Goode, *World Wonder Saved,* 32–33.

41. Max B. Nahm to George E. Zubrod, January 4, 1929, box 2, folder 1, MCNPA Collection, WKU.

42. Goode, *World Wonder Saved,* 33–34.

43. "Park Body Controls 13,000 Acres Now," *Edmonson County News,* February 28, 1929, 1.

44. The two-thirds/one-third ownership arrangement by the association and the commission eventually led to the creation of an operating committee consisting of members from both organizations and the National Park Service to manage and run the hotel and cave tours. See Goode, *World Wonder Saved,* 37.

45. Kentucky National Park Commission Meeting Minutes, October 20, 1931, MACA 35455, Mammoth Cave National Park Museum Collections, Mammoth Cave, KY (MCNP, Mammoth Cave); Mammoth Cave National Park Association Meeting Minutes, September 5, 1929, box 4, folder 3, MCNPA Collection, WKU.

46. "Sampson Names Park Body," *Louisville Times,* April 2, 1930, 1.

47. "Cave Company Sues in United States Court," *Edmonson County News,* April 17, 1930, 1; Kem, *The Kentucky Cave Wars,* 197.

48. Kem, *The Kentucky Cave Wars,* 197; Kentucky National Park Commission Meeting Minutes, December 10, 1931, 35455, MCNP, Mammoth Cave.

49. Kentucky National Park Commission Meeting Minutes, December 28, 1931, 35455, MCNP, Mammoth Cave.

50. "The Deadly Parallel," *Edmonson County News,* January 21, 1932, 1.

51. *Edmonson County News,* January 6, 1931, 3.

52. Homer Collins to George E. Zubrod, April 30, 1926, box 1, folder 4, MCNPA Collection, WKU.

53. Marshall Collins to George E. Zubrod, August 31, 1926, box 1, folder 5, MCNPA Collection, WKU.

54. George E. Zubrod to Marshall Collins, September 1, 1926, box 1, folder 7, MCNPA Collection, WKU.

55. Max B. Nahm to George E. Zubrod, October 28, 1926, box 1, folder 7, MCNPA Collection, WKU.

56. Mammoth Cave National Park Association Meeting Minutes, October 29, 1926, box 3, folder 4, MCNPA Collection, WKU.

57. George E. Zubrod to Dr. Harry B. Thomas, June 27, 1928, box 3, folder 3, MCNPA Collection, WKU.

58. George E. Zubrod to Adrian Wychgel, December 13, 1927, box 2, folder 6, MCNPA Collection, WKU.

59. "Collins' Body Is Moved to Cave," *Louisville Courier-Journal,* June 17, 1927, 5; Murray and Brucker, *Trapped!* 235.

60. "Collins' Body Is Moved," 5.

61. Ibid.; Murray and Brucker, *Trapped!,* 235.

62. George Newman to Kentucky National Park Commission members, June 21, 1928, box 3, folder 3, MCNPA Collection, WKU.

63. George E. Zubrod to Adrian Wychgel, December 13, 1927, box 2, folder 6, MCNPA Collection, WKU.

64. George E. Zubrod to A. A. Demunbrun, July 13, 1928, box 3, folder 4, MCNPA Collection, WKU.

65. "Park Commission Buying Property," *Edmonson County News,* July 27, 1928, 1.

66. George E. Zubrod to Assistant Attorney General S. H. Brown, July 21, 1928, box 3, folder 4, MCNPA Collection, WKU.

67. Mammoth Cave National Park Association bulletin, July 30, 1928, box 3, folder 4, MCNPA Collection, WKU.

68. George E. Zubrod to Huston Quin, August 2, 1928, box 3, folder 4, MCNPA Collection, WKU.

69. Max B. Nahm to George E. Zubrod and Huston Quin, July 29, 1928, box 3, folder 4, MCNPA Collection, WKU.

70. Mammoth Cave National Park Association Minutes, August 2, 1928, box 3, folder 4, MCNPA Collection, WKU.

71. George Newman to George E. Zubrod, August 6, 1928, box 3, folder 4, MCNPA Collection, WKU.

72. Huston Quin to H. B. Thomas, August 13, 1928, box 3, folder 4, MCNPA Collection, WKU.

73. George Newman to George E. Zubrod, August 17, 1928, box 3, folder 4, MCNPA Collection, WKU.

74. George E. Zubrod to George Newman, August 18, 1928, box 3, folder 4, MCNPA Collection, WKU.

75. "Park Board Objects to Cave Valuation," *Edmonson County News,* August 23, 1928, 1.

76. Mammoth Cave National Park Association Executive Committee Meeting Minutes, August 23, 1928, box 3, folder 4, MCNPA Collection, WKU.

77. George E. Zubrod to Huston Quin, October 13, 1928, box 3, folder 5, MCNPA Collection, WKU.

78. For more on Matt Bransford's hotel and African American tourism to the Mammoth Cave area, see Katie Algeo, "Underground Tourists / Tourists Underground: African American Tourism to Mammoth Cave," *Tourism Geographies* 15 (August 2013): 380–404; Lyons, *Making Their Mark;* Jeanne C. Schmitzer, "The Black Experience at Mammoth Cave, Edmonson County, Kentucky, 1838–1942," master's thesis, University of Central Florida, 1996.

79. Anonymous to Mammoth Cave National Park Association, October 16, 1928, box 3, folder 5, MCNPA Collection, WKU.

80. Ibid.

81. George E. Zubrod to Harry B. Thomas, October 19, 1928, box 3, folder 5, MCNPA Collection, WKU; Goode, *World Wonder Saved,* 88.

82. Algeo, "Underground Tourists / Tourists Underground," 380.

83. J. B. Yates to George E. Zubrod, May 22, 1926, box 1, folder 6, MCNPA Collection, WKU.

84. George E. Zubrod to Max B. Nahm, May 27, 1926, box 1, folder 6, MCNPA Collection, WKU.

85. Max B. Harlin to Blakey Helm, January 25, 1929, box 4, folder 1, MCNPA Collection, WKU.

86. John B. Rodes to Huston Quin, July 30, 1930, box 6, folder 1, MCNPA Collection, WKU.

87. The best in-depth examination of the cases involving ownership of Great Onyx Cave is Bruce Ziff, "The Great Onyx Cave Cases: A Micro-History," *Northern Kentucky Law Review* 40, no. 1 (2013): 1–48.

88. "Farmer Sues Trio for Accounting in Operation of Cave," *Park City Daily News* [Bowling Green, KY], April 19, 1928, 4.

89. Ziff, "The Great Onyx Cave Cases," 15–17.

90. Max B. Harlin to Blakey Helm, January 25, 1929, box 4, folder 1, MCNPA Collection, WKU.

91. "State Commission to Have Broad Power in Carrying National Park Program," *Edmonson County News,* February 17, 1928, 1.

92. Warnell, *Mammoth Cave,* 70, 92, 100.

93. "Sampson Names Park Body," *Louisville Times,* April 2, 1930, 1.

94. "Taxation without Representation in 1776; Condemnation without Representation in 1930," *Edmonson County News,* April 3, 1930.

95. "Park Promoters Go Into Railroad Business," *Edmonson County News,* April 9, 1931, 1.

96. "A Little Study in Genealogy," *Edmonson County News,* March 13, 1931, 1; Park Land Reaches $33 An Acre," *Edmonson County News,* March 26, 1931, 1.

97. "For Each Dollar Paid for Park Lands, $8 Has Been Expended for Something Else—What Was It?" *Edmonson County News,* August 14, 1930, 1.

98. "For Each Dollar," "Drouth [*sic*] Presents Chance For Higher Ups to Retrieve Respect," *Edmonson County News,* August 14, 1930, 1.

99. Several issues of the *Edmonson County News* in 1931 alone testify to relief efforts. See "Red Cross Will Feed the Hungry," "Blanks for Crop Loans Received," February 6, 1931; "Drought Loan Rules Announced," January 29, 1931.

100. "Ferguson's Bill Would Give Opportunity for Change in National Park Commission," *Edmonson County News,* January 14, 1932, 1.

101. "New Park Board Is Now Assured," *Edmonson County News,* February 4, 1932, 1.

102. "Mammoth Cave Commission," *Louisville Courier-Journal,* May 29, 1932, 4; "The Deadly Parallel," *Edmonson County News,* January 21, 1932, 1.

103. "Mammoth Cave a Private Club Maintained at a Public Expense!" *Edmonson County News,* June 16, 1932, 1.

104. "Yes, Joe, the New Park Board Does Have 'Connection' With the Club-Association," *Edmonson County News,* July 14, 1932, 1; "Club Stockholders Revive Dead One," *Edmonson County News,* July 21, 1932, 1.

105. Colleen O'Connor Olson, *Nine Miles to Mammoth Cave: The Story of the Mammoth Cave Railroad* (n.p.: Cave Books, 2013), 9; Warnell, *Mammoth Cave,* 69; Murray and Brucker, *Trapped!* 40–41.

106. "Park Commission Buying Property," *Edmonson County News,* July 27, 1928, 1.

107. Mark A. Theissen to Mammoth Cave National Park Association, October 26, 1929, box 4, folder 3, MCNPA Collection, WKU.

108. Ibid.
109. Milton Smith Jr. to George E. Zubrod, April 2, 1930, box 5, folder 3, MCNPA Collection, WKU.
110. *Edmonson County News,* April 10, 1930, 1.
111. "Deny Trees Cut on Cave Estate," *Louisville Times,* May 4, 1930.
112. Robert M. Coleman to George E. Zubrod, July 2, 1930, box 6, folder 1, MCNPA Collection, WKU.
113. "Group Objects to Timber Ban," *Louisville Courier-Journal,* August 19, 1930, 3.
114. Thomas H. Jones to Charles Peterson, September 18, 1934, box 1326, Records of the National Park Service, Record Group 79, National Archives, College Park, MD (RG 79, NARA).
115. George E. Zubrod to John B. Rodes, June 4, 1926, box 1, folder 6, MCNPA Collection, WKU.
116. Advertisement, *Edmonson County News,* September 3, 1927.
117. "Park Association to Buy Land," *Edmonson County News,* December 20, 1928, 1.
118. Huston Quin to Gillis Vincent, May 9, 1929, box 4, folder 2, MCNPA Collection, WKU.
119. Interview with Vernon P. Wells, 1986, Vernon P. Wells Collection, SC 1322, WKU.
120. "Oil Struck in Edmonson County," *Louisville Courier-Journal,* March 27, 1927, 8.
121. "Nimrod," "Flint Ridge," *Edmonson County News,* February 26, 1931.
122. Charlie Hunt to George E. Zubrod, January 3, 1927, box 2, folder 1; John B. Rodes to George E. Zubrod, April 6, 1926, box 1, folder 4, both in MCNPA Collection, WKU.
123. Kentucky National Park Commission Meeting Minutes, December 28, 1931, MACA 35455, MCNP, Mammoth Cave.
124. "Mammoth Cave Commission," *Louisville Courier-Journal,* May 29, 1932, 4.
125. See Neil Maher, *Nature's New Deal: The Civilian Conservation Corps and the Roots of the American Environmental Movement* (New York: Oxford University Press, 2008).
126. Jeanne Schmitzer, "CCC Camp 510: Black Participation in the Creation of Mammoth Cave National Park," *Register of the Kentucky Historical Society* 93 (Autumn 1995): 446–64.
127. "Four Forest Camps are Picked," *Louisville Courier-Journal,* May 14, 1933, 1. The other camps were added in 1934.
128. Diary of Civilian Conservation Corps Naturalist, 1934–1935, Vertical Files, MCNP.
129. Kentucky National Park Commission Meeting Minutes, July 14, 1933, MACA 35455, MCNP, Mammoth Cave.
130. Ibid., September 8, 1933, MACA 35455, MCNP, Mammoth Cave.
131. Ibid., October 20, 1933, MACA 35455, MCNP, Mammoth Cave.
132. Ibid., September 29, 1933, 35455, MCNP, Mammoth Cave.

133. Maher, *Nature's New Deal,* 141.

134. Kentucky National Park Commission Meeting Minutes, November 9, 1933, MACA 35455, MCNP, Mammoth Cave.

135. Ibid., March 9, 1934; Mammoth Cave National Park Association and Kentucky National Park Commission Joint Meeting Minutes May 28, 1934, both in MACA 35455, MCNP, Mammoth Cave.

136. Maher, *Nature's New Deal,* 138.

137. *Creation and Revision of National Park Boundaries, Hearings Before the Committee on the Public Lands,* House of Representatives, 73rd Congress, 2nd Sess. on H.R. 7360 and H.R. 4935 (Washington, DC: Government Printing Office, 1934), 29.

138. Ibid., 23.

139. Ibid., 24.

140. Legislation Pertaining to Mammoth Cave National Park, box 1326, RG 79, NARA.

141. Testimony, House of Representatives Committee on Public Lands, 73rd Congress, March 13, 1934, box 1329, RG 79, NARA.

142. "U.S. To Start Park Purchase," *Louisville Courier-Journal,* May 16, 1934, 16.

143. Mammoth Cave National Park Association and Kentucky National Park Commission Joint Meeting Minutes, April 5, 1934, 35455, MCNPA Collection, WKU.

144. W. W. Thompson to Mammoth Cave National Park Association and Kentucky National Park Commission, January 28, 1935, box 12, folder 2, MCNPA Collection, WKU.

145. Ibid.

146. Interview with Vernon P. Wells, SC 122, WKU.

147. Ibid.

148. Ibid.

149. Kentucky National Park Commission Meeting Minutes, May 2, 1935, MACA 35455, MCNP, Mammoth Cave.

150. "Park Area 'Foresters' Break Up Plows, Sink Them In River, Warrant Charges," *Edmonson County News,* May 2, 1935, 1.

151. Ibid.

152. "Holland and Ridge Waive Trials to the Circuit Court," *Edmonson County News,* May 9, 1935, 1.

153. "Holland, Ridge Pay for Plows 'Drowned' Also Damage Suits," *Edmonson County News,* May 16, 1935, 1.

154. "Plow Drowners Square Selves With the Law," *Edmonson County News,* November 21, 1935, 1.

155. Kentucky National Park Commission Meeting Minutes, October 20, 1933, MACA 35455, MCNP, Mammoth Cave.

156. W. W. Thompson to Kentucky National Park Commission, November 1, 1935, box 12, folder 2, MCNPA Collection, WKU.

157. "Plow Drowners' Pal Receives Portion of Buckshot Charge," *Edmonson County News,* October 31, 1935, 1.

158. Interview with Vernon P. Wells, SC 122, WKU.

159. W. W. Thompson to Kentucky National Park Commission, November 1, 1935, box 12, folder 2, MCNPA Collection, WKU.

160. Interview with George Childress regarding CCC, August 6, 1987, FA 81, Folklife Archives, WKU.

161. W. W. Thompson to Kentucky National Park Commission and Mammoth Cave National Park Association, January 28, 1935, box 12, folder 2, MCNPA Collection, WKU.

162. Emergency Conservation Work Annual Report, 1935, 45818, MCNPA.

163. "Forest Fires!" *Edmonson County News,* January 16, 1936, 1.

164. "We Stand Corrected! Or Do We?" *Edmonson County News,* January 23, 1936, 2.

165. "Forest Fires!"

166. Superintendent's Monthly Reports, August–December 1936, 45818, MCNPA.

167. L. P. Dossey to George E. Zubrod, October 6, 1927, box 2, folder 5, MCNPA Collection, WKU.

168. Ibid., March 15, 1928, box 3, folder 2, MCNPA Collection, WKU.

169. "Park Association Buys Dossey Tract," *Edmonson County News,* March 7, 1929, 1.

170. Superintendent's Monthly Reports, August–December 1936, 45818, MCNPA.

171. Superintendent's Annual Report for Fiscal Year 1937, box 1328, RG 79, NARA.

172. Superintendent's Monthly Report, September 1936, 45818, MCNPA; Superintendent's Annual Report for Fiscal Year 1937, box 1328, RG 79, NARA.

173. Superintendent's Annual Report for Fiscal Year 1942, box 1328, RG 79, NARA.

174. Superintendent's Annual Report for Fiscal Year 1937, box 1328, RG 79, NARA; Max B. Nahm, Fiscal Report for Kentucky National Park Commission Ending June 30, 1938, box 12, folder 5, MCNPA Collection, WKU; Schmitzer, "CCC Camp 510," 462.

175. W. W. Thompson to Kentucky National Park Commission and Mammoth Cave National Park Association, January 28, 1935, box 12, folder 2, MCNPA Collection, WKU.

176. Max B. Nahm to Arno B. Cammerer, November 19, 1932, box 1326, RG 79, NARA.

177. Ibid.

178. Executive Committee of the Mammoth Cave National Park Association Meeting Minutes, December 21, 1936, box 12, folder 3, MCNPA Collection, WKU.

179. "State Caves Bill Signed," *Louisville Times,* August 30, 1937.

180. Arno B. Cammerer to G. A. Moskey, September 16, 1937, box 1326, RG 79, NARA.

181. Superintendent's Annual Report for Fiscal Year 1942, box 1328, RG 79, NARA.

182. Joseph H. Mader, "It's America's Cave Now," *Louisville Courier-Journal Sunday Magazine,* September 21, 1941, 2.

183. "Colored Man Starts His 32nd Year as Cave Guide," *Park City Daily News* [Bowling Green, KY], September 13, 1937.

184. "Bransford Family Has Century of Years in Cave Grinding" [*sic*], *Danville Kentucky Advocate,* December 28, 1937, 1; Lyons, *Making Their Mark,* 61.

185. Murray and Brucker, *Trapped!* 241.

186. See Alyssa D. Warrick, "Underground Wilderness? Mammoth Cave and the Wilderness Act of 1964," *Register of the Kentucky Historical Society* 116 (Summer–Autumn 2018): 405–41.

187. "NPS Report Shows MCNP Visitors Benefited Local Economy by $61.6 million," *London* [KY] *Sentinel Echo,* June 7, 2109, https://www.sentinel-echo.com/news/local_news/nps-report-shows-mcnp-visitors-benefited-local-economy-by-million/article_53d888dc-3ab2-589d-9fdd-ad530730d6b6.html.

188. Warnell, *Mammoth Cave,* 73, 87–90, 108–9, 123–26.

189. Lyons, *Making Their Mark,* 62; Eke, "Where Did They Go?" 65.

190. Interview with Vernon P. Wells, SC 122, WKU.

5   Layers of Loss

1. Lindsey A. Freeman, *This Atom Bomb in Me* (Stanford, CA: Stanford University Press, 2019), 46 (first quote), 48 (second quote).

2. Dorathy Moneymaker, *We'll Call It Wheat* (Oak Ridge, TN: Adroit Printing, 1979), iv.

3. Ibid.; Thomas S. Kuhn, *The Structure of Scientific Revolutions,* 3rd ed. (Chicago: University of Chicago Press, 1996).

4. Lindsey A. Freeman, *Longing for the Bomb: Oak Ridge and Atomic Nostalgia* (Chapel Hill: University of North Carolina Press, 2015), 14–36.

5. Overholt, ed., *These Are Our Voices.*

6. Russell B. Olwell, *At Work in the Atomic City: A Labor and Social History of Oak Ridge, Tennessee* (Knoxville: University of Tennessee Press, 2004).

7. Ibid., 2–3.

8. F. G. Gosling, "The Manhattan Project: Making the Atomic Bomb," US Department of Energy, 1999, 19, https://www.osti.gov/biblio/303853.

9. Peter B. Hales, *Atomic Spaces: Living on the Manhattan Project* (Urbana: University of Illinois Press, 1997).

10. Freeman, *Longing for the Bomb.*

11. Ibid., 14–36.

12. Drew Swanson, *Beyond the Mountains: Commodifying Appalachian Environments* (Athens: University of Georgia Press, 2019), 159.
13. Charles W. Johnson and Charles O. Jackson, *City Behind a Fence: Oak Ridge, Tennessee, 1942–1946* (Knoxville: University of Tennessee Press, 1980), 47.
14. Hales, *Atomic Spaces*, 56–57.
15. Ibid., 11.
16. Olwell, *At Work in the Atomic City*, 9–26.
17. Russell Olwell, "Help Wanted for Secret City: Recruiting Workers for the Manhattan Project at Oak Ridge, Tennessee, 1942–1946," *Tennessee Historical Quarterly* 58 (Spring 1999): 52–69.
18. US Census, 1940, Roane County, Tract 73–16.
19. Richard Rothstein, *The Color of Law: A Forgotten History of How Our Government Segregated America* (New York: Liveright Publishing Corp., 2017), 17.
20. Olwell, *At Work in the Atomic City*, 20–24.
21. Ibid., 74–77.
22. Rothstein, *The Color of Law*, 28–29.
23. Thomas J. Sugrue, *The Origins of the Urban Crisis: Race and Inequality in Postwar Detroit* (Princeton, NJ: Princeton University Press, 2005).
24. See Russell Olwell, "Atomic Workers, Atomic City: Labor and Community at Oak Ridge, Tennessee, 1942–1950," PhD diss., Massachusetts Institute of Technology, 1997.
25. "Historic Cemeteries in Oak Ridge," Oak Ridge Public Library, http://www.oakridgetn.gov/department/Library/Oak-Ridge-Room/Oak-Ridge-Cemeteries.
26. "Bethel Valley Interviews: Maude Lane, S. E. Coley, Dorathy Moneymaker, Barbara McCall-Ely, Velma Blank, and Dot Anderson Bussell, 1998," transcribed by Jordan Reed, Oak Ridge Public Library, http://coroh.oakridgetn.gov/corohfiles/Transcripts_and_photos/Bethel_Valley_History/Bethel_Valley_Interviews_Final.docx.
27. Keith McDaniel, interview with James Brennan, November 2, 2011, Center for Oak Ridge Oral History, http://cdm16107.contentdm.oclc.org/cdm/singleitem/collection/p15388coll1/id/187/rec/1.
28. Daniel Lang, *Early Tales of the Atomic Age* (Garden City, NY: Doubleday, 1948).
29. "ORICL Panel: Robertsville and Scarboro Communities, Part 1," Oak Ridge Public Library, http://cdm16107.contentdm.oclc.org/cdm/singleitem/collection/p15388coll1/id/300/rec/4.
30. Freeman, *Longing for the Bomb*, 5–10.
31. Olwell, *At Work in the Atomic City*, 117–33.
32. Arjun Makhijani, Howard Hu, and Katherine Yih, *Nuclear Wastelands: A Global Guide to Nuclear Weapons Production and Its Health and Environmental Effects* (Cambridge, MA: MIT Press, 1995).
33. Ibid., 232.

34. Ibid., 229.

35. Keith McDaniel, interview with Spencer Gross, June 2, 2018, Center for Oak Ridge History, https://cdm16107.contentdm.oclc.org/digital/collection/p15388coll1/id/887/rec/2.

36. Keith McDaniel, interview with Clayton Gist, March 16, 2013, Center for Oak Ridge History, https://cdm16107.contentdm.oclc.org/digital/collection/p15388coll1/id/335/rec/3.

37. Ibid.

38. See Denise Kiernan, *The Girls of Atomic City: The Untold Story of the Women Who Helped Win World War II* (New York: Simon and Schuster, 2013).

39. See "Manhattan Project," National Park Service, https://www.nps.gov/mapr/oakridge.htm.

40. "U.S. Involvement in World War II Through the Lens of the Manhattan Project National Historic Park in Oak Ridge, TN Grades: 9–12," National Park Service, 19, https://www.nps.gov/mapr/learn/upload/MAPR-Lesson-Plan.pdf.

6 When Minds Wander Back

1. Jessi Stone, "Trying to get the most out of North Shore funds," *Smoky Mountain News*, March 6, 2019, https://www.smokymountainnews.com/archives/item/26511-trying- to-get-most-out- of-north-shore-funds.

2. Linda Hogue interview with Alan Jabbour, July 7, 2004, *North Shore Cemetery Decoration Project, Great Smoky Mountains National Park Archives, National Park Service, Oak Ridge* (GSMNP Archives).

3. J. D. Vance, *Hillbilly Elegy: A Memoir of a Family and Culture in Crisis* (New York: HarperCollins, 2016); Elizabeth Catte, *What You Are Getting Wrong About Appalachia* (Cleveland: Belt Publishing, 2018).

4. See Ron Eller, *Miners, Millhands, and Mountaineers* (Knoxville: University of Tennessee Press, 1982).

5. Stephen Wallace Taylor, *The New South's New Frontier: A Social History of Economic Development in Southwestern North Carolina* (Gainesville: University Press of Florida, 2001), 148.

6. Karl B. Rohr, "The Road to Nowhere and the Politics of Wilderness Legislation," PhD diss., University of Mississippi, 2003, 4–5.

7. Laura Kerr, "A 'Road to Nowhere'? The Political Ecology of Environmental Conflict over the North Shore Road in the Great Smoky Mountains National Park," term paper in comparative environment and development studies, Macalester University, 2006, 4–5, https://www.macalester.edu/geography/wp-content/uploads/sites/18/2012/03/kerr.pdf.

8. Ibid., 20.

9. Ibid., 35.

10. Taylor, *The New South's New Frontier*, 96.

11. Brown, *The Wild East*, 145.

12. Ibid., 97; Matthew Chisholm, "The Arrival of the Road to Nowhere: Memory and Myth in the Great Smoky Mountains' North Shore Road Controversy," *The Journal of East Tennessee History* 88 (2016): 47.

13. Brown, *The Wild East*, 147–49; Rohr, "The Road to Nowhere," 37–38.

14. "Memorandum of July 30, 1943 Fontana Agreement," October 8, 1943, North Shore Binder, North Shore box 1, Special Collections, Western Carolina University, Cullowhee (Special Collections, WCU).

15. Most of this excitement was evident in the *Bryson City Times* and the *Jackson County Journal*. See Brown, *The Wild East*, 147–49; Rohr, "The Road to Nowhere," 37–38.

16. Brown, *The Wild East*, 155–56; Rohr, "The Road to Nowhere," 42–45; "Memorandum of July 30, 1943 Fontana Agreement," 1–22.

17. Chisholm, "Arrival of the Road to Nowhere," 49–50.

18. Rohr, "The Road to Nowhere," 22–23.

19. Brown, *The Wild East*, 72.

20. Rohr, "The Road to Nowhere," 22.

21. See H. B. Ayers and W. W. Ashe, "The Southern Appalachian Forests," US Geological Survey, *Professional Paper* 37 (Washington, DC: Government Printing Office, 1905); Leonidas C. Glenn, "Denudation and Erosion in the Southern Appalachian Region and the Monongahela Basin," US Geological Survey, *Professional Paper* 72 (Washington, DC: Government Printing Office, 1911).

22. Brown, *The Wild East*, 57, 69–71.

23. Ibid., 72.

24. Rohr, "The Road to Nowhere," 23; Brown, *The Wild East*, 72.

25. Eller, *Miners, Millhands, and Mountaineers*, xxiv–xxvi.

26. Rohr, "The Road to Nowhere," 39.

27. Ibid.; Tennessee Valley Authority, *The Fontana Project: A Comprehensive Report on the Planning, Design, Construction, and Initial Operations of Fontana Project* (Washington, DC: Government Printing Office, 1950), 487–88.

28. Rome C. Sharp, "Proctor Community: Fontana Area Community Removal Profile," 4, Fontana Removal Profiles, Collection: NC3-142-29-2, Records of the Tennessee Valley Authority, Record Group 142, National Archives, Atlanta (RG 142, NARA).

29. Sharp, "Proctor Community," 4, 10–11, 13, RG 142, NARA.

30. Arnold J. Hyde, "Almond-Judson Community Removal Profile," 2, RG 142, NARA.

31. Ibid., 2–3, RG 142, NARA.

32. Ibid., 3, RG 142, NARA.

33. Ibid., 5–6, RG 142, NARA.

34. Ibid., 6, RG 142, NARA.

35. Ibid.

36. Ibid., 7, RG 142, NARA.

37. Arnold J. Hyde, "Stecoah Community Removal Profile," 2, RG 142, NARA.

38. Ibid., 2–4, RG 142, NARA.

39. Ibid., 4–9, RG 142, NARA.

40. Ibid., 5, RG 142, NARA.

41. Rohr, "The Road to Nowhere," 40–41; TVA, *The Fontana Project,* 480–81, 486.

42. *United States ex rel. Tennessee Valley Authority v. Welch,* Appellate Brief, 1945 WL 48904 (1945).

43. Ed Anthony Family Removal Profile, RG 142, NARA.

44. L. W. Ammons Family Removal Profile, RG 142, NARA.

45. Will Jenkins Family Removal Profile, RG 142, NARA.

46. Andy Chicklelee Family Removal Profile, RG 142, NARA.

47. Game Walker Family Removal Profile, RG 142, NARA.

48. Jim Styles Family Removal Profile, RG 142, NARA.

49. W. W. Jenkins Family Removal Profile, RG 142, NARA.

50. Ibid.

51. This assertion is in direct opposition to the argument put forward later by the North Shore Cemetery Association, later renamed the North Shore Historical Association, that the TVA did indeed steal the land and did not compensate the descendants for not building the North Shore Road.

52. Taylor, *The New South's New Frontier,* 98.

53. Ibid., 97–99.

54. Roy Taylor to Conrad Wirth, June 18, 1962, North Shore Road, 1943–75, DSC III-12, 1962 file, GSMNP Archives; Rohr, "The Road to Nowhere," 62, 64.

55. "Wild Society Forgets There Are People, Too," *Asheville Citizen,* November 13, 1965, A4.

56. Elbert Cox, *Wilderness Hearing on the Great Smoky Mountains National Park* (Bryson City, NC: n.p., 1966), vol. 1: 5–8; Rohr, "The Road to Nowhere, 83.

57. Rohr, "The Road to Nowhere," 82–84.

58. M. G. Roberts, in Cox, *Wilderness Hearing* 2: 33–40; Rohr, "The Road to Nowhere," 88.

59. Ben Smith, in Cox, *Wilderness Hearing* 2: 93–96; Rohr, "The Road to Nowhere," 90.

60. Gannon Coffey, in Cox, *Wilderness Hearing* 2: 127–28; Rohr, "The Road to Nowhere," 96.

61. Brown, *The Wild East,* 268, 272–73.

62. "Inflation Calculator: Money's Real Worth Over Time," 2019, http://www.coinnews .net/tools/cpi-inflation-calculator.

63. Swain County Board of Commissioners, "Economic Impact Study," 1979, 29, North Shore binder, North Shore box 1, Special Collections, WCU.

64. Alan Jabbour, Philip E. Coyle, and Paul Webb, *North Shore Cemetery Decoration Project Report* (Great Smoky Mountains National Park: National Park Service, 2005), G-57. Also available in *North Shore Road Environmental Impact Statement* (Great Smoky Mountains National Park: National Park Service, 2006), appendix G, http://paws.wcu.edu/pcoyle/Appendix_G.pdf.

65. The total number of cemeteries varies depending on the source. The figure of eleven hundred graves comes from "Attorney Plans Suit to Gain Access to Fontana Cemeteries," *Asheville Citizen,* September 20, 1982.

66. "Attorney Plans Suit to Gain Access to Fontana Cemeteries"; *Fontana Newsletter,* Winter 1996.

67. Joanita M. Hallenbach, "Decoration Day Journey," *The Mountaineer* (Waynesville, NC), August 28, 1995.

68. "Places: Hazel Creek," *Fontana Newsletter,* January 1989.

69. "Remember Me," *Fontana Newsletter,* Winter 1997.

70. Linda Hogue, "Group Walks 3.5 Miles Across Old Highway 288," *Fontana Newsletter,* Summer 1992.

71. Bob Scott, "Shared Memories Draws Visitors to National Park Cemetery," *Fontana Newsletter,* Fall 1992.

72. "Controversy Rooted in More Than Road, Includes Relocated Families," *Asheville Citizen-Times,* March 8, 2003.

73. "The Road Less Traveled," *Mountain Xpress* (Asheville, NC), March 14, 2006.

74. David Monteith interview with Alan Jabbour and Karen Jabbour, July 27, 2004, North Shore Cemetery Decoration Project, GSMNP Archives.

75. Heath Shuler interview with Matthew Chisholm, July 23, 2018, in author's possession.

76. Jesse Stone, "Finally! Swain County receives North Shore settlement money," *Smoky Mountain News* (Waynesville, NC), July 3, 2018, https://www.smokymountainnews.com/news/item/25100-finally-swain-county-receives-north-shore-settlement-money.

77. Supposedly this technique was so effective that three hundred graves were discovered after one dowsing excursion.

78. Pete Prince interview with Alan Jabbour and Karen Jabbour, August 18, 2004; Fairview-Cook Decoration interview with Ted Coyle, July 18, 2004, all in North Shore Cemetery Decoration Project, GSMNP Archives.

79. Ray Hooper, "Just a Wide Place in the Road," *Fontana Newsletter,* Fall 1989.

80. Chisholm, "Arrival of the Road to Nowhere," 65.

81. Trevor Lanier interview with Tonya Teague, August 9, 2004, North Shore Cemetery Decoration Project, GSMNP Archives.

82. Christine Cole Proctor interview with Alan Jabbour and Karen Jabbour, July 6, 2004, North Shore Cemetery Decoration Project, GSMNP Archives.

83. Julie Ball, "Environmental Feasibility Studies Expected for Road," *Asheville Citizen-Times,* April 2, 2002.

84. Chisholm, "Arrival of the Road to Nowhere," 68–69.

85. Paul Webb, *Cultural Resources Existing Conditions Report, North Shore Road Environmental Impact Report, Swain and Graham Counties, North Carolina, Final Report* (Raleigh: Garrow Associates, 2004), http://www.scribd.com/doc/27612090 /North-Shore-Road-Environmental-Impact-Statement-2004.

86. Chris Irwin, "North Shore Road Project Hearing Transcripts: Knoxville, TN," March 1, 2004, North Shore binder, North Shore box 1, Special Collections, WCU; "Fight Over Roadbuilding in Great Smoky Mountains National Park Settled," February 3, 2010, *Environment News Service,* http://www.ens-newswire.com/ens/feb2010 /2010–02–03–091.html.

87. Bob Miller, "Briefing: Great Smoky Mountains National Park—North Shore Road Monetary Settlement," March 15, 2010, *National Park Service,* http://www.nps.gov /grsm/parkmgmt/upload/North-Shore-Rd-3–15–10.pdf.

88. Kerr, "Road to Nowhere?" 5, 33–39.

89. Jeremy Markovich, "The Getaway," *Our State,* October 2018, 130–44.

7. Any Who See the Valley Would Regret Its Loss Forever

1. Michael Hembree and Dot Jackson, *Keowee: The Story of the Keowee River Valley in Upstate South Carolina* (Greenville, SC: Michael Hembree and Dot Jackson, 1995), 93.

2. Douglas Mauldin, "3 Dams Planned, Forming 2 Lakes in Oconee, Pickens," *Greenville News,* January 3, 1965.

3. *Seneca Journal and Tribune,* January 20, 1965.

4. "Era Six (1945–1972)," *Oconee Heritage Center,* http://www.oconeeheritagecenter .org/learn/oconee-history/era-six-1945–1972/.

5. James Dickey, *Deliverance* (Boston: Houghton Mifflin, 1970); *Deliverance,* directed by John Boorman (Warner Brothers, 1972).

6. Piper Peters Aheron, *Images of America: Oconee County* (Charleston, SC: Arcadia Publishing, 1998), 125.

7. David L. Carlton, "Textile Industry," *South Carolina Encyclopedia,* https://www .scencyclopedia.org/sce/entries/textile-industry/.

8. Michael Hembree, *Newry: A Place Apart* (Shelby, NC: Westmoreland Printers Inc., 2003), 41 (quote), 10, 26.

9. Debbie Fletcher, *Images of America: Lake Jocassee* (Charleston, SC: Arcadia Publishing, 2014); Debbie Fletcher, *Whippoorwill Farewell: Jocassee Remembered* (Victoria, Canada: Trafford, 2003), 134.

10. Claudia Whitmire Hembree, *Jocassee Valley* (Pickens, SC: Hiott Printing, 2003), 11, 16, 17.

11. Ibid., 123.

12. Ibid.
13. Jerry D. Vickery, *The Forgotten Society of the Keowee River Valley: A Biography of a Sharecropper, Johnny V. Hester* (Easley, SC: Barn Yard Art, 2008), 15.
14. Ibid., 15.
15. Ibid., 16.
16. Hembree and Jackson, *Keowee,* 80.
17. Ibid., 90.
18. Ibid.
19. Ibid., 94.
20. Nora Nimmons Field, *The High Falls Story* (Seneca, SC: Journal Co., 1966), 5.
21. Pearl McFall, *The Keowee River and Cherokee Background* (n.p.: Pearl McFall, 1966).
22. Manganiello, *Southern Water, Southern Power,* 11, 145–46.
23. Carlton, "Textile Industry."
24. *Farm Plat Book and Business Guide: Oconee County, S.C.* (Rockford, IL: Rockford Map Publishers, 1953), 51, http://www.oconeeheritagecenter.org/farm-plat -book-business-guide-oconee-county-sc-1953/.
25. Vickery, *The Forgotten Society,* 20–22.
26. Ibid., 23.
27. Ibid., 26.
28. Debbie Fletcher interview with Austin Gregory, March 10, 2018, in author's possession.
29. Email from Claudia Whitmire Hembree to Austin Gregory, June 23, 2018, in author's possession.
30. Hembree, *Jocassee Valley.*
31. Harry McCall interview with Austin Gregory, June 2, 2018, in author's possession.
32. Claudia Whitmire Hembree interview with Austin Gregory, May 7, 2018, in author's possession.
33. "Era Six (1945–1972)," *Oconee Heritage Center.*
34. Fletcher interview with Gregory, March 10, 2018.
35. Mike Wilson interview with Austin Gregory, March 11, 2018, in author's possession.
36. Hembree interview with Gregory, May 7, 2018.
37. Wilson interview with Gregory, March 11, 2018.
38. Fletcher interview with Gregory, March 10, 2018.
39. Wilson interview with Gregory, March 11, 2018.
40. Fletcher interview with Gregory, March 10, 2018; Fletcher, *Whippoorwill Farewell.*
41. *Seneca Journal and Tribune,* January 13, 1965.
42. McCall interview with Gregory, June 2, 2018.
43. Wilson interview with Gregory, March 11, 2018.
44. Wilma Crocker Thompson interview with Austin Gregory, October 8, 2018, in author's possession.

45. Wilson interview with Gregory, March 11, 2018.
46. A Zillow.com search (on September 25, 2018) for one-acre waterfront lots on Lake Keowee returned eight results with an average asking price of $281,750. The most expensive one-acre lot listed was $525,00 and the least expensive $179,000.
47. Wilson interview with Gregory, March 11, 2018.
48. McCall interview with Gregory, June 2, 2018.
49. Thompson interview with Gregory, October 8, 2018.
50. Alice Badenoch, *Keowee Key: The Origins of a Community* (Seneca, SC: Jay's Printing Co., 1989), 62.
51. Wilson interview with Gregory, March 11, 2018.
52. Ibid.
53. "It'll Be Under Water Pretty Soon," *Seneca Journal and Tribune,* February 22, 1967.
54. Thompson interview with Gregory, October 8, 2018.
55. *Greenville News,* March 25, 1965.
56. "Get On With Keowee-Toxaway!" *Greenville News,* May 17, 1966.
57. "And There Are Tadpoles Too," *Keowee Courier,* January 19, 1966.
58. *South Carolina Trout Fishing* (Columbia: South Carolina Department of Natural Resources), 4, http://www.dnr.sc.gov/fish/pdf/TroutBook.pdf.
59. *Greenville News,* March 25, 1965.
60. "Schumacher Blasts Opposition to Duke," *Greenville News,* March 26, 1965.
61. *Seneca Journal and Tribune,* June 30, 1965.
62. Ibid., September 14, 1966.
63. Federal Energy Regulatory Commission, "Order Issuing New License, Duke Energy Carolinas, LLC, Project No. 2503–154," August 16, 2016, 1, https://www.ferc.gov/industries/hydropower/gen-info/licensing/active-licenses/P-2503.pdf.
64. Fletcher interview with Gregory, March 10, 2018.
65. Ibid.
66. Email from Jim Richardson to Austin Gregory, April 3, 2018, in author's possession.
67. *Crescent Land & Timber Corp.* v *Williams,* 207 S.E.2d 98, 262 S.C. 671 (S.C., 1974).
68. Email from Richardson to Gregory, April 3, 2018.
69. McCall interview with Gregory, June 2, 2018.
70. *Farm Plat Book and Business Guide.*
71. McCall interview with Gregory, June 2, 2018.
72. Fletcher interview with Gregory, March 10, 2018.
73. Thompson interview with Gregory, October 8, 2018.
74. There was no evidence of public forums being announced in the *Seneca Journal and Tribune, Keowee Courier,* or *Greenville News* during the time period.
75. "Letter to the Editor," *Seneca Journal and Tribune,* January 13, 1965.
76. Philip Lee Williams, *In the Morning: Reflections from First Light* (Macon, GA: Mercer University Press, 2006), 100.

77. Alfred Turner, "Remembering Jocassee Valley [interview with Rudy Mancke]," Nature Notes, South Carolina Public Radio, Columbia, March 8, 2016, http://www .southcarolinapublicradio.org/post/remembering-jocassee-valley.

78. "Camp Jocassee: Provides Clean Summer Fun for Girls from Everywhere," *Seneca Journal and Tribune,* October 13, 1965.

79. *Seneca Journal,* July 13, 1966.

80. Thompson interview with Gregory, October 8, 2018.

81. Ibid.

82. Hembree interview with Gregory, May 7, 2018.

83. "Duke Gives Detailed Recreational Plan," *Seneca Journal,* September 22, 1965.

84. "Devil's Fork State Park," *South Carolina State Parks,* https://southcarolinaparks .com/devils-fork.

85. "Keowee-Toxaway State Park, Frequently Asked Questions," *South Carolina State Parks,* https://southcarolinaparks.com/keowee-toxaway/faqs.

86. "Keowee-Toxaway State Park, History and Interpretation," *South Carolina State,* https://southcarolinaparks.com/keowee-toxaway/history-and-interpretation.

87. "Second Phase of Jocassee Gorges Deal is Completed," *Jocassee Journal* 1 (Winter–Spring 2000): 1, http://www.dnr.sc.gov/managed/wild/jocassee/newsletters /jocvol1no1.pdf.

88. "Bonanza Forecast from Duke Project," *Greenville News,* May 28, 1967.

89. "Greenville: Gateway to Shangri-La," *Greenville News,* August 25, 1968.

90. "Keowee-Toxaway Will Be Major Tourist Attraction," *Greenville News,* June 23, 1968.

91. Wilson interview with Gregory, March 11, 2018.

92. "Maps by Topics: Economic Status," *Appalachian Regional Commission,* https:// www.arc.gov/research/MapsofAppalachia.asp?F_CATEGORY_ID=1.

93. "Poverty Rate in Appalachia, 2012–2016," *Appalachian Regional Commission,* https://www.arc.gov/research/MapsofAppalachia.asp?MAP_ID=142.

94. "Source and Methodology: Distressed Designation and County Economic Status Classification System, FY 2007–FY 2019," *Appalachian Regional Commission,* https:// www.arc.gov/research/sourceandmethodologycountyeconomicstatusfy2007fy2019 .asp.

95. McCall interview with Gregory, June 2, 2018.

96. Ibid.

97. Hembree interview with Gregory, May 7, 2018.

98. "County Revenues and Expenditures, 2018 County Profiles," South Carolina Association of Counties, August 2018, http://www.sccounties.org/Data/Sites/1 /media/publications/countyprofiles2018.pdf.

99. "Socioeconomic Data: Oconee County, South Carolina," *Appalachian Regional Commission,* https://www.arc.gov/research/DataReports.asp.

100. Thompson interview with Gregory, October 8, 2018.

Conclusion

Epigraph: Jason Boland and the Stragglers, "Big Shot Rich Man," *Live at Billy Bob's* (Image Entertainment, 2002).

1. Taylor, *The New South's New Frontier*, 5–15. See also Shapiro, *Appalachia on Our Mind;* David E. Whisnant, *All That Is Native and Fine: The Politics of Culture in an American Region* (Chapel Hill: University of North Carolina Press, 1983); David Hsiung, *Two Worlds in the Tennessee Mountains: Exploring the Origins of Appalachian Stereotypes* (Lexington: University Press of Kentucky, 1997).

2. McDonald and Muldowny, *TVA and the Dispossessed*, 7–9.

3. Taylor, *The New South's New Frontier*, 12–13.

4. Kate Tiller, "Local History and the Twentieth Century: An Overview and Suggested Agenda," *International Journal of Regional and Local Studies* 6 (2010): 16.

5. Ibid., 16–28.

6. Portelli, *The Death of Luigi Trastulli*, 15, 8.

7. Ibid., 26; Tiller, "Local History," 41–43.

8. Portelli, *The Death of Luigi Trastulli*, 52.

9. Theda Perdue, "The Legacy of Indian Removal," *Journal of Southern History* 78 (February 2012): 3–20. For more on the relationship between the Cherokee Removal and the Lost Cause, see Denson, *Monuments to Absence;* Tiya Miles, "Showplace of the Cherokee Nation: Race and the Making of a Southern House Museum," *Public Historian* 33 (November 2011): 11–34; Andrew Denson, "Remembering Cherokee Removal in Civil Rights–Era Georgia," *Southern Cultures* 14 (Winter 2008): 85–101; Malinda Maynor Lowery, "The Original Southerners: American Indians, the Civil War, and Confederate Memory," *Southern Cultures* 25 (Winter 2019): 16–35.

10. Perdue, "The Legacy of Indian Removal," 20–23.

11. Ibid., 23–32.

12. Ibid., 30–34.

13. McDonald and Muldowny, *TVA and the Dispossessed*, 3–26.

14. Ibid., 155–94. For a nuanced portrait of the complexity of Arthur E. Morgan's personality and ideology, see Purcell, *Arthur Morgan*.

15. Walker, "African Americans and TVA Reservoir Property Removal," 417–22.

16. Grant, *TVA and Black Americans*, 73–92.

17. Walker, "African Americans and TVA Reservoir Property Removal," 422–28.

18. Arnold J. Hyde, "Stecoah Community Removal Profile," 3, Fontana Removal Profiles, Collection: NC3–142–29–2, Records of the Tennessee Valley Authority, RG 142, NARA; Taylor, *The New South's New Frontier*, 83.

19. Arnold J. Hyde, "Almond-Judson Community Removal Profile," 2–4, RG 142, NARA; Taylor, *The New South's New Frontier*, 84.

20. Taylor, *The New South's New Frontier*, 84–86.

21. Sarah Mittlefehldt, "The People's Path: Conflict and Cooperation in the Acquisition of the Appalachian Trail," *Environmental History* 15 (October 2010), 643–45.

22. Ibid., 649–53.

23. Ibid., 653–55.

24. Ibid., 655–63.

25. Will Sarvis, "An Appalachian Forest: Creation of the Jefferson National Forest and Its Effects on the Local Community," *Forest and Conservation History* 37 (October 1993): 169–71.

26. Ibid., 171–76.

27. Whisnant, *Super-Scenic Motorway*, 214–34.

28. Ibid., 235–62.

29. Ibid., 267–82.

30. Ibid., 264–89.

31. Christie M. Kleinmann, "The 'Dam Talk' of Butler, Tennessee: Tracing the Stability and Change of Historical Memory in Newspaper Coverage," *American Journalism* 29 (Summer 2012): 40–43 (emphasis added).

32. Ibid., 43–47.

33. Ibid., 47–49.

34. Ibid., 47–50.

35. Stephen Wallace Taylor, "Citizens Against Wilderness: Environmentalism and the Politics of Marginalization in the Great Smoky Mountains," in Sylvia Hood Washington et al., eds., *Echoes from the Poisoned Well: Global Memories of Environmental Injustice* (Lanham, MD: Lexington Books, 2006), 163–66.

36. Ibid., 163–64.

37. Ibid., 164–66.

38. Alesia F. Montgomery, "The Sight of Loss," *Antipode* 43 (April 2011): 1828–48.

39. Taylor, "Citizens Against Wilderness," 165.

Index

Page numbers in **boldface** refer to illustrations.

Act for the Preservation of Antiquities, 11
Adams, Edmund I., 80
African Americans: agriculture and farming,
6, 40, 51, 218, 219; and the Civilian Conservation Corps, 111, **113**, 119; and Grandfather
Mountain, 223; and Mammoth Cave, 90,
103–4, 111, 112, **113**, 119, 121, **122**, 123, 124,
251n78; mentioned, 10, 229; and National
Park Service, 246n47; and Oak Ridge, 15,
127–28, 129, 133, 135–36, **137**, 138; and segregation, 15, 127, 136, 138, 218–19; and Shenandoah, 69, 88, and slavery, 90, 104, 121, 135,
142; and Tennessee Valley Authority, 50–51,
170, 218–19; and textile industry, 190
agriculture: African Americans, 6, 40, 51, 218,
219; Fontana Dam project and Fontana
Lake, 149, 156, 159, 161, 162, 163, 164, 165–66,
167–68, 219; and Great Smoky Mountains,
2, 19–20, 22, 24, 25, 34; and Keowee-Toxaway project, 186, 190–91, 192, 193, 194, 195,
197, 200, 202, 205, 208, 210; and Mammoth
Cave, 100, 105, 107, 108, 111, 114, 116, 119;
mentioned, xii, 7, 9, 13, 17, 99, 198, 212, 217,
219; and the New River Valley, 78, 79, 80;

and Norris Basin, xi, 2, 37, 40, 43, 44, **45**, 46,
47–48, 51, 52, 53, 54, 56, 57–58, 59, 60, 62, 64,
217–18; and Oak Ridge, 2, 126, 127, 128, 130,
131, 133, 134, 135, 138, 140–41, 143–44, 147,
148; and Peaks of Otter, 222; and Shenan-
doah, 22, 68, 69, 72, 76, 77
Aheron, Piper Peters, 185–86
Albermarle County, Virginia, 85
Alleghany County, North Carolina, 78, 80, 86
Almond, North Carolina, 29, 149, 161, 162,
163–64, 165, 167, 168. *See also* Judson, North
Carolina
Aluminum Company of America (ALCOA),
29, 156, 157, 162, 170
American Museum of Science and Energy, 130
American Revolution, 44, 189
Ammons, L. W., 167
Ammons, Ollis, 167
Ancestry.com, 239n15
Anderson, Isaac, 53
Anderson County, South Carolina, 197, 206
Anderson County, Tennessee, 2, 44, 46, 133
Andersonville, Tennessee, 64
Andrus, Cecil, 172
Anthony, Ed, 167
Anthony, Sarah, 167

Cox, Perry, 93, 100, 121
Craig, Walter, 58–59
Crescent Land and Timber Corporation, 185, 200
Crisp, Shirley, 27
Croghan, John, 90, 91, 94, 121
Crystal Cave, 91, 93, 98, 99, 100–103, 104, 120–21, 123, 124
Cumberland Valley, Pennsylvania, 221
Cushman, Charles, 221
Cutliff, Lewis, 124

Danforth, Scot, xiii
Davidson, Donald, 40, 63
Davis, Frank, 105
Davis, Jim, 32
Davis, Lee, 61
Davis, Otis, 76–77
Deals Gap, North Carolina, 157
Dean, Kim, 84–85
Decoration Day, 27, **28**, 29–30, 34, 62, 155, 170, 173, **174**, 175, 179
Deliverance, 185
Demunbrun, A. A., 106, 107, 110
Detroit, 47, 138
Devil's Fork State Park, 206, 207
Diamond Caverns, 91, 124
Dickey, James, 185
Dollywood, 20
Dossey, L. P., 119
Dowsing, 177, 261n77
Draper, Earle, 63
Drowning Bear, 33
Duke Power Company: and electricity profits, 210; Keowee River dam plan, 183, **184**, 185–86, 187–88, 189, 190, 198; and license for the Keowee-Toxaway Project, 199; mentioned, 15, 204, 211; and opposition, 198, 199–200, 202–3; and real estate development, 195–96; and recreation, 205, 206, 207, 208; removal process, 186, 188, 190, 192–97, 199, 200, 205–6, 209; and taxes, 208 . *See also* Southern Power Company; Keowee-Toxaway project

Dunn, Durwood, 6, 19
du Pont, E. I., 90
Dupont Chemical Company, 166

Eagle Creek, North Carolina, 162
Easley, South Carolina, 188, 194, 196
East Fork, Tennessee, 127
Eastern Band of the Cherokee. *See* Cherokee Nation
Edgemoor, Tennessee, 127
Edmonson County, Kentucky: and Appalachian Regional Commission, 14; and county court and commissioners, 96, 97, 102, 105, 106, 118, 120; mentioned, 92, 107, 108, 109, 115, 119; and oil industry, 110
Edmonson County News, 94, 106, 107, 108, 109, 110, 111, 116, 118, 252n99
Edwards, L. P., 100, 104–5, 106
Ekaneetlee Lodge, 22
Eke, Collins, 248n17
Elkmont, **44**
Eller, Ron, 161
Ellerbe, Ned, 83–84
Elza, Tennessee, 127, 129
eminent domain: definition, 9–10, 11; and the Blue Ridge Power Project, 78; and Cades Cove, 19; and Keowee-Toxaway Project, 193; and Mammoth Cave, 95, 98, 106, 114–15, 121; mentioned, 87, 234n11; and National Park Service, 221; and Shenandoah, 67; and Tennessee Valley Authority, 10, 29
England, Arkansas, 99
environmental movement and organizations, 5, 29–30, 41, 78, 86, 87, 145, 155, 179–80, 225, 228
Environmental Protection Agency, 41
Epps Springs, North Carolina, **160**
Esters, "Red Buck," 124
"everyday nature" concept, 68, 76–77, 79–82, 86, 87
Executive Order 6542, 114
Executive Order 8802, 170
extractive industries: logging and timber industry, 23, 31, 69, 107, 108–9, 112, 154, 156, 159, 161,

National Park Service *(continued)*
15, 20–21, 22, 24, 30–32, 172, 173, 175, 222;
and Mammoth Cave, 16, 92, 93, 97, 99, 109,
111, 112, 114, 115–16, 118, 120, 121, 123–24, 220,
249n44; mentioned, 7, 17, 209, 216; and
North Shore communities, 27, 30, 32, 171, 172,
173, 175, 177, 178, 180, 226; and Oak Ridge, 16;
and Peaks of Otter community, 223, **224**; and
race, 88, 246n47; and Shenandoah, 68–69,
71, 72, 74, 75, 76–77, 82–83, 84, 222
National Parks Association, 92
National Trails Act, 220
National Wild and Scenic Rivers System, 78, 80
National Youth Administration, 164
Native Americans, 8–9, 17, 30, 33, 41, 44, 90,
191, 203, 216, 229, 244n5. *See also* Cherokee
Nation; Shawnee Nation
Nature Conservancy, 84
Navy, Martha, 207
Nellenbach, Joanita M., 34
Nelson, Hershel, 51
New Deal, 7, 11, 36, 37, 38, 43, 52, 69, 152, 154,
178, 181, 189
New Entrance to Mammoth Cave, 91, 93, 94, 97,
98–99, 104, 107, 111, 120, 123
New Entrance to Mammoth Cave Hotel, 98, 99
New Fairfax, North Carolina, 162
New Hope, Tennessee, 37, 127. *See also* Roberts-
ville, Tennessee
New Loyston, Tennessee, 38, 62–63. *See also*
Loyston, Tennessee
New River Valley; and agriculture, 78, 79, 80;
and the Blue Ridge Power Project, 14, 77–80,
86; mentioned, 68, 74, 75, 82
Newfont, Kathryn, 6–7
Newfound Gap, 1, **3**, 11, 171
Newman, George, 102
Newry, South Carolina, 183, 187, 190
Nicholson, Richard, 83
Nimick Forbesway Foundation, 87
Nixon, Rob, 82
Noland, R. L., 22
Noland Creek, North Carolina, 167, 168

Nolin River, 108
Norris, George, 36
Norris, Tennessee, 36, 63, **65**
Norris Basin: and agriculture, xi, 2, 37, 40,
43, 44, **45**, 46, 47–48, 51, 52, 53, 54, 56,
57–58, 59, 60, 62, 64, 217–18; and cemetery
relocation, 38, 43, 49, 62, 64, 239n15; and
cultural change, 42, 44, 64, 213; early history,
44; mentioned, 16, 222; and race, 50–51;
removal and relocation of families, 2, 7, 14,
37, 38, 40, 42, 43, 46–47, 49, 54, 57, 59, 60,
62; Tennessee Valley Authority reports and
surveys, 38, 39, 46–48, 49, 56, 59–60. *See also*
Loyston, Tennessee; Norris Dam; Tennessee
Valley Authority
Norris Dam: and benefits, 43–44, 60, 63, 64,
66; and employment, 52; mentioned, 8, 38,
42; and the New Deal, 36, 43, 213, 217; and
race, 170. *See also* Loyston, Tennessee; Norris
Basin; Tennessee Valley Authority
Norris Dam State Park, xi, 62
North Carolina Park Commission, 20
North Shore Cemetery Association, 29, 30, 170,
173, 228, 260n51
North Shore communities; and Decoration Day,
27, 29–30, 34, 62, 155, 170, 173, **174**, 175, 179;
and Fontana Dam project, 14, 16, 17, 29, 34,
149, **151**, **160**, 161, 162, 164, 166, 169, 173, 176,
180, 219–20, 226, 228; and memory, 31, 34, 152,
154, 158, 172, 175, 177, 178; and National Park
Service, 27, 30, 32, 171, 172, 173, 175, 177, 178,
180, 226; property transfer to Great Smoky
Mountains National Park, 156–57, 169, 226,
228; removal of residents, xiii, 14, 15, 17, 31, 152,
153, 154–56, 158, 163, 164–66, 167–68, 172, 182,
220; and settlement with federal government,
32, 150, **151**, 172, 176, 177, 180, 228; and wilderness movement, 29–30, 150, 155, 171–72, 175,
178, 228. *See also* Almond, North Carolina;
Bushnell, North Carolina; Japan, North
Carolina; Judson, North Carolina; Proctor,
North Carolina; Stecoah, North Carolina;
Swain County, North Carolina

Proctor, North Carolina, 29, 31, 158, 161–62, 163, 164, 165, 177, 219–20
Purcell, Aaron D., 14, 266n14
Purcell, Caroline M., xiii
Purcell, Laura M., xiii
Purcell, Samuel S., xiii

Quallah Boundary, 33, 168
Quin, Huston, 99, 102, 105, 108, 110, 111

Raleigh, North Carolina, 150
Raley, Sillus, 59
Ravensford, North Carolina, 22, 161
Reagan, Ronald, 32, 226, 229
Red Cross, 107, 112
Resettlement Administration, 69, 83
Revolutionary War. *See* American Revolution
Richard King Mellon Foundation, 206
Richardson, Jim, 200
Ridge, Joseph, 115, 116, 118, 120
Ritter, North Carolina, 162
Ritter, W. M., 159
Ritter Lumber Company, 31, 159, 161, 170
Roane County, Tennessee, 2, 60, 133, 135
Roane State Community College, 139
Robbinsville, North Carolina, 165, 180, 219
Roberts, M. G., 171
Robertsville, Tennessee, 37, 127, 141. *See also* New Hope, Tennessee
Rochester, Bruce, 195
Rockefeller, John D. Jr., 1, 19–20, 22, 71
Rodes, John B., 96, 105
Rodgers, Serena Livingston Croghan, 94
Rogers, Michael, 43
Rohr, Karl, 155
Roosevelt, Franklin D.: and conservation, 11, 69, 114; and the Great Smoky Mountains, 1–2, 3, 10–11, 20; letters to, 58, 67, 76; and Mammoth Cave, 115; mentioned, 111; and Shenandoah, 67, 69, 76; and Tennessee Valley Authority, 43, 58
Roosevelt, Theodore, 11
Ross, Derek G., 74–75

Rothstein, Richard, 136
Rugby Colony, x
Russell, Charlie, 57
Rust, Philip Goodenow, 166–67, 168–69

Salem, South Carolina, 196
Sampson, Flem, 94, 97
San Francisco, 136
Sand Cave, 91
Sandifer, Paul, 206
Sarvis, Will, 222
Satterfield, M. Harry, 40
Sawyer's Creek, North Carolina, 164
Scarboro, Tennessee, 127, 141
Schumacher, Snead, 198
Selznick, Philip, 39–40
Seneca, South Carolina, 190, 197, 199, 205
Seneca Journal and Tribune, 185, 194, 197, 199, 202–3, 204, 207, 264n74
Sevier County, Tennessee, 20, **28**
Shackleford, Martin, 124
Shapiro, Henry D., 71
Sharp, Freeman, 51
Sharp, Gwen Hubbard, 62–63, 64, 66
Sharp, Phoebe, 56
Sharp, Rome C., 219–20
Sharp, Rush L., 53
Sharps Chapel, Tennessee, 64
Shawnee Nation, 44, 90
Shenandoah: and agriculture, 22, 68, 69, 72, 76, 77; and the Civilian Conservation Corps, 69, 112, 120; and community relations, 71, 83–85, 86, 87, 88; and Corbin Hollow, 72, **73**; and cultural history, 71, 72, 76, 79, 83, 84–85, 86–87, 246n40; and eminent domain, 67; and "everyday nature" concept, 68, 76–77, 79–82, 86, 87; mentioned, xiii, 8, 11, 16, 78, 91, 92, 95; and National Park Service, 68–69, 71, 72, 74, 75, 76–77, 82–83, 84, 222; and race, 69, 88; removal of residents, 67, 68, 72, 74, 75, 76–77, 86, 87; and Shenandoah National Park Trust, 85, 87; and Skyline Drive, **70**; and stewardship, 14, 68, 71–72, 74–75, 77,